The Way She Chose

The Way She Chose

By Mary Miller
Artist: Lester Miller

Rod and Staff Publishers, Inc.
P.O. Box 3, Hwy. 172
Crockett, Kentucky 41413
Telephone (606) 522-4348

Printed in U.S.A

ISBN 0-7399-2325-0
Catalog no. 2458

3   4   5   6   7   —   16   15   14   13   12   11   10   09   08   07

Contents

Preface

This story is based on the life of one who suffered much because of the way she chose. The temptations Sara faced are not unlike those you will face when you need to make decisions that will determine what your life and home will be like. These decisions will also affect eternal destinies. Although this story is about a young girl, the same tests and choices also come to young men.

You are making important choices at a time of life when, in yourself, you are ill prepared to make those choices. However, God has provided all that you need to guide you to a godly future in time and to a rewarding eternal destiny. The provisions are the grace of God, godly parents, and faithful churches.

At the beginning of this story, the church and the parents were somewhat lax in giving the firm direction that may have spared Sara from the tragedies in her life. The church's youth activities were not well directed or monitored, and her parents gave in too easily, which is acknowledged later in the story. However, even Sara was given enough godly guidance that she would have been spared much suffering, had she heeded the warnings.

Young people, take to heart the warnings imbedded herein. Parents, take seriously your responsibility in giving firm, Scriptural oversight to your youth as they make important decisions that affect their future. Church leaders, you are in a strategic position to provide guidance and encouragement to youth and the parents of youth as they together face the choices that determine youth's happiness for time and eternity.

Youth, ultimately you choose the way, but the effect of those choices are in the hands of an almighty God. Choose right for the sake of your future and the future of those who follow you, both for time and for eternity.

—*David Mast*

"I know, O LORD,
that thy judgments
are right, and that thou
in faithfulness
hast afflicted me."
Psalm 119:75

1.

Train Up a Child

It was a cool and pleasant summer evening in the sheltered little Germantown Valley. The breezes softly touched the small brown cottage located at its southern end. There were few homes beyond the Yoder homestead. The main road, running straight through this lush green valley, spanned a distance of about eight miles. The width of the valley was about half as much.

No more than fifteen families lived in the entire valley, and seldom, in the early 1900s, did they associate with anyone outside their small community. And even more rare were gatherings in the valley attended by anyone living outside this sheltered haven.

Their world was a small one, set apart as it

was in the hills of western Virginia. Of course, there were occasional business transactions that took the men outside, and on the rare visits to relatives or friends, their families went along. Travel was not easy and the roads were poor. More often than not, the mothers were glad to keep their little ones at home.

The Mennonite Church at large brought its influence into the valley during this time. The conference concept had been introduced in the late 1800s in an effort toward unifying the churches across the continent. The preaching of John S. Coffman (deceased in 1900) and John Funk was having a profound effect upon the churches. Although there was spiritual revival, there was also much change, some of which was not good. John and Mary Yoder were members of the Germantown Valley Mennonite Church, which had experienced revival but had not been directed in a course that would adequately provide ongoing spiritual safety for its members.

The hearts of John and Mary Yoder were filled with praise this lovely August evening in 1901. God had graciously blessed their small farm. Their home was filled with love and peace. Almost two years had passed since the happy day when they had joined their lives in one. This day was pleasant, much like that day two years ago had been. Today, August 5, their first child was born. It was the day they had looked forward to with joy, and with a tremendous feeling of responsibility. God had entrusted to their care the soul of an innocent little jewel.

Little Sara was round faced, sweet, and plump. Words could not express the joy Mary felt the first time she lifted the little one in her arms and looked into that pure and innocent face. With deep thanksgiving, John watched the mother and child. They were his own. He would offer them the tenderest care; he would protect and provide for them, both in material and spiritual things. He felt keenly the responsibility that had been added to his role in the home.

As a calm tranquility settled over the Yoder home that evening, John took up his Bible, as was their daily custom at the close of the day. After reading a portion of Scripture, the happy parents prayed. Their petition included a special plea for God's blessing on Sara's life.

As time passed, Sara grew sweeter and dearer to her parents. She was an unusually contented child. Her large, brown, expressive eyes spoke volumes, long before her little lips could form words. Before she was two years old, Sara had a little sister, and several years later, a brother.

Sara listened attentively when her mother said to her, "You are almost five years old now and able to help very much." Mother laid the new pink-skinned little bundle in Sara's arms. "New babies must be handled very carefully," she instructed, while she showed Sara how to hold her new baby brother and protect his head. "I will need lots of help, not only with tending the baby, but with washing the dishes and keeping the house clean."

"I will help, Mother," Sara replied cheerfully, gently holding the small baby. "Marie is three years old already. I am glad we have another little baby. What will we call him?" She gently touched the little hands. He grasped her finger and held it tightly. Sara was delighted.

"Father and I have decided to call him James. Do you like that?" Her mother beamed happily.

"Oh, yes." Sara touched the small fingers again. "James, James," she kept repeating, enjoying the sound of her new brother's name. He opened one little eye. "Oh, Mother! Look at James," Sara exclaimed excitedly. "Come, Marie; look! James is waking up."

The little girl ran eagerly to her older sister. There were no signs of jealousy, only joy at the presence of a new child in the home. Each child could feel the love of his parents, and each knew they were all wanted and treasured alike.

*　　*　　*　　*　　*

Fall came in brilliant beauty to the valley. Above the lush farmlands in the valley, with here and there a large oak among them, the maples on the mountainsides lent their varying hues of reds and oranges to the colorful landscape. Sara's

14

eyes were bright with excitement when Mother said, "Sara, tomorrow will be your first day of school. Here are two new pencils and a tablet for you. Your teacher will give you your books on the first day of school. Be sure to take good care of them and listen carefully when she speaks to you so that you can learn your lessons well."

Sara's excitement had lessened by the next morning when she crawled out of bed. "Mother, may Marie go with me this morning?" she asked wistfully. "Just this one day? Tomorrow I can go by myself." The big brown eyes, shining with appeal, accented the beauty of the round face and rosy cheeks of the child. Long brown braids hung almost to her waist. When Mother began shaking her head, her dimpled smile faded for a moment as she added in a pleading voice, "Must I go alone?"

"Marie is only four years old, Sara. Only children who are six may go to school. Be a big, brave girl for Mother and Father today. Remember, Father told you last evening all about your first day of school."

As she listened, the little cloud disappeared from Sara's sunny brow. Only for an instant had she felt frightened by the thought of leaving her home all alone. After all, Mother and Father would not be far away and she would soon be back. Sara had not met the new teacher yet, but all her fears were quieted by Mother's calm smile.

"Everything will be all right, or Father and Mother would not be sending you."

"Lydia will be there, won't she, and Anna and Susie and John?"

"Sure, they will all be there," Mother replied, "and lots of other children too. You will know most of them, because most of the children in school are from our church. But remember, you are not going to school to play. You will work hard at your studies most of the day, and talk and play only at recess time," Mother reminded her.

"I am sure you will enjoy school," Mother continued, "if you listen to your teacher carefully and play nicely with the children at recess. Remember, Sara, that you must not whisper in school, not even to your closest friends, even if they talk to you."

"Yes," Sara replied soberly.

When it was time to go, Sara ran out and stood beside the mailbox, holding the little tin syrup bucket in which Mother had packed her lunch. In her other hand she carried her new pencils and tablet. She wore her blue gingham dress, which Mother had ironed the evening before, while Sara had entertained James.

Now Marie will be Mother's big helper, Sara mused, casting an anxious glance toward the house. There on the front porch stood Mother and Marie. They were watching the Millers' team rounding the curve, pulling a wagon with about a dozen children on it.

Sara waved, called "Good-bye," and climbed up on the wagon. As the team pulled away and started down the road, Sara could see Mother still waving. She was glad Mother had watched her leave.

Sara looked all around her. Only when she saw Lydia, her nearest neighbor and closest friend, near the front of the wagon did her cheeks dimple and her face brighten in a smile. As she made her way toward her friend, several older children moved over, leaving room for the little first grade girls to sit together on the straw. Sara recognized most of the other children from seeing them in church on Sundays, but there were a few strangers.

At home, Mother wiped a few tears, and then took Marie's hand as her oldest daughter was lost from her sight. *Dear Father in heaven, keep Your hand over Sara. She is so young and eager to learn. Help her to learn only the good and shun the bad,* she prayed. *And help me to prepare these other little ones for the day when they too will take their first step outside the protecting walls of home.* As she committed them all to God, she stepped back inside to tend the two still at home under her care.

Brother Miller stopped the team at the railroad crossing, and then moved on past the country store, the Germantown post office, and the church. These were familiar sights. Next was the little red brick schoolhouse, situated right in the center of the Germantown Valley. Sara's heart fluttered as they entered the schoolyard and the children all climbed down from the wagon. There were twenty-four children in all. Though most of them were familiar, Sara felt strange in this large group without Father or Mother nearby.

Sara loved school, and she soon learned to love her teacher. She loved Lydia most of all, and was very happy when she learned that she and Lydia were the only first graders that year.

The first evening after school, Sara burst excitedly into the kitchen at home. She could hardly talk fast enough as she told her parents all about what she had learned and done at school. Father and Mother listened with interest, enjoying her childish pleasures and encouraging her to share all that had taken place in school that day.

Sara nearly smothered Marie with kisses; she was so glad to see her again. "In a way it was a long day," she sighed contentedly. Never before had she and Marie been separated for so long. Baby James was asleep. Sara could hardly wait for her eleven-month-old brother to awaken and see that she was back again.

"Oh, Mother," Sara began, while drying the dishes for Mother after supper, "I almost forgot to tell you something important. Lydia told me that her mother said she may stop off here tomorrow evening if it is all right with you. She would like to play with baby James. You know she doesn't have any younger sisters or brothers. She would like so much to have a new baby in their home." Sara felt sorry for her friend, who was the youngest in her family.

"Surely," Mother replied. "I would be happy to have Lydia visit here with you awhile tomorrow afternoon. You may tell her in the morning that it is all right with us."

"She said her father will stop here for her at about five o'clock, on his way home from the gristmill. I am glad she may come," Sara said. "She loves babies as much as I do. I am so glad we have babies that I can help to care for."

Sara was an intelligent and eager learner. Her lessons were easy for her, and she spent much time reading. She learned many things as her first year in school progressed, including some things that were a burden to her godly parents. They soon began to notice a very independent spirit in their oldest child. "Sure, we want her to develop into a competent adult." Her father expressed his concerns to her mother. "But she must first learn subjection to authority and dependence on others."

There were only a few children in the Germantown school who were not from Christian homes. The bad habits of these few, however, were naturally seen and imitated by some of the children from Christian homes.

Father and Mother Yoder were shocked one evening to hear their innocent little girl take the Lord's Name in vain. It was on a Wednesday evening while they were preparing for prayer meeting.

"Sara, please help Marie to tie her shoes," Mother had called from the living room.

Marie had mischievously pulled her foot from one side to the other, making it impossible for Sara to tie the shoe. For a while, Sara had wrestled playfully with her; then, grabbing her foot and holding it tightly, she uttered those awful words she had heard at school. Mother walked into the little girls' bedroom just then. Sara's face turned red. She could not face Mother. She felt guilty.

"Sara!" her mother exclaimed in a shocked tone. "I am very sorry to hear you using the Lord's Name in vain." Mother took the little shoe and, holding Marie's foot firmly in her hand, said, "Marie, when Mother asks Sara to help you, you must not kick as you were doing. That was not nice."

Tears came quickly to the little girl's eyes. "You should tell Sara you are sorry," Mother admonished her. "It makes it very hard for her to help you when you act this way."

"I am sorry," Marie sobbed, burying her face in Mother's lap.

Sara was sitting on the bed with tears streaming down her cheeks also. "I am sorry I was so impatient," Sara said brokenly. "And I am sorry too that I said bad words. They just came out before I thought. I know you do not want me to talk that way."

Mother put her arms around the two tearful little girls, glad to see them broken-hearted for their wrongdoing.

John and Mary Yoder had set before their children an example of humility and repentance. The children had, more than once or twice, heard their parents admit that they had done wrong in becoming impatient or in neglecting to do something they felt they should have done. They freely confessed their sins, thus finding peace. The children had early learned this release of guilt when they knew they had displeased their parents. They were establishing a conscience that would help them in responding to God when they became aware of their accountability to Him.

"Marie," Mother instructed, "go out to the living room and ask Father to help you undo your braids. Mother will come soon to comb your hair." Marie jumped off the bed and ran immediately to Father.

"Sara," her mother began gently, taking her young daughter's hand in hers, "it is very naughty to use the Lord's Name the way you did. I hope it will never happen again."

Sara's upturned eyes filled with tears. Her lip quivered. She felt very badly for displeasing her mother.

"God knew that people would be tempted to swear and take His Name in vain," Mother went on to explain. "Long ago, God gave His people the commandment 'Thou shalt not take the name of the LORD thy God in vain.' In the New Testament, He also reminds us to reverence His holy Name.

"Father and I want our home to please God, so we are not pleased when you speak that way. You see, it is Satan who wants you to use God's Name in vain instead of worshiping God and using His Name reverently. I know you want to please God," Mother said, smiling into Sara's tear-filled eyes. "Jesus died for us so we would not need to live in sin. We must always ask God to help us. While you are young, Mother and Father will help you to remember not to do things that are wrong. When you are older, you will need to take the responsibility yourself not to do wrong things. If you have bad habits now, it will be hard for you to break them when you are older."

Sara sobbed on Mother's shoulder for a while after meekly receiving the punishment that she knew she deserved. Now she felt relief. Her wrongdoing had been taken care of. Then those

22

big, expressive eyes so filled with sorrow were dried, and she looked up into Mother's eyes with confidence that she had been forgiven. Once again her cheeks dimpled and a rosy smile brightened her face, and the incident was forgotten. Sara quickly dressed for church while Mother braided Marie's hair.

The Yoders were soon on their way to prayer meeting. Sara sat quietly beside Mother during the service. After dismissal, while Mother and Father visited with neighbors and friends, Sara talked quietly to several of her school friends. One by one the people left. Only a few remained.

"Good evening, Sara," the minister greeted her with a smile, offering her his hand.

"Good evening, Brother Mast," Sara replied, shaking hands with him.

"How is school?" he asked.

"Oh, I like it very much," Sara answered brightly. "I have so many friends at school, and we are learning lots of new things."

"That is good," Brother Mast responded kindly. "Have you learned to read and write?"

"Yes," Sara answered his question eagerly. Then her face clouded as she remembered some other things she had learned at school. "Mother told me," she said, her voice scarcely above a whisper, "sometimes I learn things that I shouldn't. I don't want to do those things, but I forget sometimes."

"I will pray for you so you won't forget, Sara," he promised.

Sara felt relieved. She would try harder, and Mother and Father and the minister would all pray for her. Young as she was, Sara was learning to have great faith in prayer.

"Sara," Brother Mast went on, "will you pray for me also? Satan tempts me to do wrong things sometimes too."

Sara looked trustingly into the eyes of the older man, whom she had learned to respect. "Y-yes," she faltered, "I will pray for you. I didn't know you were ever tempted anymore." From that evening on, Sara began to faithfully pray for their minister.

One Sunday morning in May, soon after six o'clock, Father came in from the barn. "Mother," he called from the back door, "we'd better get the children up early. We're going to have to walk to church today. The horses are both sick this morning. Ranger seems no better than he was yesterday. Now this morning Frisk is getting lame in his hind legs—just as Ranger started to last week. I don't believe we should plan to take the buggy today. Do you feel able to walk?"

"Yes," Mother answered. "It is only three miles. But we will have to start earlier. I wouldn't want to have to rush, and James is getting so heavy that you will be tired from carrying him before we get there."

"Oh, I'll make out," Father answered cheerfully, walking across the kitchen. "He is heavy, but I have a strong back. Besides, he is big enough to walk some of the time."

"Sara, Marie," Father called, "it is time to be getting up. Get dressed as quickly as you can."

Sara rolled over. The sun was just coming up, shedding a soft glow through the white curtains at her east window. She dressed and helped Marie with the buttons down the back of her dress. Both little girls appeared in the kitchen with happy smiles a few minutes later. They went to the washstand behind the kitchen door and scrubbed their faces, ears, and necks.

Mother brought James out of the bedroom and set him in the highchair that Father had built. Then Mother set breakfast on the table. The large white bowls looked pretty on the bright, blue-checked oilcloth. The steaming oatmeal in the big bowl smelled good. Everyone gathered around the inviting table and sat silently while Father read a chapter aloud from the Bible. Together they bowed their heads and thanked God for His blessings to them. Even little James was quiet.

"Children, we will walk to church today," Father announced while he served them with oatmeal. "The horses are both sick. You must hurry and eat so we can get ready to go as quickly as possible."

...s were delighted. They had not walked to church since Marie could remember. Sara often told her of the good times they used to have walking to church before James was born. Then Father used to carry Marie, and Sara walked beside Mother—unless the Millers walked too. Then she would walk with Lydia just ahead of Mother and Sister Miller. Now the oatmeal disappeared rapidly. They had never been late for church and were determined to be there on time today.

With each one cooperating, it was not difficult to be ready to leave by eight o'clock. "This will give us an hour and a half before time for the service to begin," Mother stated with satisfaction.

Father nodded approvingly. "And we will have plenty of time to freshen up a bit and relax to prepare our hearts for worship," he added.

As she started out across the front porch ahead of the rest, Sara shouted, "The Millers are walking today too!" Happily she joined Lydia out in front of the house.

The rest of the family hurried out, and after friendly greetings the two families walked down the road together. "It is a beautiful day," Brother Miller exclaimed, "so we decided to walk once again."

Father explained why they were walking.

"Too bad about the horses," Brother Miller

sympathized with Father. "I certainly hope they get better soon."

The Millers and Yoders arrived in good time and enjoyed the morning worship service with about seventy-five or eighty brethren and sisters.

"It would be closer to go home by the railroad tracks," Father suggested after church. Brother Miller agreed, so the little group followed the tracks south through the green fields of young corn and grain on their return home.

"Let me carry James awhile," Brother Miller offered after they had walked a mile. Father gladly consented. Sister Miller took one of Marie's hands, while Mother took the other one. Lydia and Sara walked on ahead.

"Mother, may we take off our shoes and stockings?" Sara asked awhile later. "It is getting so warm."

"Yes, you may, if Sister Miller doesn't mind Lydia taking hers off," Mother replied.

"May I, Mother?" Lydia asked.

"Yes, it is warm today, and this isn't as public as the road. I think it would be all right," her mother agreed.

The two girls clasped hands and ran about a hundred feet toward the curve ahead, so that their parents would not get ahead of them while they stopped to take off their shoes. They were puffing when they sat down on the tracks and began untying their shoestrings. Their faces were bright with the fresh air and sunshine and the joy of walking with friends.

Their parents followed slowly with the little ones, engrossed in their discussion of the encouraging morning message. Suddenly John stopped and listened. What was that he heard? And what caused the slight vibration of the tracks under his feet, the very tracks on which the girls were sitting a hundred feet ahead? Yes, it was a fast train approaching from around the curve up ahead! He sprang into action before the others had noticed anything.

The two carefree children heard nothing but their own happy chatter. Nor did they see Sara's father flying to their rescue at the risk of his own life. The train was rounding the curve now; the girls looked up. Suddenly the train whistle blew a warning, loud and clear. At the same instant, both mothers dropped to their knees under the trees beside the tracks. "O God," they cried helplessly, "save the children. Save the men, if it be Thy will."

Sara heard the whistle and the clatter and rumble of the train. "Lydia!" she cried, starting to rise to her feet. Just as suddenly, she was swept off her feet by the strong arm of her father and was rolled down the bank into the wooded area in the gully below. He also grabbed Lydia, threw her off the track, and jumped to safety himself just as the train whizzed by.

Brother Miller, who had followed him, also jumped to safety and slid down the bank. Silently they waited while the train roared past. Then the two thankful fathers gathered up their frightened little girls.

"Father"—Sara's bright eyes looked into his— "I didn't see the train in time. How did you get here so fast?" Her cheeks were flushed with excitement. She clasped his hand, still trembling. "Father, if you hadn't come, I couldn't have gotten off in time."

"I know, Sara, I know," he answered shakily. "And I was afraid I couldn't get here in time either."

Sara still clutched her father's hand. "Weren't you afraid the train would run over you, Father?" she exclaimed, her eyes wide with wonder. Her father was a brave hero.

"Sara, I wasn't thinking about me. I was thinking about my little girl," he replied.

Sara was deeply touched by those tender words. She loved her dear father more than ever before. He had actually risked his life for her!

The little girls' mothers joined the others with tears of joy. "Oh, Sara," her mother cried, pressing her oldest child to her breast, "I thought Father would not make it in time, but God helped him and spared you and Father both. Thank the Lord!" She examined Sara's scratched knees and arms, which were bruised and bleeding.

"They don't hurt too much, Mother," the

small girl explained. "Father had to get us off fast, or we would have been hurt much worse."

"That is right," Mother agreed. "Father had to do this to keep you from being crushed beneath those iron wheels. It was his love for you that caused him to be so rough with you. He knew you would be bruised and scratched on the rocks and brambles, but he wanted to spare you worse pain."

"Oh, Mother, our shoes!" Lydia cried. "They are still back there on the railroad track. I hope they didn't get smashed."

"They're probably all right, if they were between the rails. I'll run back and get them," Lydia's father offered. Quickly he dashed back, and soon he returned with two pairs of shoes and two pairs of stockings. They were not hurt at all, and each girl happily took her own.

As they walked along now, the girls stayed close to their parents. Sara clung to Father's hand. While the bruises ached and the abrasions burned as they walked along, she was thinking seriously. *Father had to hurt me a little to keep me from getting hurt badly. And I am glad he did. I have a wonderful, wonderful father.*

"God is like Father," Mother explained later. "He watches over us and protects us, but sometimes He allows us to suffer to keep us from greater pains."

Sara could not comprehend all the truth of

her mother's statement, but she often pondered it; and later in life she understood more fully the meaning of Mother's words.

Soon after school started again that fall, Sara experienced the joy of having another little brother. Father asked the girls what they wanted to name him. Sara and Marie agreed on Joseph, one of their favorite Bible characters, and Father and Mother were agreed. The new baby was named Joseph.

For eighteen months Joseph added joy and delight to the Yoder home. Then he suddenly became ill. For several days he was very sick. Sara, an industrious eight-year-old, helped her mother all she could to take care of Marie, James, and six-month-old Lois, and to fix the meals. With the help of Marie, she folded the clothes and did the ironing after school. She helped Father make the rows in the early garden and plant peas and onions and lettuce. She made oatmeal for breakfast and potatoes for supper, and Marie and James willingly set the table, while Mother tended to Joseph.

Often as they worked together, all three children would pause to kneel in the kitchen and ask God to heal their little brother if it was His will. Nearby, Mother gently rocked Joseph and sang softly. When the end of the week came, Sara was very tired, and Mother was too. Finally one evening Joseph seemed to be sleeping soundly, and Mother tiptoed to his little bed in the bedroom and softly laid him down. Then she quickly tucked the other children into their beds and tried to get some rest.

Each time Mother got up to tend Lois through the night, she also tiptoed softly to Joseph's bed and checked on the small boy. He seemed to be resting well, and she did not want to awaken him.

At the usual time in the morning, Mother had breakfast ready. Not a sound had yet been heard out of Joseph. Before he sat to the table, Father went into the bedroom once more to check on the sick child. When he returned to the kitchen several minutes later, he had a strange look on his face. Sara noticed and wondered about it. Father walked to Mother and said something very softly to her. Then Father and Mother went to the bedroom together. When they returned to the kitchen, Father and Mother found three silent children waiting for them with questioning eyes.

Mother wept softly while Father explained to the children that God had taken their little brother to heaven. "Now he will not suffer anymore," Father said. "We will miss him, but God knows what is best. We must try to think about how happy Joseph is, safe in the arms of Jesus." Father cleared his throat. Marie and James looked at Father questioningly, but Sara took a deep breath and quietly burst into sobs. She understood that Joseph had died.

Many people came to visit and bring food to help Mother with meals for the family and guests. Sara was numb with grief. How she had loved Joseph. Lydia came over with her parents, but the little girls did not play. It was a long day, but finally, when everyone had left, Father read the Bible and prayed just as usual before bedtime. Then while Father went to tuck James and Marie into their beds, Mother began feeding Lois.

Sara lingered in the kitchen. "Mother, I don't feel like going to bed this evening," Sara confided tearfully. The young girl had never faced a real sorrow before.

"Shall we wait till Father is finished getting the younger ones to bed," Mother suggested sympathetically, "and have a little talk with him? Then I think you will want to go to bed and sleep awhile. You will get too tired if you do not sleep tonight."

Sara nodded, snuggling closer to Mother's comforting arm, which was around her. She could hardly talk past the lump in her throat.

"God is good, and His wisdom is so much greater than ours," Father explained when he came to sit with Sara and Mother. Father and Mother talked a long time with Sara about death and heaven and God's wonderful provision for those who love Him. Then Sara was able to smile and was willing to go to bed. Her fears and questions had been stilled by the calm

serenity of her parents. Her reverence and trust
in a loving and just God was strengthened, and
she fell asleep peacefully.

*   *   *   *   *

Sara's school years passed rapidly. Seven years
was considered a good education in the early
1900s, especially in small towns like Germantown. After that, the girls got their education in
the kitchen and about the house with Mother as
teacher. Many domestic arts were learned: weaving, spinning, quilting, knitting, and sewing,
along with the daily duties of cooking, gardening, canning, washing, and cleaning. The boys
spent their teenage years with Father, learning
the techniques of farming which included ani-
mal care and many means of survival in clearing
land and making use of natural resources.

The fall that Sara was thirteen, she watched
Marie and James go off to school without her.
Mother needed a helper, and Sara learned many
valuable lessons that winter. In addition to the
two children who were going to school, two were
at home, besides Sara. Lois was now five, and
David was one.

When Ruth joined the family that winter, the
children numbered six. Mother was not very well
after Ruth was born, and she was especially glad
for the help of a big girl at home.

All winter long, Sara filled the place of Mother's helper. There was washing and cooking

and cleaning and sewing to do. She was glad for a tiny baby to care for too, and many busy days passed as she faithfully fulfilled her duties.

"I'm glad I'm out of school while there are still babies at home," Sara remarked to Mother one balmy spring day. "I didn't have as much time to help with caring for the babies who were born during my school years." Sara was now going on fourteen. She and Mother were planting potatoes in the garden plot while Lois sat on a blanket nearby holding Ruth and watching David, who was busily playing with a stick horse in the yard.

"Babies always make more work," Mother replied as she went to fill her small bucket with more potatoes, "but they are surely worth the effort. I am glad too that you are getting some experience in being responsible to care for the little ones."

As Mother observed her first child, she noticed with a sense of deep joy, as well as awesome responsibility, how rapidly the tender bud was blossoming into lovely young womanhood. Her deep brown eyes, her long brown hair, and her fair skin were as beautiful as they had been when she was a child, never having been spoiled by the vanities of the world.

To her parents' great joy, Sara gave her heart to the Lord later that spring. She was an intelligent child and had listened attentively as her

THE WAY SHE CHOSE

parents taught and instructed the family during their daily devotional times as well as by their precept and example in the daily duties of life. After Sara received Christ as her personal Saviour, she was even more conscientious than before. She had always been a tender-hearted child. Now her love for her Saviour kept her humble and sweet. There were times when the tempter got a victory in her life. But of these Sara always repented with bitter regrets and sought God's help to live in greater victory over sin.

2.

The Teenage Years

"Mother, I am so glad I will be home with you and the younger children again this year," Sara exclaimed with shining eyes on the first day of school that fall. "But I do miss being with my school friends too."

Marie, James, and Lois were walking out the driveway. Sara picked up David and held him up at the window to wave to the children. How vividly she remembered her first day of school as Lois, the new first grader, turned and waved.

"Bashful little Lois. I'm glad she has an older brother and sister to go with her today. It was hard for me to go alone on my first day," Sara murmured. "But not as hard as it would be for Lois. She is so timid."

Sara stopped for a moment to talk to baby Ruth as she passed her playpen. She was delighted when the baby quickly pulled herself up and begged for her. "Be careful, David," Sara said, restraining her little brother's arm. "Touch Ruthie gently. She isn't very big yet." Carefully guiding David's hand, Sara lovingly laid it softly against Ruth's cheek. "That's right," she encouraged. "We must be very gentle with little sister." David smiled and patted the little pink cheek softly while Ruth smiled and prattled happily to him.

"Someday Ruthie will be big enough to play with me," David said. "Then I will share my toys with her and give her a ride on my back the way Father gives me rides."

Sara chuckled. "You love baby sister, don't you?" *By the time Ruth is big enough to safely ride on David's back,* Sara was thinking, *she'll probably be too heavy for him.* But David would not understand that now. The important thing was for him to learn to love her and handle her gently. Sara set up the ironing board where baby Ruth could watch her and where she could talk to Ruth while she ironed.

Mother was busy baking bread, and there was a big ironing to do. The little cottage rang with joyful praises as Mother and daughter sang together while they worked. Their home was filled with joy. The baby played happily, at times watching Sara move and turn the clothes across the ironing board. And David played with some blocks of wood nearby, building a barn and barn-yard for his pretend animals. The morning passed quickly and pleasantly for the Yoder family.

"How nice it is to have my big girl home from school!" Mother exclaimed when Father came in for dinner. Father's smile of satisfaction pleased Sara and warmed her heart. She lowered her eyes modestly, not wanting to glory in the praises of her parents.

"I'm glad you have the help you need again this fall," Father agreed. "Before Sara was out of school, I often thought it would be nice for you to have help. But good hired help is hard to find, since many of our young sisters are beginning to work in factories where they can earn more."

"Oh, I made out all right," Mother said with a sweet smile. "You always were very helpful when I needed it most. As scarce as money was those first years, we could hardly have afforded help if it had been available. You could have used a hired man on the farm too, before James was old enough to help."

Father nodded as he replied, "It certainly does help since James can do the milking. And even though he is only ten, he did well handling the team with the cultivator this past summer. And Marie does well taking care of the chickens." Father looked across the table at David sitting on his stool. "Soon David will be old enough to

THE WAY SHE CHOSE

come out and feed the calves and help with a few other little chores." David smiled happily at his father as he cleaned out his bowl.

"Yes, even at two he can run a lot of little errands for me in the house," Mother agreed with a smile.

As soon as the noon meal was finished, Sara cleared the table, putting away the food and washing the dishes while Mother put David and Ruth to bed for naps. Father dozed awhile in his big chair before going out to finish picking corn. When he awoke, Sara was back at the ironing board.

As Father walked out to the field, he mused thankfully, *Sara is a helpful, cheerful daughter. She is so much like her mother.* As his habit often was when he thought of one of the children, he prayed for her. *Father in heaven, I thank Thee for Sara. Keep her ever true to Thee. Guide her and keep her from the snares and pitfalls of the enemy of our souls. May she always be a consistent example to the younger children. Bless those in school today, and the little ones in the house with Mother.*

Days and weeks passed rapidly. The Yoder children enjoyed the quiet farm and family life. Each doing his share brought a spirit of contentment in the home.

If only such tranquility could have continued! But into the peace of each home in the Germantown Valley rose the awful specter of war. Even in this forsaken valley, the news finally came that "the whole world was at war." When rumors reached the valley that the United States had declared war on Germany on April 6, 1917, the peace-loving people began to have serious thoughts about how their own little group would be affected.

Brother Mast continued to faithfully preach and teach. "The Christian's duty," he reminded them, "is peace and love to all men. There is no alternative for love for our enemies and non-resistance to evil. If we are called upon to fight for our country, we must suffer rather than take up arms."

The time did come when the young men were drafted. For a time some could claim exemption by paying a three-hundred-dollar fine. Some hired someone else to take their place. Then convictions grew, and the brethren no longer felt it was right to hire another to take their place. "It is not consistent to hire one who has no convictions against fighting. It is the same as taking part ourselves."

Then another problem arose. First they were *encouraged* to buy war bonds to raise money for the war chest. Then the government *demanded* that they help the cause of their country by buying them. Again, for conscience' sake, the Christians could not participate, and so they were labeled traitors.

As the war continued, and more and more men were drafted, the government made less allowance for the conscientious objectors, who would not fight. A few men in the valley gave in to the pressure and signed up. Others went into hiding.

One day Sara came in from doing her chores to find Mother crying. "What has happened?" Sara asked in great concern.

"Father is gone," Mother replied in a strained voice.

"But—where is he?"

"I don't know."

Sara had known that Father was in danger and did not go out of the house more than necessary. Neighbors were becoming angry that the Mennonite young men and boys were not out on the battlefront with theirs. Several men had been tarred and feathered, and some barns had been painted yellow to show that those men were not helping their country.

Sara knew all that, but somehow it was hard to take it personally. Until now . . . "But where is Father?" she repeated anxiously. "Has . . . has something happened to him?"

"He is hiding," Mother answered. "But I do not know where. He saw men coming in the lane, and he went out the back door on the run. He had told me he has a place to hide, and that I am not to know where it is."

"What did the men want? Did they see him go?" Sara could hardly think straight for the fear in her heart.

"They did not see him. They just asked if there are any young men in this house old enough to sign up for the draft, and I could answer them 'no.' They left without any more questions."

Mother quickly dried her eyes and got up to finish fixing supper. Sara still stood motionless, hardly able to grasp the impact on their family that Father's going away would have. "Father said he won't be far away," Mother added comfortingly. "He has told James where he will be so that James can take him food and water early each morning."

With Father away, more of the chores fell on Sara. She worked willingly, doing more than her share. The cows needed to be milked, the firewood cut, and so many other chores attended to. Marie and James helped after school as much as they could, while Lois helped Mother in the house.

The dreary winter days dragged on. In many homes the father or older sons were missing. There was much need. But almost worse than the lack of adequate food was the continued tension between the Mennonites and their neighbors.

Finally the war ended. Fathers and sons came home to their weary and hungry families. Father came home, pale and gaunt from his months of hiding. Spring came and gardens were planted. Life somehow began to resume a semblance of normality.

Some of the Germantown young people, happy in the release from wartime tensions, put forth new efforts to arrange for social gatherings.

More and more often, Sara neglected her daily Bible reading and prayer, justifying herself with the excuse that she did not have time. Communion with the Lord did not seem nearly as important as it once had. Rather, she began to find greater satisfaction in the opportunities to be with friends at church or at the occasional youth socials.

Sara and her best friend, Lydia, often had confidential chats about which of the young men each would choose. Such subjects had been topics of conversation among the older girls while they were still in school, and they became part of social life at church as well. Lydia would beg Sara to tell her whom she liked. But Sara was not sure herself. "Oh, there's really no one in the Germantown Valley that takes my eye," she replied one day. "Maybe somebody really special will come along one of these days!"

"To this forsaken valley?" Lydia laughed. And so the girls would talk and dream, hurrying the time when they each would be old enough to have a special friend. Such discussions were unchecked by the church and only weakly addressed by parents. This paved the way for failure in courtships and marriages.

As summer changed to fall and fall to winter, Sara, now seventeen, began to grow restless and dissatisfied. Certainly life must hold more for her than never-ending work day after day—weaving and quilting and sewing and washing. With the colder weather and poorer road conditions, the social activities among the youth came to a stop and Sara's restlessness increased.

Life at home became more and more of a drudgery, rather than the pleasure it had used to be. It seemed the work in a big family was never finished! And the long winter days seemed especially lonely with all the other older children in school.

"Mother," Sara complained one January morning, "my bread never turns out as good as yours. I would rather always do the sewing or ironing and let you bake."

"But, Sara, you must learn the art of making good bread also, and yours has been turning out better each time you try it. I think I should iron today," Mother said firmly.

"I guess I would like to learn, if everyone can put up with my efforts," Sara finally agreed reluctantly.

"I haven't heard anyone complain," Mother

said, smiling at Sara as she set up the ironing board.

"Mother," Sara began when dinner was over, "may I walk over and visit Lydia Miller awhile? I haven't seen her for so long, except at church. I would enjoy so much to have a good visit with her again." She glanced hopefully at Mother, who was back at the ironing board.

"Well, now that the baking is done, I believe I could spare you," Mother replied thoughtfully. Then she looked up as Sara coughed hoarsely. "But what about that cough you have?" she asked. "I really don't think you should be out this afternoon," she decided. "It is so cold and damp; I believe we will see snow flying before evening."

Mother, sensing Sara's disappointment, added, "I will be happy for you to go some other time. I know that you and Lydia haven't seen much of each other lately and that these winter days can seem long to girls your age. Next year when Marie is out of school too, the two of you can enjoy being together more."

"I wish I would still be in school," Sara blurted out. "It isn't fair that I had to quit at thirteen and Marie will be sixteen before she quits!"

"You know why we have allowed Marie to stay in school," Mother said patiently, even though Sara had already heard the explanation many times. "She does not learn as fast as you did, and we felt she needed the extra time in school."

"Well, at least you could allow me to go to Lydia's today!" Sara insisted perversely.

"Not this time," Mother returned firmly. Mother, considering the matter settled, went to the bedroom to check on Ruth, who had suddenly begun to cry.

Sara sighed and walked over to a stack of mending that Mother had laid aside while she was ironing. Rebellious thoughts churned inside her, making her feel miserable. Sorting through the stack, she chose several shirts that had lost buttons, and sat down with the button box to find buttons to match.

As she worked, Sara heard Father kick off his barn boots and hang his coat in the pantry. *I wonder why he has come in so early today. It won't be time for supper for a long time yet.* Sara looked up when Father entered the room and drew the old hickory rocking chair up in front of the fireplace.

"I am not feeling very well," he explained, "and that wind is so bitter. I think I will spend the rest of the afternoon near the fire."

"Is it going to snow, Father?" Sara asked, looking out at the gray, overcast sky.

"I think it will tonight," he replied. "But I'm not expecting it to this afternoon." Father pulled his chair nearer to the crackling wood fire, enjoying the warmth as well as finding pleasure in the warm feeling of seeing his oldest daughter dutifully mending the family's clothes. *She has been a faithful, obedient daughter—a good worker,* he mused with a feeling of satisfaction.

As he rested, John Yoder had no idea of the struggle going on in Sara's mind, nor her reason for inquiring about the weather. If he had, he would not have considered her such a faithful and obedient daughter.

"Father," Sara began again after a while, "it *is* cold outside. But if I bundled up well, it wouldn't hurt me, would it?"

"No, I don't suppose it would," he agreed readily, entirely oblivious to her scheme and the rebellion that was in her young heart. "A crisp, cold wind would do you no harm if you were dressed for it. You are strong and healthy." He smiled. "But why would you want to go outside? There are no chores for you to do. I did all I could before I came in. When the children come home from school, I will go out again and help finish them up."

"I wasn't thinking about doing chores, Father. I was wondering . . ." She hesitated. Her eyes dare not meet Father's. She began again. "I was wondering if I could run over to the Millers awhile. It has been so long since Lydia and I have been together on a weekday, because we have been so busy all fall and winter. They live close. I wouldn't be outside long. May I?"

48

Though Father knew nothing of Mother's answer a few minutes before to this same question, Sara felt afraid to meet his steady gaze. She felt guilty. Never did he and Mother oppose one another. When one spoke to the children, the other always stood behind the decision that had been made. Suddenly Sara hoped he would say no. How could she go to the Millers after Mother had just said she should not go? Father would never say yes if he knew Mother had just said no.

Father paused a long while, looking out the window. "Where is Mother?" he asked.

"She is with Ruth," Sara answered softly.

"Yes, Sara," he answered at last. "You may go. I am sure Mother won't mind. You have been a faithful daughter. You deserve a little vacation." He looked at his oldest daughter fondly.

Sara's heart pounded. Reluctantly she laid her mending aside. *What have I done? Father's confidence in me makes me feel terrible. I don't deserve it. Oh, I wish he had said no.* Slowly she walked over to the pantry to get her coat. She felt deceitful and wicked. She no longer had any desire to see her best friend just across the field. Why had she ever thought she could get by with this?

Then Sara thought of Mother. Mother would soon be coming out of the bedroom. She quickly struggled to get into her coat. *I do not want to be here when Mother steps out but I do have permission to go.* She tried to ease her conscience.

But Mother will wonder where I am going, and then Father will find out what I have done. He will sooner or later, probably. But right now Sara wanted to be out of the house. She could not face the exposure of her deceit with Father and Mother both looking reproachfully at her.

Father continued to compliment Sara, "Not every girl your age is able or willing to help as you have helped your mother this winter. We appreciate this, and if there is nothing pressing to do just now, I'm sure Mother would agree that you should have a little free time."

Evading Father's eyes, Sara headed for the door. His praise gave her no warm feeling; rather, it made her feel more wretched. *It's good Father doesn't know how rebellious I feel,* she thought morosely.

As she reached the door, Mother stepped out of the bedroom. In response to Father's last words, she said pleasantly, "Yes, the mending can wait. The work is all caught up. Sara certainly does deserve some free time. What would she like to do this afternoon?"

Sara's hand seemed frozen to the doorknob. Her face burned. She felt glued to the spot.

"Sara is going over to see Lydia for a while. I was just telling her I am sure you would agree that she deserves some free time," Father explained to Mother.

Mother looked at Sara standing at the door

dressed for the cold outdoors, and suddenly a look of disappointment and sadness clouded the happiness on her face. Slowly she said, "Father, I had asked her to wait to go to Lydia's until another day because of her cold. I will be glad to give her time off to read a book or rest, or anything she would like to do inside."

Father turned surprised and stern eyes toward Sara. Immediately her eyes dropped. She could not stand the hurt in the usually kind and loving gaze.

"Sara, I am deeply disappointed that you would ignore Mother's decision, and then try to secure my permission without my knowing that Mother had already given you an answer." Father's kind and yet stern tone of voice brought quick tears to Sara's eyes.

"I—I wanted to go so badly, Father," Sara faltered. But how flimsy that excuse sounded now. How childish. With shame, Sara began to unbutton her coat.

"You knew better than to ask me to go to visit Lydia without explaining what Mother had already told you," Father rebuked her. "I realize that it is not often that you go to visit your friends and that you would enjoy more fellowship among the young people. But deceitfully getting what you want is very wrong and will never bring you any real happiness."

Hot tears burned Sara's eyes as she hung up

her coat and sat down on the sofa. She picked up the shirts she had been working on. "I am sorry, Mother and Father," she said humbly. "I will try to be more cheerfully obedient. I knew I shouldn't have asked your permission, Father, after Mother had said no. I knew if you had heard what Mother had told me, you would have been in full agreement with her."

"That is right, Sara. You are forgiven. Let's kneel together here and talk to the Lord about it," Father suggested, "Sara, you pray first." The three knelt together there in the living room. Knowing what her father expected of her, Sara prayed brokenly, confessing and asking for strength to be a faithful daughter. Father and Mother prayed in turn, asking the Lord to keep their daughter from the devil's snares. They also asked for wisdom for themselves so that they would know how to meet the needs of the young souls in their home.

When Mother started mending again, Father asked Sara, "Want to play checkers till the children get home from school? Or, Mother, you could play with her and I can watch. You need to relax too."

Sara did not really feel like playing checkers, but she dutifully got the game and set it up.

"You two go ahead and play," Mother said pleasantly. "I can relax while I work at the mending."

After the third game was finished, the schoolchildren burst in the door. "It's really getting cold out there," James announced, rubbing his hands. "Feels like snow."

"Yes, it does," Mother agreed with a welcoming smile to the children. "All of you go change your clothes, and then you may have a snack."

When the children had gone to their rooms, Mother asked Sara, "What shall we have for supper?"

"I don't know," Sara replied listlessly. "I don't feel hungry for anything."

"It is probably your cold making you feel that way," Mother sympathized. Going to Sara, she felt her forehead. "I don't believe you have a fever," she murmured. "But you should plan to go to bed early tonight so you are sure to get plenty of rest."

"Oh, I'll be all right," Sara responded shortly. She went to the cellar for a pan of potatoes. Why did she feel so despondent? Was it her cold, the weather, or what?

When Sara started peeling the potatoes, Mother walked out to the springhouse. Looking around thoughtfully, she spotted the cream. *Just the thing,* she mused. *I'll take some fresh cream in to whip. We will open a jar of peaches. Perhaps Sara's favorite dessert will help her feel like eating.*

Father stood up, reluctant to leave his warm chair and the warm house. While the children were in their rooms changing their school clothes for barn clothes, Father put on his coat and boots. "Are you in the kitchen alone this evening?" he asked Sara. "Should I let Marie stay in to help you?"

"No," Sara replied impatiently, "the old woman just went for something at the springhouse. She'll help—"

"Sara!" Father's voice shocked her into a keen realization of the great disrespect she had just shown toward her dear mother. That was a term Sara had often heard in her school days, but never before had she used it, nor heard it used in her home. Tears of remorse splashed into the water with the potatoes she was peeling. *Oh, why did I answer that way?* Sara could not understand herself. Why had she twice disrespected her dear Mother this miserable afternoon?

Just then Mother entered the kitchen, humming a happy tune. She was carrying the fresh, foamy cream and a dish of butter.

Oh, I hope Father doesn't say any more! Sara panicked. *Never would I want Mother to hear what I said. I'd rather take a whipping.* Sara cringed. She had not been spanked for years. But right now nothing would hurt worse than for Mother to know how disrespectfully she had spoken of her.

Without a word, Father turned and walked toward the door. Sara looked around. None of the schoolchildren had come out of their rooms yet. A flood of relief swept over her. Suppose they had heard her and she would hear them use that expression themselves sometime, saying that they had learned it from their oldest sister.

"Are you feeling better?" Mother asked Father as he stood at the door.

"Yes, sitting by the heat this afternoon has helped some, I believe," he replied. His voice sounded sad and heavy, Sara thought. "Send the children out right away so we can finish the chores early," he added.

Sara kept her face turned toward the window. *I must control myself better*, she decided. *I am only making myself and those I love unhappy by acting this way.* Hot tears blinded her eyes.

In the days that followed, Sara put forth real effort to be more cheerful and submissive to her parents. She began spending more time in her private devotions. *O Father in heaven*, she prayed fervently, *I have not been spending enough time with You! I'm truly sorry. Help me do better.* Fellowship with her Lord grew sweeter as she more earnestly sought His help to live above self and sin. By His grace, her life was enriched and sweetened. She grew stronger in the faith, earnestly seeking to set a good example for her younger brothers and sisters.

*   *   *   *   *

There was much excitement in the small Germantown Valley the day the news began to circulate that the Millers had sold their farm. A new family was moving into Germantown soon. It was, however, a sad day for Sara. Such a move meant that Lydia, her closest friend, would be moving to a distant state. In Sara's almost eighteen years there had been only a few small changes in the comfortable little community, and they had not affected her greatly. She could remember only one time that a new family had moved in, and that was in her early school years. She found it hard to imagine how life could go on without Lydia, the one with whom she had shared all her confidences since her early years!

"Father, do the Benders have anyone my age?" she asked hopefully. Perhaps the new neighbors would have a girl near her age and she could make a new friend, though she was sure that would never make up for the loss of her dear friend Lydia.

"I don't know," Father replied. "But they have ten children under eighteen years of age, so there is a good possibility that they will have children near the ages of most of you," he said comfortingly.

"Oh, I hope the oldest is a girl," Sara replied, "to fill the vacancy Lydia will leave."

"That would be nice," Father said, smiling at Sara's eagerness. "Brother Miller did say that this farm is just what the Benders need to keep all those big boys busy."

Sara looked crestfallen as she voiced her assumption, "I suppose that means then that only the very youngest are girls!"

Mother smiled. "Just because he has some big boys doesn't say there isn't an older girl. We had better wait and see before we form too many opinions."

They had only a few days to wait. The Benders had sent their household belongings ahead of them on the freight train, and they followed soon afterward on a passenger train pulled by a large steam engine. The train depot was in the center of Germantown, right across the road from the small country store. And so, on the day they arrived, the Benders' horse-drawn wagons, loaded with household supplies and farm equipment, drew the attention of everyone in Germantown. Rattling south along the dirt road came the two large farm wagons behind four big Belgium horses. The wagons were loaded with furniture and some farm items. Several boys were seated on top of the furniture, and walking beside the wagon were several more boys leading some cows and goats. A horse-drawn carriage carrying the rest of the family followed these.

From every house in Germantown, someone watched this unusual procession. Father was working in the strawberry patch near the road.

"Howdy, neighbor," Reuben Bender called out, halting the team he was driving. "You must be Mr. Yoder. Your farm joins the Miller place, doesn't it?"

"Yes, I'm John Yoder, and our farm adjoins the Millers'," Father answered. "Welcome to Germantown Valley. We hope you will like it here."

"Oh, we will," the big, husky man assured him in his booming voice. "It looks as though crops do well here. That is just what we are looking for."

Inside the house, Sara hid behind the heavy curtains inside the windows, well concealed from view. She could not hear all that Father had said, but she did hear him say, "When we moved here, we were basically interested in a Bible-believing and Bible-practicing church, and we believe we have that here." Sara was eagerly searching the faces of the Bender children who were peering from the carriage windows, as well as that of a tall, dark-haired young man by the side of one of the wagons. A few long strides brought the young man across the dusty road to the edge of the field where Father stood talking to Mr. Bender.

"Good evening, Mr. Yoder." His deep bass voice sounded plain and clear through the open window. "Glad to meet you."

Sara watched the young man admiringly as he spoke to Father. *So handsome and manly looking,* she breathed to herself. *Wonder how old he is!* She was ashamed of herself for entertaining such thoughts, because her parents had taught her better than that. But what could be wrong with noticing the fine qualities of a young man? She wished with all her heart that Lydia were here to share this moment! Lydia had laughed at the idea that a "special somebody" could ever come to this valley! Sara allowed her inappropriate thoughts to continue to wander, further obstructing her ability to think right in relation to the sacred subject of courtship and marriage.

Sara continued to scan the children she could see. If only there would be a girl her age. She was sure that the two or three oldest children were boys, and she could see a few little girls. There did not appear to be any older girls. *Lydia and I will write,* she tried to console herself, swallowing her disappointment bravely. *But writing is not like having a friend right here I can talk to.*

"Come on, son," the older man called, "we'd better be moving on. It won't be many hours till dark. We have lots of work to do before we will have beds to sleep on tonight." The procession moved on.

"Imagine traveling all the way from Minnesota on a train with all that stuff!" Sara watched with interest. But her thoughts were with the memories of the last day she had spent with Lydia, helping to load their wagons.

Soon Father came up to the porch. Sara left

her lookout by the window when Father called in the back door, "Mother, our new neighbors have arrived."

Mother walked to the kitchen door, where all the Yoder children joined their parents to hear what Father had learned about the new family.

"It is late to be arriving," Mother remarked in concern. "There is no furniture in the house, and there will be supper to fix."

"I wondered if we would have something here to help them out this evening," Father suggested. "I want to go over and help them unload in a few minutes. Would you have anything handy to send along?"

"Surely," Mother agreed thoughtfully. "We have several apple pies baked, and we could spare that dish of potato salad. We could also send them one of those rolls of summer sausage hanging out in the smokehouse, and a few loaves of bread."

"Maybe some of the children could walk over with me to help carry the food. Or would you like to go along, Mother?" Father asked.

"Not this evening. I am almost too tired, and you will want to stay awhile to help. I'll go another time."

"I want to go. I want to go too," the younger children cried.

"Not this time," Father answered kindly. "I think we will take some of the older children.

You may go when Mother and I go over to visit some evening soon."

Sara was hoping her parents would suggest she could go. And they did! "Sara, you carry this large pie," Mother suggested, "and Marie the bowl of potato salad. James, maybe you should go too, to carry the bread." Father went to the smokehouse to get a roll of sausage.

"Won't you need help preparing supper here?" Sara asked, trying to hide her eagerness to accompany the others.

"No," Mother assured her. "Lois can give me the help I need this time." She handed the food to the three oldest children.

When Father returned with the roll of sausage and a bowl of fresh, creamy butter, the four started down the road the Bender wagons had traveled half an hour earlier. It was a pleasant evening and the Yoders enjoyed the walk, arriving just before the sun dropped below the hill behind the home of their new neighbors.

A wave of homesickness for the former residents of the old farmhouse swept over Sara as Father knocked at the door. He had to knock loudly several times before he got anyone's attention. Even then, when the door finally opened, the commotion inside almost drowned out their voices. Mrs. Bender opened the door wide and invited, "Step inside."

"Reuben," she called, "see who is here." The

big, husky man made his appearance from behind several big boxes and chests.

"I can't find a lamp," he explained, lifting several more lids. "It will soon be dark. Say! That
pie looks good, and I'm hungry. I could eat it all
myself, but I'd have to get to it before the boys
do!" Reuben laughed and continued his search
for a lamp.

Several small children scampered in the back
door, all talking at once. "Someone is here! They
brought us some supper! It looks like the man
Father talked to along the way."

"Quiet! Quiet!" Mrs. Bender silenced them,
very much embarrassed by their noisy remarks.

A girl who appeared to be a little younger
than Marie peeped over the chest her father had
opened. Then the tall, dark-haired young man,
whom they later learned was the oldest son,
looked up from the bed ends he had been adjust-
ing in the adjoining room. "Hi!" he called. "Say,
what's all this? A feast, on our first night in
Germantown! This is going to be great! What
great neighbors! I know we will feel at home and
love it here."

Mrs. Bender had relieved Father and James
of the food they carried, placing it on the table
in the middle of the living room. Before she
reached Sara, her oldest son had stepped
through the bedroom door and walked toward
the young ladies.

"We certainly thank you kind people," he said graciously, reaching for the delicious-looking pie. Taking the large pie plate in one hand, with the other he firmly squeezed the hand that offered it to him before Sara had time to draw it back. "We want to learn to know you folks. We will be seeing more of you," he said, looking straight into her eyes until Sara lowered hers, blushing. Even though she enjoyed his attention, she felt embarrassed. She was not accustomed to this familiar kind of attention from a young man and wished she could still the strange stirrings within her.

"Are these all your children?" the young man inquired with a sweeping glance at the three young people.

"No," Father answered. "There are three younger ones at home with Mother."

"If they are all as good looking as these young ladies, you have a mighty nice family," the tall boy responded, fastening his admiring gaze again upon Sara until she again looked away in embarrassment. The young man apparently enjoyed seeing her blush, she decided.

Reuben Bender stood up and began introducing his family from the youngest to the oldest. "And Jacob will be eighteen next week," he finished.

Sara again glanced up, meeting Jacob's eyes. *He is only a couple months older than I am,* she thought.

"We must go," Father said, after helping to carry in the last pieces of heavy furniture. He started toward the door. The light had faded while they were inside, and now evening twilight had turned to a starlit night. "Come and see us," Father invited cordially as he stepped outside.

Jacob followed Father to the door and held it open for the rest. As Sara walked past him, he said softly, "Please come again." Sara quickly stepped across the porch to join her family, glad that no one had seen the special attention he had shown her.

The Yoders walked home quietly. Mother and the younger children were waiting eagerly to hear more about the new neighbors. "We don't want to judge them too quickly," Father began slowly, after telling a few details of their evening with the Benders. "But I cannot approve of the way they talk. They are friendly enough, but very casual in appearance and speech. In associating with them, we want to be careful to be a good testimony for our Lord in areas of speech, dress, modesty, and a proper reserve.

"When I tried to bring spiritual things into our conversation," Father continued, "I found little spiritual interest in that home. Hopefully we will find it different after we learn to know them better."

3.

The Oldest Son

At ten minutes after nine on Sunday morning, the Yoder family arrived at the Germantown Valley Mennonite Church. Quietly they went inside, took their seats, and waited reverently for the service to begin at nine-thirty.

Sara and Marie took their usual places among the young girls on the third bench. Mother walked to the front bench with Lois and Ruth. James and David sat on either side of Father. Several other families were coming in. Soon there were half a dozen girls on the bench with Sara and Marie Yoder.

The back door was constantly opening as the Germantown people gathered for worship. Sara could hardly refrain from looking back to see who was entering. The Reuben Bender family was on her mind. It was almost nine-thirty, and she was quite sure they had not yet arrived, that is, unless they were all seated behind the third bench. Sara was sure they had not come in though, because each time the door opened, the footsteps were familiar.

Sara wished the Benders would hurry. Seldom was anyone late for the worship service without a very good reason. Sara found herself making excuses for the new family. They had just moved in and were hardly settled yet. They were on a big farm, and it would take some time to get everything organized properly.

The singers at the singers' table began to sing the opening song, and the congregation joined in. The first two songs were sung. Still only the regular members were there. Surely something must be wrong; Sara was convinced of it. To miss a church service, or even to be late to one, was as unheard-of in the Yoder home as to forget mealtime. It was something that just did not happen.

At quarter till ten the door opened again. There was a lot of shuffling, whispering, and moving about in the rear of the building. As the superintendent began reading the Scripture that introduced the Sunday school lesson, Reuben Bender walked to the front and took the seat next to Father and the Yoder sons.

Two of the Bender girls made their way to the bench where the girls sat. Several smiled and made room for them. The strangers were a few years younger than the rest of the girls on the bench, and their conduct soon proved that they should have been sitting with their mother.

Brother Mast brought a very inspiring message. Sara noticed Reuben Bender's head nod several times. It was not the first time she had ever seen a brother sleep in church, but never before like this. By the middle of the sermon, his chin was resting on the front of his shirt. Several times she thought she heard him snore. Sara tried not to glance in his direction anymore. His poor wife must be dreadfully embarrassed. Sara excused him, telling herself that Mr. Bender must be very tired. But she could not imagine her father sitting in that position in a church service, no matter how tired he was.

There were other faithful members watching the Bender family that morning too. Some wondered, *How spiritually-minded are these people? What contribution will they make to the Germantown Valley church? Are they really interested in church building?*

There was an unusual commotion in the rear of the church. Several fathers looked back disapprovingly to see if their sons could possibly be involved. But neither Mr. nor Mrs. Bender seemed to notice that it was their children who

were moving about, whispering, and even writing in the hymnbooks.

Sara heard the commotion too, and, though
it was very distracting, she did not look back.
Instead she bowed her head and prayed for an
open heart to receive the message from God's
Word. Then she made a sincere attempt to keep
her mind on the message.

Following dismissal, there were warm hand-
shakes and friendly greetings. Everyone wanted
to meet the new family. They were welcomed
into the neighborhood, and into the church, as
everyone's thought was that the Benders would
surely want to be a part of the church and that
they would apply for church membership soon.
Of course their young people would mingle with
the Germantown young people and later in life
intermarry with the group they would then be a
part of. Since this was to be expected, some parents immediately felt a deep concern for the obvious spiritual needs in the Bender family. Other
more careless ones did not immediately sense
the danger.

"Where were you members before coming
here?" kind Sister Mast asked, without a thought
of causing embarrassment.

Mrs. Bender began to fumble for words. "Well,
we haven't been members anywhere for a few
years. Ever since we moved West, we have not
found a church we were satisfied with. We are

hoping to settle down now and join the church.
I realize it is high time to get our young people
established in a church."

"Will you folks come with us for dinner?" Mary
Yoder invited cordially, greeting Mrs. Bender.

"Oh, there are so many of us," Mrs. Bender
began to apologize.

"That is no problem," Mary assured her. "I
enjoy large families. We want to become
acquainted with you folks. Are you pretty well
settled in?"

"Oh, I guess," Mrs. Bender laughed, "considering that we just arrived. Things are still a
bit mixed up, and some things are misplaced.
We have moved so often. I just hope we can stay
settled awhile now." She added the last words
with a slight hint of weariness. "I think I will love
it here in this quiet little valley."

"We hope you will," Mary replied warmly. Her
smile was sincere and heartwarming.

The Benders and the Yoders enjoyed a good
dinner of mashed potatoes, beef roast, and gravy.
They visited a long while around the table as they
enjoyed the first course, and then there was
dessert—apple pie with cream. Even the hearty
appetites of all the Benders could not exhaust
Mother Yoder's generous supply of good food.

"Who baked the delicious pies?" Jacob asked,
taking his third piece.

"I believe Sara did this time," Father answered

when Sara modestly remained silent. "But Marie's are just as good. Unless I am here and see who does the baking, I never know for sure if it was Mother or one of the girls."

"Any girl who can bake a pie like this is ready to start housekeeping, I'd say." Jacob let out a whistle of delight, forking up another large bite of pie.

Sarah blushed self-consciously. Jacob was looking straight at her, apparently enjoying the color that rose in her face.

"There is a lot more responsibility in house-keeping than just knowing how to bake good apple pies," Father said soberly.

Throughout the afternoon, Father tried to steer the conversation to spiritual things, but at such times Mr. Bender had nothing to offer. However, when such subjects as farming, fishing, or recollections of school days were brought up, he was very talkative, saying quite a few things that Sara was sure her father did not approve of.

"You all come over," Reuben invited as they were leaving at about four o'clock in the afternoon.

"Yes, we want to do that sometime," Father replied.

"Let your young people come over and spend the evening sometimes," Mr. Bender urged. "I think it would do ours good to be with yours."

Father smiled. "Your children are welcome

to come to our home sometimes too. We normally do not allow our children to be away many evenings. We like to spend most of our evenings together as a family."

"Well, we're neighbors, and I do hope you'll let them come over often," Reuben said. "Our youngsters came from a much larger community than this, where there was a lot of activity. There were plenty of social gatherings to keep them occupied. I believe they will miss their old community too much if we don't keep some activities going here."

"Our young people enjoy going with us to visit the elderly and helping where there are needs in the church. Occasionally we have a young folks' singing or some other such social activity," Father kindly informed Reuben Bender.

Finally the Benders went home, the younger ones riding in the horse-drawn carriage with their parents, the older ones walking.

"Children," Father began very soberly after their guests were gone, "I do not wish to talk unkindly about our new neighbors, nor to judge them too quickly, but I am afraid they are not the best company for you. I was sorry to hear Mr. Bender speak so lightly and jokingly about his misbehavior in school. The things he bragged about getting by with, he should rather be ashamed of. I hope the children will not follow his example in our school."

Mother nodded in agreement. She too expressed her disappointment in Mr. Bender's attitudes. "You children should be kind to them whenever you meet them and not talk disrespectfully about them," she continued the warning, "and we want you to accept them in your play. But be very careful if their speech and conduct is questionable. Be sure to do what you know is right."

"Maybe the children will not be like their father was in school," Sara contributed quietly. She was willing to believe the best about the Benders until they had proven themselves unworthy of that trust. "Maybe they will see the inconsistencies in their parents and want to do better. Don't you feel that sometimes it works that way?" Sara turned her eyes to her father, hoping that he did not sense her real reason for defending the family.

"Yes, Sara, that could be the case. We trust it will be that way with the Bender children, but often it isn't." Father thought a bit before continuing. "Those children do seem nice in a lot of ways. And respectful. But they have been raised in a very different environment than you have been and have habits that we won't be able to approve of. We trust they will learn to appreciate the safer environment our church here has endeavored to have for our young people. I certainly hope they will get the nurture and care here that they need to grow into spiritual and happy young people.

"Remember, they are not a part of any church. We thought the parents were, by how they appeared. But they have not been for years. As far as I know, none of the children have ever made a start in the Christian life," Father continued. "I do not want to see any of you shunning or avoiding them, or in any way causing them to think you feel too good for their company. Yet I do want you to be careful not to become close associates, so that you do not acquire any of their undesirable habits, their looseness in conduct, or their lack of reserve."

Mother nodded her head in agreement with what Father was saying. "The Bible says," she injected, "that 'evil communications corrupt good manners.'"

"That verse means that we become like the people with whom we associate," Father continued. "Mother and I want you to choose your closest companions carefully, as those choices will affect your entire lifetime, and even your eternal destiny. We will try to help you in these very important decisions."

Father had often reminded the children before of the need for carefulness in their close associations. His concern was not new to them. But this time it was in direct connection with their next-door neighbors, which made the admonition doubly necessary and serious.

The Yoders were quiet and sober as they prepared for the meeting that evening. Sara thought about the Benders. She had, for reasons known only to her, a very warm spot in her heart for them. She pitied any child who did not have the opportunity of growing up in a good, sound Christian home. She appreciated her parents and all the teaching they had given her and her brothers and sisters. *But the Bender children apparently have not had the opportunity of a good Christian home like ours,* she reasoned with herself. *They do need help, yes. But we can't judge them and say they can't do well, just because of their parents.* Sara felt a twinge of guilt. She felt she was almost making her godly father's concern invalid by her choice to defend the Benders.

They are Mennonites, she reasoned further. *It is unfortunate that there has been no sound church in the past years that they felt comfortable with.* Somehow Sara felt sure that things would soon be different, now that the Benders were in an established Mennonite community. The children all seemed so eager for the fellowship of the Christian young people.

Sara continued to reason with herself as she prepared for church. *Perhaps when we become better acquainted with them, we will see more spirituality there than we now think. We are not accustomed to their ways. Maybe we are not understanding them.* Sara hoped that this was true. She felt sure she could see in the eyes of the tall young Bender boy a look of sincerity. She was sure that behind his laughing countenance there lurked an honest desire for what was right and good.

Sara mused over the past afternoon. Jacob had seemed so gentlemanly and kind. He had very gently helped his mother into her sweater and offered to carry his sister's Bible and purse. He had given up his rocker when his father entered the room, offering it to him and going to sit with the Yoder boys on the wooden bench. His voice was so deep and kind. Sara continued to dwell on what she considered Jacob's fine qualities, hardly realizing that her infatuation for him was coloring her attitudes.

She thought of the girls. They too had seemed very polite and helpful. They had offered to help with the dishes without being reminded to do so. Their total bearing was different from the rowdy commotion the Yoders had heard that first night in the Bender home. *They were just arriving from a long, hard trip then,* she thought, wanting to excuse them. *On the other hand, maybe*—she struggled to be realistic—*maybe they were just trying to make a good impression today.*

Sara's thoughts troubled her as a battle of loyalties waged within her. She could hear Father's clear warning. But she did not want to think unkindly about the Benders, and especially not about the polite and handsome boy her own age. *But you had better heed your father's warning.* The voice of conscience pressed upon her, intruding into her feelings of defense and good-will for the new neighbors.

How should she feel? Sara herself could sense a definite lack of spirituality in the Bender home; that was not hard to see. *But they all seemed so nice and polite and friendly today. They just haven't had good spiritual teaching; that's the problem . . .*

A shrill whistle rang through the quiet evening air, cutting short her troubling thoughts. James walked to the front door. "Hi!" he called out. "Come on in."

"No, thanks," Jacob Bender answered. "We thought maybe you and a couple of your sisters would walk to church with us." The four oldest Bender children were waiting outside.

Quickly Sara brushed back her hair and placed her covering neatly on her head. She was eagerly on her way to the living room when she heard Father say, "No, son. I do not want any of you to walk. Maybe some other time. This evening it is too late. You will not be able to get there on time. Why, it is nearly time to start with the carriage. If the Benders wanted to walk, they should have started earlier."

James turned and walked out onto the porch.
"No, Jacob, I guess none of us will be walking
this evening," he called. "Father has the carriage
hitched and is about ready to start. It is plenty
late for walking. Maybe next time."

As James stepped back in the door, Father
called down the hall, "Come, girls; it is time we
get started. Mother and Ruth are already getting
into the carriage."

Sara, Marie, and Lois followed Father and
James to the carriage. The three girls got into the
back seat of the two-seated carriage. Ruth sat
between Mother and Father in the front. James
and David sat on the floor of the carriage with
their feet on the step. Father clucked to the
horses and started for the Germantown Valley
Mennonite Church.

As they passed the Bender young people,
Father pulled lightly on the reins. "I'm sorry that
we are too crowded to offer you a ride," he
called.

"We'd rather walk," Jacob replied. "We are
enjoying the fresh evening air."

Sara wished she could have said, "See, he is
not only polite and mannerly, but he also enjoys
nature." But she thought she had better not. No
doubt Father would say that Jacob was just trying to impress them, and she did not think she
could bear right now to hear such an indictment!

The Bender young people were late for

church that evening. Their parents and the younger children did not come at all. After the service, most of the young people gathered outside the front door. It was interesting to have a few new ones in the group.

"We want you all to come over on Friday evening for a get-acquainted party," Jacob informed the friendly little group. To those who inquired about the party, he answered, "We are going to make ice cream and play some games."

The young people liked this good-natured boy and crowded around to hear all about the get-acquainted party. The other Bender young people were talking excitedly too. "Everyone from ages twelve to nineteen is invited," Jacob added jovially. "We will have a good time." The party of Friday evening was the big topic of conversation among the young people the rest of that Sunday evening. Every young person was interested and wanted to be included.

"You all walk home with us," Jacob called as James walked with Sara and Marie across the churchyard. It was time to go home, and they were walking toward their carriage. Father and Mother were already waiting with the younger children in the carriage.

"Oh, I don't believe that Father would want us to walk, since it is this late," James answered. "Maybe next Sunday morning we can walk. We will see."

"Oh, come on tonight," the older boy coaxed. "Do you have to ask your father about everything you do?

"Come on, Sara," Jacob tried again. "You will if your brother does, won't you?"

Sara's pulse quickened. "I would enjoy walking if Father doesn't care," she answered eagerly. "I'll ask him."

Sara hurried to the carriage ahead of the rest, hoping to secure her parents' permission. After all, there would be a large group walking. Perhaps they would be allowed to walk this time.

But Father answered firmly, "No. Tell James and Marie to come. We are ready to go home. It is late."

Sara walked back across the churchyard. "James and Marie, Father wants us to ride tonight," she said quietly, trying to still the irritation that wanted to rise within her. "He is ready to go now."

"Aw, it would have been so much more fun if you all could have walked with us," Jacob remarked disappointedly as the Yoder young people walked away from the group.

The Yoders started home. "Mother!" Marie exclaimed. "The Benders are having a party, and all the young people twelve and over are invited."

"Yes," Mother answered quietly, glancing at Father. "We heard about it. But twelve is pretty young."

Father turned to look at the children. Sara noticed for the first time a few deep lines across his forehead. "That would include James, Marie, and Sara," he replied thoughtfully.

"Yes," James responded hopefully, standing on the step beside David. Never before had he—at not quite thirteen—been considered old enough to join the young people. He had gone on social visits only if Father and Mother were along also.

"May we all go?" he asked eagerly. For several moments Father did not answer. Sara searched his face, willing him to give a positive answer.

"We will see," he said at last. "Mother and I will talk it over."

Every child in the Yoder home knew there would be no use in asking again until Father and Mother had had time to talk the matter over. Nor at any time would there be any use in begging their parents to decide in favor of the gathering. The subject was therefore dropped verbally, but the party was not forgotten.

Friday night came, and the three oldest children were ready to leave for the Benders. Father had checked with the Benders to be sure there would be adult supervision, and he and Mother had decided to allow them to go this once. "But don't expect such permissions to be granted often," Father advised.

Before they left, the Yoder children were

instructed clearly as to what their parents expected of them. "And we expect you to be home promptly at nine o'clock," John Yoder finished his admonition to the three eager young people. "Mother and I have confidence that you will conduct yourselves wisely while there. If you should ever prove unworthy of this trust, your privileges will be greatly restricted."

Father turned to James. "Son, you are too young to be joining the young folks in their gatherings. I would not allow you to go except that we do not want the girls to walk home alone, even though it is not far. Please remember that I want the three of you to all walk home together."

"Yes, Father," James answered, feeling more grown up than he ever had before. After all, he was going along mainly as an escort for his sisters. James felt honored!

"Be sure to act like a Christian young man," his father added.

"Yes, Father," James answered again. "I will try to be all you expect of me."

John and Mary looked with concern on their three excited young people. The glowing face of Sara sent a dart of indecision through the anxious mother's heart. Were they doing the right thing in allowing their precious children to mingle so freely with such spiritually careless neighbors? But what could they do when most of the other brethren seemed not to share their concern about this gathering at the Benders'?

"Good-bye," Sara called gaily. "We will be back at nine." It was now nearly seven. The young people were expected to gather at the Benders' at seven-fifteen.

"We will need to leave at quarter till nine," Sara told her younger brother and sister, "to be home by nine. That gives us exactly one and a half hours to be with the young people." Remembering the concerned faces of her parents, Sara assured herself that she would make sure they got home in time.

"Maybe we could be there a few minutes longer if we walk fast," James laughed, eager to be with the group.

None of them realized how fast the hour and a half would pass, not knowing all the Benders' had planned for that evening. Socials held at the school on Saturday or Sunday evenings were not new. But such a gathering in a home and on a weekday evening was a more rare experience, not only for the Yoder family, but for a number of other homes in the Germantown Valley group as well.

Some of the young people had come in buggies, some had walked, and a few had come on horseback. Most of them were already there when the Yoders arrived. The boys were laughing uproariously, pushing and shoving each other around good-naturedly. They were just ready to begin cranking the first freezer of ice cream. When the first freezer was finished, another one was brought out. The girls joined the fun with light-hearted giggles as they piled on the ice and salt for the boys who were turning the freezer. Soon after eight o'clock both freezers were finished.

"Now let's play one or two games while the ice cream sets for a while to stiffen up," Jacob suggested. "We have packed it well, so it should get firmer before we are ready to eat."

"We have to be home by nine o'clock," James whispered to Jacob. That was less than an hour away now, and he did not want to miss out on the homemade ice cream!

"Nine o'clock!" Jacob exclaimed. "Why so early? Anyone else have a set time when they have to be home?" he asked the group.

Several said they were to be home by soon after nine or at least by nine-thirty. A few others said their parents would expect them by nine-thirty or ten, but had not set a limit. There were a few who declared, "It doesn't make any difference. Just whenever the party is over."

"All right, at eight-thirty we will eat ice cream," Jacob announced. "What shall we play until then?"

The Germantown young people looked at each other. They had gotten together very seldom to play games before, and they waited to see what new games the Benders might suggest.

When no one suggested any, the Benders suggested blind man's buff and whisper down the line. There was lots of laughter and commotion, but everyone enjoyed the games. At eight-thirty the ice-cream freezers were opened and everyone was served. Suddenly, in what seemed like an incredibly short time, Sara noticed the time. "It is ten minutes till nine. We must go," she said to her brother, who was seated nearby.

"This has been a short evening!" Jacob exclaimed regretfully, when he noticed the three Yoders getting ready to leave.

"Yes, it has," Sara agreed with a smile. "We have enjoyed it very much." Then she turned with a warm smile to Mrs. Bender, who had appeared in the kitchen doorway. "Thank you all for the nice time," she added.

Again Jacob went to the front door and held it for them to pass through. Again Sara managed to be the last one. Jacob stepped outside with them. "You all come often, please," he begged. "I hope you won't need to leave so early the next time." He stood close to Sara.

"Thank you," Sara replied politely, reluctantly stepping across the porch.

"And you all come down some evening," James called back as he and Marie walked out across the yard.

"We will," Jacob replied, following Sara across the porch. "I'll walk you all out the driveway," he offered. "There are several stones that you may stumble over. I'm sorry that our lantern is not unpacked yet."

Sara quickened her steps to join Marie and James. As she did so, her foot landed on a big loose stone. The stone suddenly rolled, and she lost her balance and fell. Jacob was at her side immediately. "Careful, young lady," he said. "Let me help you back on your feet." Then, as he helped her to her feet again, he whispered, "I hope I'll have the chance to do that again some-day. Only I hope you won't hurt yourself."

James turned back. "Coming, Sara?" he asked.

"Yes," she answered, quite out of breath. She was thankful for the darkness so that James would not see her face, which she was certain was crimson.

"The young lady stumbled, and her brother was nowhere near to assist her," Jacob playfully chided James. "So another young prince came to her rescue." He turned to Sara again, saying, "Please come again." Then, as she hurried away, he added, "I must go back to my guests."

Sara was silent as they hurried home as fast as possible. What did Jacob mean by all the con-sideration he was showing her? Her heart beat faster than the run home warranted. Was Jacob the very special young man that she sometimes dreamed about? How could she know that Jacob was merely plotting to break down her natural reserve so that she would be drawn to him regardless of his questionable character?

Father and Mother were waiting in the living room when the children burst into the house, breathing heavily. They had had to run most of the way to be sure they were home by Father's deadline of nine o'clock.

"Oh, we had a wonderful time," Marie panted, her dark, expressive eyes sparkling with the joy of youth.

"Yes, we did!" James agreed. "The Benders are really nice, friendly people. I think we will really like them for neighbors," he added with enthusiasm.

"It will be such fun to get together like this once in a while," Marie continued.

All the while Sara had remained quiet. After the exclamations of excitement quieted down a bit, Father asked, "Just what did you do that was so exciting?"

"First we froze ice cream," James replied. "And then we—"

"We played some games," Marie interrupted. "And—"

"Wait, children, wait. Only one at a time, please." Their father laughed. "I can't tell what either one of you is saying when you both talk at once."

Marie waited quietly while James explained, "We ate the ice cream at about eight-thirty. We had played only a few games before that."

"But they were just getting ready to play some more," Marie added when her brother paused. "Oh, it seemed we had to leave so early. Everyone else was having such fun, and all the other young people were planning to stay longer than nine o'clock."

"We're glad you had a nice time," Father began. The smile had left his face, replaced by a troubled frown. "Didn't you do any singing?"

James and Marie both shook their heads.

"I am disappointed about that," Mother said. "I thought you always sing when you are together." She looked inquiringly at Sara, who had as yet not said a word.

"Yes, Mother, we usually do, at least some of the time," Sara replied. "The last time we were at the Millers' house—you know, the week before they moved—we spent much of the evening singing. And the evening that we were here, we did too. I always enjoyed the singing together very much."

"But, Mother, you wouldn't expect us to say 'Now we want to sing awhile,' when the party is in someone else's home, would you?" Marie asked.

"No, I would not expect you to do that," Mother assured her. "Although I don't think it would have been improper to suggest it, if there was opportunity. Especially since the Benders are new here and don't know how the German-town young people usually conduct their get-togethers."

"But, Mother, the whole evening was all planned," James explained. "We could hardly have suggested doing something else without seeming rude."

"I see," Mother replied understandingly.

"What kind of games did you play?" Father inquired with interest.

The younger two described the games they had played. "And when we were leaving, they were just getting ready to play a game called 'let's get acquainted,'" Marie added. "I don't know for sure what it was like. They talked about going out in the yard to play it. It was something about choosing partners and walking around the yard, introducing yourself, and then trading partners with the first couple you met coming back, and walking around again, or something like that."

By the time Marie had finished her description of the game, Father was frowning his disapproval. "I am not so sure that is a proper way for Christian young people to introduce themselves," he commented soberly.

"She may be mistaken about that," James spoke up. "We did not stay till they finished explaining how to play. Maybe everyone walks around together instead of pairing off in twos. I am not sure either how that was." He appeared willing to cast the Benders in the best possible light.

"Well, maybe I could approve of the game if that were the case. But I believe it would still be wiser to stay in the lighted house to play instead of out in a dark yard," Father answered slowly, his concern apparent in the tone of his voice. "Playing games in the dark is very questionable. When you are with the young people, or at any other time, be very careful of your conduct, or you will regret it in later years. Out on the lawn in the dark may present more temptations to carelessness of conduct," he warned. "Loose conduct in youth often causes years of sorrowful reaping."

"Were their parents involved all evening with the young people?" Mother questioned, looking at Sara for an answer.

"Yes, they were there, but not in the room with us. It really was very crowded," Sara answered.

James hardly heard a word his parents had been saying. He had suddenly recalled the strange look he had seen on his sister's face in the Benders' yard. Just now it came to him that if the young people had been going to walk around the yard in pairs to be introduced, that oldest Bender boy would surely have wanted the first walk with his oldest sister.

He looked at her quizzically now, fancying he

knew why the red glow still tinted her cheeks. The thought amused him. "I'd say that oldest Bender boy was just waiting for his chance to walk Sara around the yard," James quipped, as he watched Sara for her reaction.

Sara did not look up, but her cheeks burned. She knew that James was looking right at her, and she knew why he had said what he did.

"Anyone could see how eager he was by the way he held her hand in the—"

"James!" Father stopped him by a word, looking sternly at the two young people. The Yoder children were allowed some good-natured teasing, but never about boyfriends or girlfriends or the like.

Now Father faced Sara squarely. "Sara," he asked calmly and purposefully, "will you tell us what your brother is referring to?"

Sara kept her eyes lowered. She could not face her father. Knowing that he had always been fair and understanding gave her courage, finally, to explain. "When we were leaving the Benders," she began with some embarrassment, "I stumbled and nearly lost my balance. Jacob happened to be standing there, and he helped me to my feet." Sara felt very uncomfortable. That much was the truth, but what she was leaving unsaid made her feel guilty of deceiving her parents.

"That is what any gentleman would do," Father replied, looking directly into the eyes of his son. "To use an apparently innocent incident to infer something that is not honorable is deceitful," he rebuked him.

James wilted under Father's rebuke, and Sara felt even more guilty. How much had James heard? He did not say more. If he knew all that was done and said, he had good reason for his remarks. *I am the one guilty of deception,* she realized with a sharp pang of conscience. Sara knew she should do some explaining, but when she did not even understand herself, how could she explain? Why had she allowed such familiarity? Furthermore, why had she lingered and given him the opportunity? Sara felt condemned. She had intended to tell it just as it was when Father had asked, but it was too hard to put into words, especially in front of the other children.

Sara was not sure how long Father continued watching her. She did not dare to look up until he asked, "Well, children, let's get our Bibles and read a chapter before going to bed. We won't sing this evening, since it is already late. And we already sang with the little children before they went to bed."

Several weeks passed. The young people, especially the Benders, were again talking about having a party. When Marie mentioned it at home, Mother suggested to Father, "Let's invite them to have it here. That way we can give them some guidance and try to keep the young people's gatherings headed in the right direction."

"Maybe if the Benders see how our gatherings are conducted, it will help them in planning another one," Father added. "I think that is a good idea. Only I do not think the young people should start planning weekday get-togethers every couple weeks."

4.

A Lifetime Promise

Sara was finding it harder and harder to be cheerful around home. Her father's confidence in her made it even more difficult. She knew she would never feel right until she told her parents that she had deceived them by omitting part of what had actually happened at the Benders that evening. But for the first time in her life, she felt they would not understand.

For one thing, how could she admit her guilt without also condemning Jacob? She knew that her parents would be more than unhappy if they knew about the liberties that Jacob had taken with her. Such liberties would not be proper even in courtship. She knew also that she should not be savoring in her heart the warm feeling she had enjoyed at his special attention. Jacob was not a member of the church, and her parents had expressed implicitly, judging by the fruit of his life, that he was not even a Christian.

I should have avoided contact with Jacob, she chided herself, remembering the evening at the Benders. A*nd I could have, if I had not lingered behind James and Marie. But I tried to release my hand,* she reasoned. *I did not appreciate his actions.* But all her excuses did not quiet the burden of guilt in her heart. She knew very well that she had enjoyed his attentions and that she was trying to hide those feelings from her parents because she knew they would not approve.

John Yoder was concerned that his children have a well-guarded Christian life. This was his first and foremost priority. But he was also concerned that they have a well-balanced social life. So when the older children reminded their parents again of their earlier promise to have a youth gathering at their home, Father promised to talk it over with Mother. Before long they came up with a plan. "We could have another gathering for the youth at our home in two weeks," Father proposed, "which would make it a month from the last one."

"Oh, good." Marie rejoiced, eager for the opportunity to be with friends again. But Sara said nothing.

"We will announce it right away so that the Benders won't get the idea to plan another one before then," Father continued. Invitations were sent out, and the young people cheerfully accepted the invitation.

But the following Sunday, the Benders invited all the young people home to dinner with them. John and Mary Yoder considered this invitation for some time before reluctantly consenting. They learned that, although several other families were also hesitant, all were planning to allow their young people to go. The Yoders had never before felt that they needed to keep their children from joining in with the Germantown youth activities, and they did not want to deprive them of that social exchange now.

"'Remember the sabbath day, to keep it holy,'" Father admonished as the three oldest of his children started down the road to the Bender farm on Sunday.

After dinner the girls cleared the table while the boys carried chairs out onto the lawn. Sara was greatly relieved to learn that they planned to spend at least part of the afternoon singing. She stepped out onto the porch with a pan of scraps for Rover, the Benders' dog. No sooner had the door closed behind her than Jacob was there. He stepped up to her and said in a low voice, "Sara, may I take you to church tonight? My father said I may have the buggy. They aren't going, and the others can walk if they want to go." He looked wistfully into her eyes. "Please say yes," he urged pleadingly. "It would make me so happy." He waited hopefully.

Sara smiled, a bright dimpled smile. She was pleased. This tall, handsome young gentleman had captivated her fancy. But her mind was awhirl; what should she do? She took several deep breaths and did some quick, serious thinking. She knew that her parents would not approve of her beginning a friendship with Jacob for several reasons. For one thing, she was not quite eighteen; and for another, her parents preferred that their children wait till they were closer to nineteen to date. But the most important reason, she was sure, was that they did not consider him a Christian. Another reason was that Jacob was not a member of the church.

Sara remembered also the counsel Father had shared with Marie and her lately. "When it comes to courtship," he had said earnestly, "never go with a young man, not even one time for one date, with any other purpose than finding a good Christian life companion."

Sara had not known the Benders very long, and she did not know Jacob well enough to make such a decision. *But suppose I refuse and he chooses another girl,* her thoughts argued. *He may not want to wait for me when there are other girls around!* She could hardly bear that thought. She wanted this handsome, gentlemanly young man, and she wanted him badly! But her parents . . .

Jacob was waiting. She must answer. If only he had waited a little longer to ask. Sara kept her eyes on the bowl she carried.

"Please," he repeated in a soft, beseeching tone. He reached for her hand, but Sara drew it back. Jacob dropped his hands by his side and waited patiently.

"No," Sara answered hesitantly, "not tonight." Quickly Sara turned and walked across the porch, leaving Jacob standing alone, disappointed and very much taken aback by her refusal. What Sara did not know was that he had already dated many girls and was not accustomed to being refused.

Sara entered the house by the side door after emptying the scraps. Her hand trembled as she closed the door behind her. She liked Jacob; she did not want to hurt his feelings. *He did respect me*, she reasoned. *Why didn't I just explain? Why didn't I just ask him to wait awhile? He will probably find another girl, thinking my answer is final!*

With all her conflicting thoughts, Sara still felt she had done right in refusing, at least until she had time to talk it over with Father and Mother. She was glad, however, that she had not really given him a final no; she had simply answered, "Not tonight." She clung to the hope that he might wait for her and ask again.

Several times during the afternoon, Sara sensed that Jacob was watching her. At such times, she would glance down quickly at her song book, her face feeling flushed. Sara could not keep her mind on what she was singing.

The young people began getting rowdy as soon as the singing was over, and the visiting was light and frivolous. Sara motioned to James and Marie that it was time to start home.

After church that evening, Sara went immediately to the carriage. Mother and Father soon came out, Father carrying a sleeping Ruth. He placed her gently on the seat, and he and Mother climbed in. Before the other children came out, Sara took the opportunity to tell her parents about Jacob. "Mother and Father," she began hesitantly, "today Jacob asked if he could bring me home from church this evening."

They waited a moment in silence. When she said no more, Mother turned and faced her oldest daughter, replying, "I guess it is evident what your answer was, since you are here in the carriage."

Sara nodded. "I wasn't sure you would approve, so I told him no. Maybe I should have just asked him to wait awhile."

"You were not really sure we would approve? I am afraid you were quite sure we would *not* approve," Father stated firmly. "And I am very glad you did not accept his offer of friendship. He is not a member of the church, and you are too young. Those are two good reasons why we do not approve."

Mother smiled encouragingly at Sara. "We are glad you had maturity enough to refuse him, and we hope you will not encourage his attention now. Would you have liked to say yes," Mother asked, "if conditions were right?"

"Yes, I would have," Sara replied, looking at her parents frankly. "He seems like a gentleman, and even a Christian. I hesitated to turn him down. Would it have been right to tell him that I will be glad to accept if he waits until he is a church member?"

"No," Mother answered quickly. "This is a most important step in life. You need to let it rest now and wait for God to show His will for your lives. Perhaps you both will change your minds when sufficient time passes."

"I am glad you waited, Sara," Father added. "You will want to spend much time in prayer before making such a serious decision. I am glad you mentioned this to us." Father cleared his throat. "You have felt attracted to this young man ever since they moved here, haven't you?"

"Yes," Sara admitted honestly, glad to have it all out in the open. It was easier to express these feelings when James and Marie were not around. They were younger and would not understand her feelings. Father and Mother understood and wanted what was best for her. Why had she not shared before?

"He has such a kind voice and seems to be a real gentleman," Sara continued. "I believe that he is a Christian but that his parents' situation has discouraged and confused him. He was brought up differently than we were, and he may do things at times that I do not approve of. But he seems sincere, and he respects my wishes."

"Be slow to come to those conclusions, Sara," her father warned soberly. "Your feelings are normal, but you must keep them in control. A big help in doing that will be to stay close to the Lord and to be open with Mother and me.

"I sincerely hope Jacob proves to be all you believe he is, whether he shows any further interest in you or not. But don't even consider a special friendship with him until he is a member of the church and has proven himself to be a faithful Christian for some time. I am sure you can sense a real lack of spirituality in the Bender home, particularly in the father."

"Yes," agreed Sara, "I am aware of that. But I believe Jacob is sincere. I feel sorry for him—and for all the children," Sara added quickly. "Father, you have been such a help to me. I think if Jacob had a father like you, to give him training like that which we have had, he would be a different boy. If we give him a chance here in our church setting, I believe he will change a lot." Sara had done a lot of thinking and reasoning in her immature mind about all this, and she was quite sure that the way she felt was the way it was.

James and David started toward the carriage, followed by Marie and Lois. Nothing more was said about the Benders.

The younger children were tucked into their beds, and the older ones had lit their candles and headed for their bedrooms, but still Sara lingered in the kitchen. She walked over to the dry sink and dipped water from the water bucket. Slowly she drank it.

Father and Mother returned to the kitchen, sensing that their oldest daughter wanted to talk. That something had been troubling Sara for the past weeks had not escaped their attention. She had been too quiet and withdrawn. They longed to help her.

"Father," Sara began in a trembling voice, "that Friday evening when we came home from the first party at the Benders' house, what I said about Jacob was not entirely true. It was true that I stumbled and he helped me up. But I am afraid I was deceitful in the way that I pictured it. Jacob did hold my hand longer than necessary." Now the tears were flowing freely. It was humbling to admit her failure, but oh, what a relief it was to her mind and conscience!

Father and Mother waited for her to finish.

Sara went on to tell her parents about other inti-
macies, which seemed so commonplace to Jacob.
He seemed to think nothing of taking physical
liberties, while Sara had always been taught that
such were not appropriate for Christian young
people outside of marriage.

"I am glad you have felt free to speak to us
about these things," Mother said warmly, tears
on her own cheeks. "These are things every
young girl needs to avoid lest they lead to other
things she is not able to control."

Again Sara's parents had a long talk with her
about the dangers and temptations she would
face in life. They tried hard to impress on her
that Jacob's freedom to touch her did not speak
well of his character. It could even indicate that
he was used to such familiarities with girls and
was using physical attraction to make Sara desire
him against her better judgment.

Sara mentioned that Jacob had respected her
wish that afternoon. He had not taken her hand
on the porch when he understood that she did
not approve of his conduct.

"That is commendable," Father agreed. "But,
as I have said before, you cannot be too careful
of the associates you choose as close companions. Give him time to prove himself to be the
kind of godly young man that you would want
for a husband. You will want one who will be a
spiritual leader in your home, one submissive to

the church, one interested in serving God rather than self and pleasure."

"After he joins the church, would you have any objection to my accepting his friendship, if he should ask again?" Sara asked with a slight flush on her fair cheeks. "Isn't courtship a way to get better acquainted? And I could help him to gain convictions to raise his standards."

Father and Mother looked at each other for some time before either spoke. Sara could sense the love and concern of her parents. Finally Father said, "We could not agree to that until he has proven himself faithful for a good amount of time. Also, we are asking that you wait until you are past eighteen and a half to begin courtship. Remember, Sara, such important decisions affect us for life, as well as for eternity."

* * * * *

More than a month had passed since Sara's confidential talk with her parents. It was a warm August morning. Sara awoke to the singing of birds outside her window. The world was bright and peaceful this Sunday morning.

The other girls were still asleep. Sara crept softly out of bed and dropped to her knees. She heard Father and Mother moving about in the kitchen. Marie rolled over in bed. Ruth started chattering out in the front room. *What are they doing up so early?* Sara wondered.

In an attempt to draw her mind from the things

about her, Sara began repeating several familiar Scripture verses. Then she tried again to pray. But she could not concentrate on prayer, nor even on the fact that it was Sunday morning and her favorite day of the week. She could only think that today was her birthday—she was eighteen years old. Might her parents relent and allow her to begin dating? Most of the girls in their community began courtship even before they were eighteen. Why must her parents be so old-fashioned as to suggest she wait until eighteen and a half to date?

Jacob Bender had not asked her for another date since the time on the Benders' back porch. But Sara felt sure that he would sometime again, maybe sometime not too far away! His interest in her was evident. He had never shown special interest in another girl. There had been several youth gatherings since that Sunday in June at the Benders', and he had always talked to Sara and shown a special interest in her. *Maybe he will ask me again, now that I am eighteen,* Sara mused. *I'm sure he knows it is my birthday. If he asks me now, I will consent,* Sara determined.

Father and Mother did not definitely say that I may not date now, she thought, trying to justify her decision to accept his friendship. She knew that even if she were now eighteen and a half, her parents would not approve of the friendship. She purposefully chose to overlook her parents' injunction.

A deep sigh escaped the lips of the girl on her knees by the bed. She knew in her heart that she was being rebellious and that she did not have peace about her decision. But Sara chose to ignore the pleadings of her conscience and enjoy the pleasure Jacob's special attention brought to her.

Marie rolled over again. Sara knew that her sisters would soon be getting up. She tried once more. *O Father, she cried* from a divided heart, *help me this day to keep my mind on Thee and on Thy Word. Help me to do Thy will for me. Do not allow other things to crowd out good and pure thoughts.* Sara wished fervently to have God's favor on her life, just as she fervently wished to have Jacob Bender. But which desire was greater, she hardly knew herself. *Why can't I have both?* she reasoned stubbornly, not willing to give up her desire for Jacob's friendship.

The clock struck six-thirty. Sara started. *Have I been on my knees half an hour already? And I haven't really spent many minutes in prayer.* She felt ashamed, but pushed aside the feeling of guilt. Her sisters were moving about the room now, getting dressed.

O God. She tried again. *I thank Thee for Thy blessings to us. Father, show Thy will for our lives. I pray especially that You would speak to my heart through the message today. And please lead Jacob and me together if it is not against*

Thy will. Sara stopped and took a deep breath. Was it right to ask it that way? *Should I have just asked for God's will? I know I would be happy with Jacob, and I could be such a help to him too. Jacob seems so sincere. He just hasn't had a fair chance in life.* Again troubled thoughts filled her mind as all her teaching from the past flooded into her consciousness. *Is he really sincere? He is an adult. Couldn't he want the Lord's will enough to be a part of the church regardless of what his parents do?*

Sara had some serious doubts that her prayer had reached God. Was she herself sincere and living as close to the Lord as she should? Somehow she did not feel the closeness to the Lord that she had once had. Troubled thoughts turned over and over in her mind. She remembered other times she had wanted something so badly, something her parents restrained her from having. She knew the ensuing results when she had resisted, as well as when she had submitted. She wanted to submit to God and feel that deep assurance that He was guiding her life. But if that meant giving up Jacob. . .

How vividly Sara remembered the day she had deceived Father, hoping to obtain his permission to go and visit with Lydia Miller. And how she had regretted that later. Why should this come to her now? She was not trying to deceive anyone, but she must make her parents understand how very much having Jacob meant to her. They would surely accept him after they saw how well it would work out! But still Sara felt confused and troubled. She arose dismally from her knees and began to quickly dress and comb her hair.

Soon Sara joined her sisters and Mother in the kitchen. "Happy birthday!" they all greeted her lovingly. Sara's heart felt too heavy for happiness, and she responded with a half-hearted "Thank you."

Mother noticed with concern. She had been observing other things lately as well. Sara was not her usual frank and cheerful self. It seemed more difficult for her to open up and have a good talk with her parents. Mother grieved as she looked on, determining that she must make an opportunity to have a good heart-to-heart talk with her oldest daughter soon. It was obvious that something was troubling her.

Throughout the morning worship service, the fierce struggle continued in the young girl's heart. Her desire for God's will and a satisfying worship experience competed with her desire to relax and please the flesh and her own selfish desires. Sometimes Sara felt unsure which was uppermost in her mind. How she wished she could have both!

Why can't I talk with my parents? she wondered, as Brother Mast preached on and on. They had often spoken to her about her relationship with the young people, especially since she had told them about her interest in Jacob. She had received much good advice and encouragement from them. But more and more Sara felt herself yielding to the temptation to believe that her parents were not trying to understand her and were trying to make it hard for her. *They are to blame if I have withdrawn from them,* she reasoned rebelliously.

"Who can remember where the devotional reading was taken from this morning?" Father asked at the dinner table.

"Romans 5," James responded promptly.

"And the sermon text?" Father asked next.

"Hebrews 11. The faith chapter," Marie answered immediately.

Only Sara remained quiet as Father continued to ask more questions about the morning worship service. She tried to think but could not remember a thing that had been said all morning. She sat with her head lowered, a feeling of shame resting heavily upon her heart. *I missed a lot,* she concluded as the rest of the family shared truths that they had gleaned from the message.

One thing she did remember vividly. Several times she had looked back, and each time Jacob's eyes were on her. What was he thinking? After church she had not gone out the back door. She was not sure why. *If only I could be sure.* Sara puzzled over her strange, mixed-up feelings. She spent most of the afternoon in her room, reading.

"I am eighteen now," Sara stated resolutely to no one in particular. It was late in the afternoon, and she was carefully combing her hair before going to the kitchen for supper. "If Jacob should ask for my friendship again, I will accept. We can try it awhile. I can change my mind later if I decide we should not be sharing this special friendship. How else would I know? If I turn him down again, it might discourage him completely, and he might turn away from the church." With this important decision made, Sara started out the hall to join the others in the kitchen.

Soon supper was over and the dishes cleared away. The Yoders started for church in the carriage. The service meant little more to Sara than the morning service had. She felt frustrated. She did not know what was wrong.

After dismissal, Sara lingered awhile to give Jacob an opportunity if he wished to speak to her. When she saw him standing inside the back door, she deliberately walked past him. She did not look up at him but slipped quickly outside.

"Sara." He detained her, stepping out beside her. "Sara, you are eighteen today?"

"Yes." She beamed and blushed.

"May I have the pleasure of taking you home tonight?"

Sara looked up into his pleading eyes. Quickly

she replied, "Yes," before she would lose her courage.

Sara waited while Jacob hitched his horse to the carriage. Suddenly she said, "Please, Jacob, I want to go and say a word to Mother first."

"Is that necessary?" he asked, a little impatiently.

"Oh, I don't know. But I want to. That is the way we do things in our home."

Sara walked quickly to her parents' carriage, her heart beating fast. Only Mother and Ruth were there. Marie had started out that way, but was detained by a friend. Sara was relieved. She wanted to talk to Mother alone. She was not sure what she wanted to say. She was not even sure now that she wanted to ride home with Jacob. She felt frightened. *Why didn't I ask Mother first?* she chided herself. She truly wished she had. Likely Mother would have said no, and Sara felt now as though she would have welcomed that answer. *Why did I think I am mature enough to make my own decisions, just because I am eighteen now?*

"Mother, I am going home with Jacob Bender. I mean, he is bringing me home tonight." She rushed through her announcement. Sara felt uneasy. Mother was not smiling in approval, as Sara had felt sure she would not. The young girl turned to hurry back to the other side of the churchyard.

110

"Sara," Mother called to her quickly. "Wait till Father comes. We want to talk to him about this first."

"No, Mother," Sara replied with determination. Her sharp answer brought quick tears to her mother's eyes. Never before had Sara so openly defied her mother and hurt her in such a manner! Sara felt a sharp pang of guilt. She suddenly wished she could back out of all this, but Jacob was waiting, and Sara had reason to believe it was with a bit of impatience. She could not keep him waiting any longer. She could see him now, pacing from one side of his carriage to the other, all the time casting anxious glances her way.

Apologetically, she said in a softer tone, "I must hurry, Mother. He's waiting." Sara took a step away when she noticed Father coming toward them.

"Please, Sara, wait just a minute," Mother pleaded. Then she asked, "Why didn't you tell us before that he had asked you?"

"Mother, he just asked after the service tonight. I didn't know."

"Then you haven't even taken time to pray about it before you gave him your answer?" Mother asked with concern.

"Yes, Mother, I was praying about it even before he asked," Sara assured her desperately. "Father said I might date when I am eighteen and a half. Until then we will just be together occasionally and learn to know each other. That will help us know if we want to start a regular courtship."

"But didn't Father also say," Mother reminded her, "that you may date a young man only if he is truly born again?"

"What makes you so sure he isn't?" Sara demanded impatiently. "I think he will ask for church membership soon. Just give him time."

"Do his actions and conduct prove that he is a Christian?" Mother asked.

Without answering, Sara quickly slipped around behind the carriage just before Father arrived. Jacob came to meet her. He reached for her hand, but Sara drew it back. Jacob looked puzzled and walked quietly beside her. She did allow him to help her into the carriage. He seemed pleased, and Sara felt sure he would always respond to all her wishes as soon as he knew what was expected. He had been raised so differently from the Germantown people.

Sara's troubled conscience was soon forgotten. Jacob's jovial personality drove all serious thoughts from her mind, and she enjoyed the evening very much. Jacob took the long way home, an old logging trail along the river. "Just to give us more time to talk," he explained. He walked the horse very slowly. Once he stopped by the river for a few minutes, until Sara asked him to please keep going because her parents would be concerned about her. Immediately he clucked to the horse and it moved on.

Sara knew that her parents would have time to be in bed, and she fervently hoped that they would be. Why should they wait up for her? *They must soon learn that I am an adult,* she reasoned. As Jacob said, she was going to have to learn to make her own decisions and not depend on her parents forever.

Jacob refused her invitation to come in. "Not this time," he said.

"May I come for you next Sunday evening?" he asked eagerly as he walked with Sara to the porch.

"The young folks here usually start out by seeing each other every other week," Sara explained.

He looked puzzled. "Must we do everything the way everyone else does?" he asked.

"I'd rather," she replied simply.

"Did you enjoy the evening?" he asked. Before she could answer, he added, "I have enjoyed it immensely and look forward to more."

He watched Sara's face closely. She was nodding her head and smiling. "You may come for me in two weeks if you wish," she said, showing her deep dimples.

"I will be here. Good night, Sara," Jacob said fondly. "You have given me great pleasure. I will see you in two weeks. I am sorry for the times I have offended you by the differences in our understanding of what is proper. Forgive me. I am willing to learn. I want to do what is right. It was all so different in our community and in my home. You will be a big help to me." Jacob rushed on as Sara watched him with trusting eyes. How could she know, in her innocence and immaturity, that his were empty words?

Looking into his troubled eyes, Sara longed to reach out to him and comfort him. But she refrained, saying only, "You are forgiven."

"I'll be seeing you," he replied. He turned to walk out to his rig. He swung himself up as he spoke to his horse, and was rapidly leaving by the time Sara walked across the porch and clasped the door handle.

The living-room light was still burning, but at least the children's rooms were dark. *The children must be in bed.* Sara was glad. But she wished her parents were also! She knew they must be waiting for her in the lit living room. Her cheeks burned. *Oh, I wish Mother and Father had gone to bed. I could meet them much more easily in the morning,* she fretted, entering the house slowly. She made her way even more slowly to the living room, where an oil lamp was still burning on the library table.

Sara's head throbbed. Her thoughts were in such turmoil. She had had her good time—she had been so happy while Jacob was near. But

114

now—now the reckoning with her loving parents was upon her.

When Sara entered the room, Father sat reading his Bible and Mother was nodding drowsily in her chair. Sara saw traces of tears on Mother's cheeks.

"Sara," Father began, glancing at the clock, "it took you exactly one hour longer to get home than it took us. I would like to know where you have been."

Sara glanced uncertainly at the clock. Surely it could not have been that long! "We came right home without going anywhere else," she replied honestly. "We did take the river road instead of the direct road here," she explained as Father watched her sternly.

"Then you didn't stop anywhere?" he asked with unusual sternness for Father.

"No," Sara replied. "I mean we didn't stop *in* anywhere. He did stop to look at the river a short while."

"I wish you would tell him, if there are any more rides home with him, that you would rather come directly home and do your visiting here." Father spoke firmly, but kindly. "It is not good to be out riding around at night. And to take a largely unused road at night was certainly not a wise thing to do. I am very disappointed in you, Sara."

Father's words, as well as the hurt look in his eyes, brought quick tears to Sara's eyes.

"I trust if he, or anyone else, ever asks to bring you home again, you will ask for time to pray about it first, as well as to counsel with your parents and the ministers."

Mother spoke up from where she was sitting. "I'm bothered that Jacob chose to bring you home by way of the old logging road. And at night! It may be a lovely drive in the daytime, but why drive it when it is almost dark? I am wondering too about your stopping at the river. Why would you stop at the river when you couldn't see much of it anyway?"

"I don't know why he took that road. More time to talk, I guess. And then he was just talking and we stopped at the river. I soon asked him to bring me on home," Sara responded.

"I'm glad you did that."

Sara was still standing, feeling very uncomfortable as she shifted wearily from one foot to the other.

"Sit down, Sara," Father advised. "We want to talk some things over. I am convinced you cannot have thought things through. All of us do things impulsively sometimes and wish later we wouldn't have. Often this causes serious regrets."

"We want to help you, Sara. You are so young yet," Mother added earnestly.

Father again took up the conversation. "I would like to suggest a few things for you to think about before you go any further with your friendship."

Sara reluctantly drew up a chair near her parents. She was so tired. How she longed to go to bed and sort out her own confused thoughts. But her respect for her parents constrained her to comply with Father's wishes.

Father bent toward her. "Sara, I sense a lack of spiritual interest in Jacob. And the fact that you did not take time to consider, get counsel, or pray about this decision shows a lack of maturity on your part. Courtship is for spiritual and mature people because its purpose is for marriage and that only.

"Before you go any further, I want you to honestly answer a few questions. First of all, do you want a husband who is a Christian, who will be a godly leader in your home? Would Jacob make a godly father for your children, should God bless you with little ones? Did your time spent with him tonight enrich your Christian life and draw you closer to God, or did it drive serious thoughts aside for an evening of pleasure?"

As Father faced her searchingly, Sara wondered if he expected her to answer all those questions now. After he waited several minutes in silence, she faltered, "Father, it is too soon to know everything yet. Isn't courtship also to learn to know him? He is young, but he really seems sincere."

When Sara said no more, Father continued, "Surely, courtship is to learn to know your friend—his interests, ideals, and personality. But before courtship even begins, you should know whether or not he is a Christian. You already know how careless he is in his speech and what a casual approach he takes to church life. Marriage will not change those things; only true repentance will do that. You must not continue your friendship until he has experienced those changes and has proven himself to be faithful."

"But, Father, he hasn't had a chance," Sara argued miserably and stubbornly. "I don't want to discourage him. He wants to do right. I want to help him."

"No, Sara, you cannot help him by lowering your own standard of holiness. You cannot afford to keep company with one who is not a child of God. You will help him most by refusing his friendship until after you have seen evidence of a real change of heart.

"You are risking the loss of your own devotion to God by keeping company with such a young man. It is a path many other young girls have taken and later reaped years of bitter regrets. You are young. You need the help and discernment of older Christians. You are making an important decision. You are, in fact, choosing your path—the path you will have to walk for many years, the path that will affect the destinies of eternal souls. The way you choose now will determine the divine joy or bitter anguish of your home."

Sara stood up, greatly agitated. She did not wish to disappoint her loving parents. But they did not understand! They did not know Jacob as she did. "May I go to bed now?" she asked, tears streaming down her cheeks. "Can we wait until another time to discuss this?"

Mother stood beside her daughter. "You are tired," she agreed. "Why don't you spend several days seeking God's will, and then we will talk with you again."

"Good night, Sara," Father said. "Remember, we want only what is best for you."

"I know," Sara replied in a trembling voice. "Good night."

Father got up stiffly. Soon he and Mother went to their bedroom.

Sara went to her own room, totally exhausted. After dressing quickly for the night, she fell into bed without even kneeling to pray. How differently things looked now than when she was with Jacob.

Sleep would not come. Sara had dreamed for years of the happy days of courtship under the blessing and approval of God and her parents. Why, oh, why did it have to be so different than she had thought it would be? Were her parents selfishly unwilling to give up their oldest daughter? No, she knew that was not true. Was she really taking her own way and resisting the will of God for her life? She did not think so. It was just that her parents did not understand. Why must she suffer this trial? For the rest of the night she tossed and turned, unable to find peace.

During the next week Sara did ask God to lead her and Jacob. She had more discussions with her parents, trying to help them to understand her feelings. "Jacob needs me," she explained over and over. "He doesn't have anyone to help him to grow spiritually but me."

Father and Mother made desperate attempts to change Sara's mind. But she would finally lapse into silence and remain quiet while they kept on talking. What a feeling of misery grew upon her as the days passed.

The two weeks passed and Sunday came again. Again Sara struggled to know what she should tell Jacob. She had told no one that she had promised Jacob he could come again. *Should I ask him to wait awhile? But suppose he doesn't wait for me.* She could not bear that thought. Why should she have to give up his friendship? Father and Mother had not told her in so many words that she could not ride home with him again. She was glad for that because she did not want to openly disobey them. As it was, she felt guilty enough for not taking the advice that she knew was given in love. But she did not have the heart to tell Jacob not to come for her that evening.

As soon as the dishes were finished after dinner, Sara went to her room. "Don't wake me for supper, Mother," she called back before she shut her door. The long afternoon dragged by. Some of the time Sara could sleep, but most of the time she spent reading or trying to pray.

When she heard the rest eating supper, she started to dress for church. Suddenly she heard a light tap on her door, and Mother opened the door and stepped in, without waiting for a "Come in."

"Sara," she asked, "are you expecting someone, that you are getting ready so early?"

"Yes, Mother, Jacob is coming," Sara stated. Then she hurried on, "I had already told him I would go with him tonight. I don't want to break my promise. Please don't say I may not go. I need to just this once so that we can talk things over."

Disregarding Mother's pleas and tears, Sara left her standing in the bedroom and hurried out to meet Jacob as soon as he arrived.

As they rode slowly along, Sara explained her parents' concerns to Jacob. "Maybe we should wait awhile," she said finally. "I promise that I will still consider your offer of friendship after you are a member of the church."

Jacob was plainly upset. "Sara, I know that my father is bitter against the church. He has never been able to settle anywhere, so I guess now we children will suffer for it. Everybody expects the Bender boys to turn out bad. They don't want their children to associate with us.

How can we ever amount to anything that way? No one will trust us. We'll never have a chance to prove ourselves because we are Reuben Bender's sons."

Sara was shocked by his outburst. "No, Jacob. It isn't as you say. You can prove yourself and then people will trust you. It's not that we think we are better than you. But . . ."

"Sara, please, can't we just forget it and be friends? I need you, Sara. Or are you afraid to trust me too? Don't you believe I really want to do what is right? Haven't I always respected your beliefs and tried to do what you asked, even when we saw things differently?"

It was not a pleasant ride to church. "Don't give me an answer now, Sara," said Jacob. "I will meet you right outside the back door after church, and you can tell me then if you will let me take you home."

After the service, Sara did meet Jacob just inside the back door. She never was quite sure how it happened. Had she intended to, or did it just happen? Or was it because God was leading in their relationship and worked it out for her? She really had not decided beforehand whether she would meet him or just slip out some other door. But here she was, and Jacob was there to meet her. He reached out his hand and smiled. "I am so glad you came," he said, relief in his voice as they shook hands. "Let's step outside."

No one else had come outside yet. Sara could not think. "Shall we go right away?" he asked in a kind voice. "We can talk as we ride."

Sara followed him to his carriage. She felt no need to tell her parents where she was. They would know. *It isn't fair to him not to at least talk things over,* she reasoned as he helped her up into the carriage. Sara watched as Jacob tightened the harness straps. Then he walked around the carriage and hoisted himself up beside her.

They were on their way. Jacob was exuberant. He took her presence at the back door of the church to mean that she had decided to continue their courtship.

"Why are you so quiet?" he asked after a while. "You aren't letting your parents' disapproval of our friendship influence you, are you? Sara, don't you know we are for each other? I am so happy when I am with you. Please tell me you won't allow anything to come between us."

"I just don't know," Sara said softly.

"This is what you would want if no one opposed it, isn't it?" Jacob asked, looking at her.

"Yes," she answered quickly, "but . . ."

"Then let's go on enjoying our friendship," he suggested. "After all, we are adults and must make our own decisions. My parents are pleased. You said that you are asking God to lead us. I have been praying too every day for His leading." Jacob's voice was low and controlled.

THE WAY SHE CHOSE

How could she mistrust him? "But, Jacob, you are not a member of the church yet," she ventured after a bit.

"Sara, I told you I gave my heart to the Lord years ago. I am a Christian. I have just been waiting for Father to get settled somewhere, and then I'll be a member."

"Why haven't you applied here?" Sara asked hesitantly, not wishing to annoy him.

"I will. Can you trust me?"

"Jacob," she pleaded, "please take me straight home so we can think this over and pray about it. Then we will talk about it later. My parents had not left church yet. I want to get home and go to my room before they come tonight. That way maybe I can sort out my confused thoughts before another interview with them."

"I will do as you wish, Sara," Jacob assured her in his most considerate, convincing tone. Loosening his hold on the reins, he gave the horse a light touch of the whip. Immediately it stepped up its pace.

Sara breathed a sigh of relief.

Jacob turned to look at her, saying, "Sara, will you promise me one thing? Then I will wait until you are ready to continue. You may take all the time you want, and I will wait for you." He stopped briefly as the horse trotted steadily on. Sara's heart began to pound erratically. She was afraid of what he might be going to ask.

"Promise me," he began very persuasively, "that you will marry me sometime. It doesn't have to be right away if your parents think you are too young. We will consider their wishes. Just give me your promise that you will be mine."

Sara drew a sharp breath as she twisted her fingers in her lap. Was what he asked more than fair? The carriage turned in the Yoder lane. The house was still dark. What should she say? Suspense hung heavy over them both as Jacob waited patiently for her answer.

She did not want to lose him. He was so kind and thoughtful of her. He did want to do what was right, even though his father was a hindrance to him. Dare she also discourage him? Sara felt desperate. She could see another pair of buggy lights coming along the road; it was most likely her parents.

"Will you promise?" Jacob repeated. His voice was soft and pleading, breaking into her troubled thoughts.

"I will," she promised as she jumped lightly from the carriage.

"Thank you, Sara. Now you are mine. I will wait for you as long as you wish. I won't come in tonight so that you can go straight to bed. Sleep well!"

Sara headed for the house without looking back. Had she really made such a promise? A lifetime promise with such far-reaching implications?

Inside the closed door, she glanced out the side window. As Jacob was leaving, her parents were driving in.

Quickly she fled to her bedroom. The moon lighted her room well enough that she was able to dress for bed without lighting the candles on her chest. *The other girls will have a snack before they come to bed,* she consoled herself. *If I get to bed quickly, I won't need to face them tonight. Mother and Father will likely think that I discontinued our friendship, since I came home so quickly. They won't need to know about my promise right away.*

126

5.

The Wedding

Summer passed into fall, and fall turned to winter. Sara had little contact with Jacob other than at church or at the youth social gatherings and singings. Father and Mother watched Sara very closely so that she would not have opportunity to meet Jacob through the week. Occasionally he passed their place when she was doing outdoor chores. Each time they met, his glances were full of meaning, and the ones she returned him were the same.

"Sara," Father asked one mild February morning, "would you mind hitching the horse and going to the store for me? I need some roofing nails to replace the tin on the chicken house roof."

"Sure, I'll be glad to," Sara responded, happy

to get out of the house for a little while. "Can Mother spare me?" she asked.

"Yes, I checked. I would have sent James, but he is at the back pasture fixing the fence."

Sara did not often have such an opportunity. She enjoyed housework, but for months she had felt uncomfortable and restless around Mother. *Mother asks such heart-searching questions,* she sighed as she hurriedly slipped into her jacket. *Mother seems to see right through me, and she always seems to know when I am disturbed about something!* Sara knew that Mother and Father were not satisfied with the evasive answers she had given them about the relationship between Jacob and herself. And many and long had been their discussions, especially after Father stipulated that Sara was not to take up a special friendship after all at eighteen and a half but that she must wait until Jacob was a church member and had proved himself for several months.

The four-mile ride to the Germantown General Store did not take long. She pulled up to the hitching rail in front of the store and was tying her horse when she heard a soft voice near her. "Good morning, Sara. What brings you here?" Willing fingers took the rope from her hands and finished the job.

"Jacob!" Sara could not hide the pleasure in her voice.

"Sara, it has been almost six months! When

128

can we start seeing each other again?" He looked long and deep into those big, troubled eyes.

"I am past eighteen and a half," she replied. "But I am very sure that my parents still would not approve of our starting to see each other again." She had never had the opportunity to tell Jacob that her parents were still insisting on his being a church member in good standing.

"I will be nineteen in June," Jacob responded. "Why do they think we should keep waiting?"

"I don't know," Sara replied with a sigh. Her conscience, though somewhat dulled the last months, still made her feel uncomfortable. She certainly did know why her parents did not approve of their courtship.

"Couldn't we have a few dates now? Then we could wait until you are closer to nineteen to get married. Your parents shouldn't object to that, should they? I think they are being unreasonable, making us wait like this. We have respected their wishes. Shouldn't they trust us enough to give in a little too? I thought that after I applied for church membership they would look at things differently. But it seems they still don't trust me."

Sara did not know what to say.

"Do they know that we are promised?" Jacob asked eagerly.

"I haven't told them. I thought it would work better to wait until after we are dating again," she explained.

Jacob nodded. "I didn't tell my parents either, although I know they wouldn't object. But if my brothers found out, they may let it out before we are ready!" Jacob chuckled.

Sara's throat constricted. She must tell Jacob about her parents' continued injunction. But would he be angry? She hoped not. "Jacob," she began hesitatingly, "I guess I never had the opportunity to tell you that my parents still feel very strongly that you must be a church member for several months before we can date again."

"The nerve of them!" Jacob exploded. But then he quickly calmed himself and responded pleasantly, "We have waited so long already. Guess we have to wait a few more months to keep them happy. Then you will be all mine!"

Sara nodded, thankful that he did not seem more annoyed.

Jacob spoke again. "But I was thinking that if your parents are requiring us to wait that long, who knows how much longer they may make us wait to get married! We might just have to make up our own minds and disregard their wishes." Jacob smiled at her. "I will be taken into the church as a member the middle of March, the preacher says. Please, may I come see you then?"

Sara flushed. She wanted to say yes, but she knew her parents would still not be pleased with that. "Oh, Jacob wait for at least a month after that," she pleaded. "Maybe my parents will agree to it by then."

"I have waited so long already. Why can't we just date? That would make it easier to wait." He looked tenderly at her. "You are planning to keep your promise, aren't you?"

"Yes, Jacob," she whispered softly. "I'll be as good as my word. I will keep my promise."

"Good," he responded with evident relief. "You aren't sorry you made it, are you?"

"No-o-o," she replied, feeling unsure of herself. "Jacob, I must get the nails Father asked for. He is waiting for them." She looked up at him. "It is only because I don't like doing things without my parents' approval that I prefer to wait."

Jacob looked at her boldly. "What would they do if I just came to see you on Sunday afternoon and took you along to church?" he asked.

"I don't know," Sara finally replied.

"May I try it?" he asked eagerly.

Sara's conscience was no longer tender as it had once been. She had ignored it too often. "Yes," she responded. "Let's try it once and see." She had begun to absorb the kind of reasoning that Jacob so often used.

Quickly Sara went in, picked up the items she needed, and hurried home.

Jacob came the next week, and the next. Sara took her own way, disregarding her parents' pleading and tears. She did not find any happiness in it, but she seemed powerless to change the course that she had set herself upon. She had made a promise and she would keep it. She did love Jacob, and somehow she felt sure that once they were married and settled in their own home, it would be a happy home and she would be at rest. Jacob was so kind and considerate! But oh, how much she wished for the approval of her parents on their plans before she left her childhood home.

"Sara—" Father's voice was full of love and kindness, yet heavy with the burden that was on his heart. Sara had just arrived home from a Saturday evening social.

"Father, I wish you and Mother would just go to bed rather than wait up for me every time I go somewhere," Sara interrupted before Father could say more. Oh, how she longed to go straight to her room.

"No, we can't do that," he replied. "We are too concerned about you to rest anyway! I don't know where we have failed you, Sara, that you have chosen this course. We have tried to teach and train you in the fear of God. We have warned you of the consequences of your choice and will continue to do so as long as you are under our roof."

Sara sat down with a deep sigh. Every time she was with Jacob was spoiled before she could even relive the blissful memories of the time she had spent with the handsome young gentleman soon to be her husband.

"Sara, I must share something with you that I heard at the general store today, and I sincerely hope you take heed. Mr. Blackhouse says that Jacob still buys cigarettes."

"I don't believe it," Sara returned heatedly.

"Why he told me, I don't know. I didn't ask for the information," Father went on. "He knows that you and Jacob are dating and seemed surprised that any of our members would smoke. I did inform him that Jacob is not a member."

"But, Father," Sara hurried to explain, "I know he used to smoke, but you know he made a confession. I think we should accept that. If it is true that he still buys them, it must be for his father."

"We also have reason to believe he is drinking," Father continued earnestly. "I talked to Brother Mast about it, and he is planning to look into it."

"Father!" Sara was exasperated. "I wish everyone wasn't so eager to believe everything they hear about him. Jacob is trying to live down his father's reputation."

"Sara, beware!" Mother warned. "You are not accepting facts. We wanted you to wait until Jacob had proven himself faithful for at least several months. But you did not listen."

"The young man does not need to live down his father's reputation. He is making his own by the things he does and says." Father spoke very firmly. "You may not go with Jacob anymore until he proves that he is faithful. You may not have him come here. While you are under our roof, you must obey. It will not hurt you to wait a few months. If the reports we are hearing are not true, it will soon be known. If they are, you will be glad you waited."

Sara burst into tears and rushed to her room. She refused to listen anymore.

Brother and Sister Mast stopped in at the Yoder home late one evening toward the end of the next week. "Sara, we would like to speak with you privately," Brother Mast requested. "There are a few things we feel we must share with you."

Sara reluctantly walked to the front room with the minister and his wife. She closed the door behind her and took a chair across the room from them.

"Sara, we are very sorry to have to tell you this, but we are not sure about the character of the young man you are keeping company with. We want to trust him, but we continue to hear unfavorable reports. We have talked with him, and he denies each accusation. We want to give him the benefit of the doubt, and yet we must be cautious."

Sara sat rigid, not saying a word.

"We have asked him to wait another six months to be received into the church fellowship. We had planned to receive him on confession of his faith next week, but now we have

asked him to wait until fall Communion time."
Brother Mast looked at Sara kindly before going
on. "He said he was baptized soon after his con-
version, before they moved out West, but he has
never joined a church because, he says, he was
waiting for his father to settle somewhere. We
want to trust him, but we would like to ask you
to discontinue your friendship with him until
after he is a member here. Then if he has proven
himself, you will be free to start again."

Sara pressed her lips into a thin line. "He is
discouraged already because no one trusts him.
I think if I did that, we would be doing him more
harm than good. Why may I not continue to
encourage him to do right, during that waiting
period?" she burst out.

Brother Mast was shaking his head. "That
would not work for his good, or for yours," he
returned. "No, we feel you should not be seeing
him at all during the proving time."

"Brother Mast," Sara replied, her voice trembling with emotion, "I know there are lots of
scandalous reports circulating. But they are not
true. Some even say he was drinking and carousing with some of the community boys down at
the store last Saturday night. But he wasn't. I
know, because I asked him about it on Sunday.
He said it wasn't true and was very hurt that I
would even believe it enough to question him
about it."

The Masts left with heavy hearts. Sara had not responded as they had hoped she would. "Perhaps there is some truth in what Sara says," Brother Mast admitted to his wife. "It does seem that many people are eager to repeat gossip about one who has failed, and add to it too, even after he has truly repented. We want to be slow to believe everything we hear, and yet we need to take the necessary precautions."

"Jacob should certainly be willing to submit and prove himself, if he is sincere," Sister Mast added thoughtfully.

A few more days passed. On Saturday morning, when Sara went out to bring the cows in for milking, she had an unexpected opportunity to meet Jacob. The cows were in the back pasture, and Jacob was out early, also bringing their cows in for milking. Sara told him about her conversation with her parents and the visit from the Masts.

Jacob was angry, vehemently denying all the accusations. "Sara," he begged when he had cooled down sufficiently, "you won't let me down, will you? You do trust me, don't you? It was bad enough when they said they wouldn't take me into the church, and now they try to turn you on me too!" Jacob paced back and forth restlessly as his herd of cows started for the barn. "Why don't we just get married and put an end to all this fuss?"

Sara's mind whirled. "Jacob, this is so sudden," she began. "I hardly know . . . I do want to do all I can for you. I do trust you. But can't we just be patient and try to live down the rumors about you? We want to have a wedding with the approval of the church, and we will have to wait until you are a member. Let's not do anything rashly, anything that will put us out of favor with the church and with my family. I want to marry with their blessing."

"But, Sara," Jacob reasoned stubbornly, "everybody seems determined to ruin our friendship. They will soon convince you that it won't work. Let's go on and get married and show them that it will work! I promise you that I will bear all these false reports patiently, without any retaliation. I will not smoke or drink. I realize now I shouldn't have done those things when I was younger, and I have truly repented of them. I want to be a sincere Christian, but it is hard with a father like mine. If you will just stand with me, I will prove my faithfulness and will soon be a respected member of the church. Will you trust me?" His voice was pleading.

"Yes, Jacob, I trust you. I am sorry that you have been falsely accused. I know it is hard, but let's bear it patiently now and prove that your character is above reproach," she encouraged him. In the end, they agreed together to discontinue dating for a few weeks until this storm blew over.

Sara moved to where the cows were waiting. "I must get these cows to the barn, or Father or James will soon come looking for me," she called back to him.

Jacob smiled patiently at her. "I'll meet you here in the pasture as often as I can," he promised, turning to follow his cows to their barn.

Sara hurried the cows along the path toward the barn. Father was waiting. "They must have been clear back at the woods," he remarked, watching Sara closely.

"They were," she returned honestly. She was glad her meeting with Jacob was out of sight of the house and barn.

In the next few weeks, Jacob walked carefully whenever there was any danger of being found out by the Germantown people. When he wanted any of his forbidden pleasures, he found them outside the valley. He used every opportunity to give his testimony in church, or to humbly confess his weaknesses. He attended regularly, was always on time for church services, and was always ready to take part in any church work. The members were favorably impressed. By mid-May, the ministry reversed their stand and Jacob was received as a member. Many of the brethren took an interest in this promising young man, offering him much encouragement. But what pleased Sara the most was that her parents finally allowed her to date with their blessing.

Sara was able to sing again as she went about her work. Jacob and Sara announced their intention to marry, and Sara shared freely with her parents their plans to be married sometime soon. They did feel sure now that Jacob was sincere, and Sara tried gratefully to be more submissive and open with her parents. Together she and her mother sewed her wedding dress, Sara in eager anticipation of the day when she could be married. But even though Jacob was now a church member, her parents encouraged her to continue to go slow. "You are still young," Mother reminded her. "Jacob just turned nineteen, and you will not be nineteen until August."

Jacob had other ideas. He was continually urging Sara to set a date. "I am a church member now," he said hopefully. "Is there any reason your parents keep insisting that we wait?"

Sara shook her head uncertainly. "Only that they didn't want us to get married so young," she returned. "But maybe they will consent now. My wedding dress is made, and we know what we want. Really, I don't know why they want us to keep putting it off."

"Tell them we are going to get married next week, and see if they will give their consent," Jacob urged one Sunday in mid-July. "You are mine, and I am tired of all this waiting!"

"I'll try, Jacob," Sara promised with some misgivings.

The following week Sara's parents were shocked when Sara informed them that she and Jacob were planning to be married on Saturday. "We have been to Brother Mast and asked him to marry us. Since we are both members in good standing with the church, he consented to do it if we have your permission," Sara hastened to explain.

"But, Sara, you are only eighteen. And Jacob is young too," her mother had protested. "Couldn't you wait at least until next summer when you both would be almost twenty?"

"We can't wait till then, Mother." Sara had said hurriedly. "Jacob is tired of all this waiting! He has bought a house, and I'm sure he doesn't want it to sit empty for so long. Nor would he want to live in it by himself."

"Sara, this all seems so hasty to Father and me. Are you waiting on God to lead in your lives, or are you trying to find your own way? We would much rather you would wait until you are older."

Sara shook her head. Her mind was made up. They had waited long enough already; Jacob had said so emphatically. "Reuben Bender is leaving in two weeks to go out West for several months," she offered as her last argument. "We would like to have our wedding before he leaves."

Mother sighed deeply. "Oh, Sara, I wish you wouldn't be in such a hurry. Give Father and me time to talk about it."

That evening Father sat down with Sara in the kitchen. "Sara, Jacob cannot even get a marriage license at his age without his father signing."

"Oh, that is why we must do it before Reuben goes West," Sara assured them. "Jacob thought of all that. And his parents fully approve of our marriage. We are just waiting for you to give your consent."

She looked at them with her chin tipped up. "Furthermore, if you don't give your consent, we will get married anyway, even if we have to go to the courthouse to do it!"

"Oh, no!" Mother remonstrated. "You want to have our ministers marry you."

Father looked at Sara soberly. What had ever happened to the sweet and submissive daughter that she used to be? Must they give in to her now, to let her learn in bitter tears that the way she was choosing would be a painful way? Father bent his head in silent reflection. There seemed to be no other way at this point to deal with this stubborn daughter. So the consent was reluctantly and hesitantly given; the decision was made. Sara was greatly relieved.

On Saturday morning preparations began early, with Marie and Lois helping Mother to prepare the house and the wedding dinner. Sara rushed about, hardly able to fix her mind on what needed to be done. The wedding service was to be at 11 o'clock.

All morning Sara's heart sang. "Jacob will make a wonderful husband and provider," she exclaimed to Mother. "He is a hard worker. He will be a good Christian father." She did not notice at first that Mother did not seem to share her enthusiasm. "He is so sincere. He has just had a rough time, but that will make him strong!" She looked at Mother when Mother made no response. It was then she noticed that Mother's eyes were red and tired and her face looked haggard.

Mother must be thinking how much she will miss me, Sara reasoned, still jubilant in the knowledge that her parents had finally given consent to their wedding. Yet down deep in Sara's heart was a nagging awareness that all was not well. Somehow that consciousness took some of the joy out of the wedding preparations.

The Yoders and the Benders and Brother and Sister Mast would be the only wedding guests. They were all invited to stay for dinner in the Yoder home. All the Germantown young people were invited to supper and to spend the evening.

"I pronounce you husband and wife," Brother Mast was saying. The wedding ceremony was completed. Sara had waited anxiously to hear those words. Now as her small hand was clasped in the big, rough one of her husband at this solemn moment, a flood of thoughts washed over her, overwhelming her.

She was entering a new era of life, the way that she had chosen. There was a finality in those words "as long as you both shall live" that sent a thrill of joy and fear through her being. She had chosen to walk out of the watchful care and protection of her parental home, and now she was entrusting her life, her spiritual well-being, herself with all her needs, to this young man. Would he meet those needs as tenderly and lovingly and fully as her parents had? Would he care about her eternal good and make decisions in the light of eternity as her parents had these past almost nineteen years?

Of course he would! Sara tried to still the anxious racing of her heart. He only needed a little time, a little encouragement and experience to become all that she hoped he would be. She would trust him.

In the thrill of her anticipation of marriage, Sara had not sensed the overwhelming reality of what had just taken place as she did at this awesome moment. A slight trembling passed through her entire body, and Jacob looked into her eyes and smiled—a big, carefree smile. Sara tried to return it but found she could not. *I must get hold of myself,* she thought desperately, willing the tears that threatened to spill over to remain hidden behind her eyelids.

In the evening after the young folks had all gone, Jacob and Sara looked again at the gifts piled on the dining-room table. The kettles from her parents and the set of dishes from his would be among the most often used items. But there were many other useful gifts from their friends: things for the kitchen, a quilt, towels, some sheets, a butter churn, and a few tools that would come in handy.

Sara thrilled as she touched one item after the other. These gifts were the things she would begin housekeeping with. "Some evening this week, all the families from our church will come with a 'surprise shower,'" Sara informed Jacob, who was not yet accustomed to all the German-town practices.

"Is that right?" he said in a pleased voice. "Back where we came from, wedding gifts came only from the guests who were invited to the wedding."

"Our homes are too small to invite everyone from church, so this has always been our prac-tice here. That shower will consist largely of food," Sara added.

"Shall we load up the wedding gifts tonight yet?" Father asked, stepping into the room where Jacob and Sara stood talking. "Or shall I just drive you over and bring these things next week?"

"Oh, I'd like to take them now," Sara spoke up quickly. "Then they will be out of Mother's way too."

"I have the team hitched out there," Father

said, and he and Jacob began carrying the gifts out to load them in the back of the carriage.

The little two-room cabin on the small place Jacob had bought was only a mile from the Yoder home. Sara thought it would be nice to be close to both sets of parents. She held the box with the dishes while Father drove carefully. Jacob held a lamp. Before many minutes, all the gifts had been carried in and placed in a corner of the kitchen–living room combination. "I will put these away next week," Sara decided. "It is getting late tonight."

The few pieces of used furniture left lots of space in the two small rooms. But Jacob and Sara were happy. There had not been money left for a horse or more furniture just now, but Jacob had a good job. They would soon have everything they needed, Sara was sure.

The first week of married life was so full of interesting happenings that the time passed swiftly for both Sara and Jacob. Sara had all her wedding gifts to put away. A food shower by the folks from the Germantown church took up one evening. And just the everyday chores, without her mother or her sisters to help, took longer.

During the next few weeks Sara settled into a routine that fit both her and Jacob's schedule, and she found she had time on her hands. The house seemed so empty and quiet without the chatter of younger brothers and sisters or the encouraging interchange with her parents.

"Housekeeping for just two doesn't keep me busy enough," she said to her mother one November day as she helped her mother with the mending. "You got behind in your work helping to get ready for my wedding, and you still have not caught up."

"The younger girls help more since you are not here," Mother replied softly, giving Sara a warm smile. Sara returned Mother's smile and then glanced out the window to where Marie and James were working together to rake the last of the leaves out of the yard to mulch the garden.

She and Jacob had spent one Sunday, soon after their wedding, with her family. And another Sunday they had spent with the Benders. Sara would have loved to spend more days with her mother, but Jacob did not seem to fully appreciate her mentioning it.

"Why don't you go spend the day with my family?" he would return.

Sara would just look at him, hardly knowing how to express the difference she felt between the two families. She just enjoyed so much more to be with her own godly parents and brothers and sisters. This blustery November day was the first time Jacob had given his consent. Sara had walked the mile home to spend a day with her mother while Jacob spent a long day on the mountain, logging. He usually did not get home until late in the evening. It was so good to be back in the warmth and comradeship of her family home.

"Do you mind being alone all day when Jacob is at work?" Mother asked as she sewed a patch on James's overalls.

"Not much, until it gets late in the evenings," Sara responded hesitantly.

"Is it usually late before he comes home?" Mother questioned with concern. "When he was still working for his father, we often saw him leave to go home before six o'clock."

"I guess he is working longer hours now so that we can get a few more things we need." Sara was reluctant to say more. She had often wondered herself why Jacob was not home until long after dark. How could one see to cut logs in the dark? But she had never asked Jacob such questions.

After the schoolchildren came home, Sara gathered her outdoor wraps for the walk home. "It has been a good day, Mother. I enjoyed it so much," she said sincerely.

"Come anytime," Mother invited warmly, looking closely at her oldest daughter. The last few times she had seen Sara, she had been troubled by the dark circles under her eyes. Mary Yoder thought she detected a look of sadness, almost like fear, in her daughter's face. But she would not question her. If Sara had struggles and wished to share them, she would know that her mother was ready to listen. *She is still young. Perhaps the adjustments to marriage are harder than she expected.*

The concerned mother hoped that nothing more serious than that was wrong. But her heart told her otherwise. If all was well, Sara would adjust easily.

How could she know the physical and emotional pain that Sara endured at the hands of a rough and inconsiderate husband? How could she know about the ensuing sleepless nights and Sara's many secret soul-searchings? She could not, because Sara would never tell her.

"Oh, John," Mary confided to her husband that evening, "I'm afraid Sara is not happy. I wish we had not given our consent for her wedding. We should have insisted that they wait longer!"

John stood alarmed as his wife burst into sobs. "What has happened?" he asked after a moment.

"I don't know of anything, really. I just *feel* that all is not well," she said tearfully.

"I agree that we should have insisted Sara wait longer. We allowed ourselves to be persuaded to make a hasty decision because it did seem as though Jacob was doing better. We felt sorry for him, his home situation being what it was, and didn't want to discourage him. But we should have taken a more definite stand before they even started to date. I fear we will live to see the day that we regret our decision most bitterly." John Yoder expressed the deep concern on his heart. "We will need to do all we can to encourage them both."

"We trusted him. And our ministry did too. They were satisfied with Jacob's commitment when they received him into church fellowship," Mary commented sorrowfully.

"Has something in particular happened," John asked, "that makes you feel he cannot be trusted? Did Sara say something when she was here today?"

"Not really. But couldn't you see how sad she seemed? She tried to be cheerful, but it didn't seem natural. Something is troubling her, but she did not mention what. Other than that Jacob often doesn't get home till late in the evenings."

"Maybe she is just lonesome, Mother," Father suggested. "She was used to having a big family around."

After praying fervently for their daughter and her husband, the burdened parents went to bed. But sleep did not come easily for Mary that night. For hours she lay awake, her thoughts a continual prayer for her oldest daughter.

Sara turned her steps slowly homeward. As she walked in the lane, a deep longing welled up in her heart. She still trusted Jacob as she always had; at least she tried hard to convince herself that she did. *He has fierce struggles because of his weak home life and past,* she excused him. *I must not let it trouble me as I have. I must keep close to God myself and be a cheerful, supportive wife. Jacob will need lots of help. But . . . if only he would be the spiritual leader in our home. I thought I was marrying a Christian man . . .*

The realization struck her like never before. The deep unmet yearning in her heart for a strong provider, a caring and loving protector, and a spiritual leader almost overwhelmed the young woman as she entered the door of their little home. She had hoped she could depend on Jacob to be that leader.

Her little home . . . She did have that, and how she loved its every nook and corner. She would make it as cozy and homey as possible. Jacob would respond to her love and do his part. He must! He would become stronger in his Christian life, and . . . But why did he seem instead to be losing ground? Why did her dreams of a strong, happy Christian home always end with such nagging doubts and fear?

I hope he can soon find a job on a farm, as Brother Mast suggested, instead of working with that logging crew. If only Father had enough farm work to hire him. But he doesn't. And since his father quit farming, there is not work for him at his home either. What can he do? He has to have work.

I'm afraid it is a rough crew of men he works with. Her troubled thoughts continued to churn. *Jacob needs lots of nurture and help to grow in his Christian life.* This startling fact was becoming more evident to Sara every day as she began to notice some bad habits he was picking up. Or was he? Were these habits he had had from his youth and had tried to keep hidden from her before they were married? Sara refused to dwell on these thoughts. She wanted to trust Jacob fully, as she had in the past year when everyone else had seemed to doubt his integrity.

Sara forced herself to sing as she prepared supper. She positively must be prepared to encourage him. A worried, strained atmosphere would not help matters.

An hour later the young bride stood hopefully at the kitchen window, watching for her tall young husband to return. She could picture him rounding the curve, hurrying in his eagerness to get home to his new wife. She would go out to meet him!

As Sara donned coat and boots, she thought about Jacob's wish for a horse and buggy. So far they had walked to church and to the store for supplies. It was a few miles, but they were young and strong.

Sara grabbed a lantern and walked to the end of their long lane to wait. The sun had already set an hour ago. As she waited, Sara began to realize how cold she was. The night air was biting cold. She could not continue to stand here and wait. With deep disappointment she walked back to the house. Jacob would be late again.

Entering the house, she checked her supper. It too was getting cold on the back of the stove. She put more wood on the fire and tried to coax more warmth to heat up her supper and her own cold hands and feet. Then she sank down into the chair near the kitchen window. Picking up her Bible, she found the place she had been reading in the morning. *Time will go faster if I read awhile,* she decided. Her mind was not at rest, and she could not concentrate. *Logging is such dangerous work, but Jacob is quick and strong.* She tried to calm the restlessness in her heart. She bowed her head. She did not know how long she had been praying when there were heavy footsteps on the front porch.

"Oh, Jacob!" She met him at the door. "You are so late tonight. I worried a little that something had happened to you."

"Don't do that," he scolded gently and then laughed. "I'm here. Let's eat."

"The potatoes are stiff," Jacob grumbled as he hungrily shoveled in the food, "and the gravy is too thick."

"I'm sorry." Sara felt hurt. "They were not this way at six o'clock. I didn't know you would be two hours late, or I would have made supper later."

"Well, I didn't know it either, or I would have told you," Jacob retorted tersely.

Sara glanced at Jacob's sullen face, and then turned her head. She could not swallow. She had never seen him look this way before. Tears came to her eyes. Sara had not meant to start an argument; she had only wanted to explain. Of course the food would taste better if they could have eaten right away after it was ready. But the evenings she had waited a little longer to start supper, he had come home on time. When supper was not ready when he got there, he had been very impatient.

Silence filled the room for several minutes—a heavy, threatening silence.

Jacob sighed as he pushed his plate away. "I'm tired. Let's go to bed."

"Shall I clear the table first?" Sara asked, attempting cheerfulness in spite of the tremble in her voice.

"Do as you like," he replied carelessly, starting toward the bedroom without offering her any assistance. "I am going now."

For several minutes, Sara wiped tears, trying to calm herself as she put the food away and wiped the table. Things were soon neatly in order in the front room. *I will wait and wash the dishes in the morning,* she decided as she walked out the back door with the empty water bucket. Sara looked up at the starry sky as she pumped the water. *O Father, help me to be calm and cheerful,* she prayed, realizing her desperate need for help.

Jacob is tired tonight. Logging is hard work. I must not be hurt so easily. That probably irritates him too. Sara carried the heavy bucket of water back into the house, closing the kitchen door softly behind her. Shivering from the cold, she backed up to the wood stove for just a few moments to warm herself. It was then she noticed the nearly empty woodbox. *Oh, I should fill that tonight yet, or I won't have wood to make a fire in the morning.* She grabbed her coat and made several trips to the woodpile behind the house. *There, that much is done for the morning!* she thought as she carefully dumped the last load into the box.

With fresh courage in her heart, Sara entered the bedroom a few minutes later. Jacob was still awake. "What kept you so long tonight?" she asked him softly. "I know that you must be very tired. Twelve hours is long to do such heavy work as logging." She spoke gently, in a truly caring tone.

"Yes, it is hard work," he replied, ignoring her first question.

"Was there something unusual that came up at the last minute, or was there just more work that needed to be done?" she continued, hoping for an explanation. Jacob had always talked freely of his job before.

"Oh, Sara, can't the questions wait till later so I can get some rest?" There was a strong undercurrent of impatience in his voice. Sara understood that the real truth of the matter was that he did not wish to answer her questions!

For a long time Sara lay perfectly still, struggling with her emotions. She did not want Jacob to know just how hurt she felt. She worried a great deal before falling into a troubled and restless sleep; and she awakened early, long before dawn.

The troubled feeling was still with her when she awoke. What was wrong? Then she remembered the evening before. *But surely it will be different this morning,* she reasoned hopefully. Jacob was only tired last evening. *Everything will be all right when he awakens this morning.*

When the early dawn began to cast a soft glow in the north window, Sara got up quietly. It seemed strange to be getting up alone. Jacob had always been ready to go to the kitchen with her. She hesitated in the doorway. *Should I call him?* Slowly she pulled the bedroom door shut behind her. She would let him sleep a little longer this morning. *I will fix a big platter of pancakes first; then I will call him*, she decided.

Secretly, Sara wished she could rid herself of the nagging fear that persisted in her mind—a fear that she could not admit even to herself. *Everything will be fine. His personality will improve with time. He is feeling a little pressed with the responsibilities of his new job.*

Half an hour later, over the good aroma of pancakes, liverwurst, and maple syrup, Jacob smiled proudly on his young wife. "You should have called me," he chided with a grin. "I ought to have built up the fire for you."

"I wanted you to get a little more sleep," she said sincerely. "I didn't mind. I had filled the wood box last evening and carried in a bucket of water. So I was able to handle breakfast alone."

Jacob smiled sheepishly. "You're a good girl, Sara. I knew I had chosen the best girl in Germantown," he complimented her, feeling a great deal of pride in his own ability in making such a wise choice.

The months passed. Winter brought bone-chilling cold. Sara carried many an armload of wood into the house in an effort to keep reasonably warm. Jacob continued coming home at any hour. More often than not, it was late, and then he was nearly always in a bad mood.

"Really, Jacob, do you need to work such long days?" Sara questioned one evening in spring. Then she added hesitantly, "Your paychecks don't seem to reflect any extra hours on them." Immediately she wished she had not said a word.

Jacob stared at her for one awful moment of silence while the color heightened on his face. "And who do you think you are, that I would have to give account of my every minute to you?" he asked in a cold, hard tone. "All right, I work ten hours a day, just as I always did. What I do after six o'clock is my business."

Sara caught her breath in a sharp gasp of surprise. She had not meant to anger him. She had had no thought that her question would stir up such a response.

But the response . . . Now her fears were no longer just fears; they were reality. If he was not working those last three or four hours before he came home, then what *was* he doing?

"Do you understand?" he asked her in the same icy tone.

Sara wondered if he expected an answer, but to relieve the silence she said, "Yes, yes. I guess I do." Her voice was expressionless. Her thoughts were troubled. What had he meant?

In the long, agonizing silence that followed, Sara began to admit to herself the real truth— that her marriage was a disappointment. Jacob Bender was not the sincere, kind, considerate young gentleman that he had posed to be. Could he even be trusted? Sara's mind flitted back to many scenes of the past. Had he really changed back then, or had she simply become blind to his faults? But no, her parents had also come to believe that he had changed. They had agreed to her marriage. The ministers had received him into the church as well, thinking him truly repentant and sincere.

Many thoughts troubled the young bride. They had scarcely been married for ten months, and so far married life had held none of the glamour that she had so often dreamed of. Jacob had not reformed, nor even made any effort to do so, that she could tell. Rather, he was becoming more and more difficult to please. Gone also were his charming ways, those little efforts to please her. But most troubling of all was his continued lack of interest in spiritual things.

Sara's young heart bowed with new fears. Surely, surely he would soon change. He would see the need to repent and be at peace with God, and things would be different again. Maybe it would take more time. To Sara, used to the love and affection of a godly home and the carefulness to honor God's Word, there seemed to be nothing to do but hope he would do better.

But the hurt was very deep. He did not share her elevated view of the church, nor did he share her views of godly home life. She knew he had been brought up differently than she had been. She had known, but she had not reckoned with the difference it would make in her own home. She had built her hopes on the assumption that he had changed, that he was sincere, and that he would also want a godly home. Now she was beginning to realize that he had deceived her. The realization was very painful.

Sara bravely struggled to hide her tears in his

presence, knowing that such weakness angered him. Supper was over and Jacob went to bed. Sara followed as soon as she had gotten the kitchen into some kind of order.

The next morning, as soon as Jacob went out the door, Sara turned her back on the stack of dirty dishes and fled to her bedroom. She was sobbing great, heart-rending sobs as she dropped to her knees. She would go to the Lord with her problem.

She had determined that she was not going to run home and tell Mother about every difference or problem in her home. But she knew that her family was aware that not all was well. They knew that Jacob was not attending church regularly. They also knew that he did not spend many evenings at home. James or Marie often dropped in after their supper and found her all alone. They did not talk about what they saw but just offered encouragement with the simple words, "We are praying for you." Sara was so thankful for their unchanging love and concern.

Such remembrances flooded over her now as she knelt by her bed. "Father in heaven," she cried out, "I have been rebellious. I have wanted my own way. I have not sought Your will, nor received the advice I was given. Father, I'm sorry." She repented in bitter tears. "Please help me to be faithful, to make the best of my wrong choice, and to be a good, submissive wife. Just don't let me stray away from You. And, Father, please speak to Jacob. Draw him with Your love. Deal with him in tender mercy."

For a long while the heartbroken, contrite young wife agonized in prayer before finding rest for her soul. She began to raise her head, peace again softening the crushing disappointments she was facing daily. Her hand fell on a jacket that Jacob had carelessly flung across the bed before leaving, and through the lining she felt a bulky package.

What is in that pocket? Sudden pain, like a knife thrust, flew through her as she drew out a half-finished package of cigarettes and realized the truth of her suspicions. Sara groaned and replaced them. Could she possibly stand any more? *Surely he isn't smoking! He promised. He promised at the same time that he would also stop drinking. If he broke one promise, will he also break the other?* The young wife had no assurance that he would not. None at all.

The past twelve months spread in vivid panorama before her. The many conversations with Jacob came back to her now: his assertions of good intention, his seeming devotion to her, his thoughtfulness, his apparent sincerity . . . Everything appeared in bold relief now. How she still wanted to trust him, even as she had trusted him then. But the bare facts glared at her, and facts cannot be denied.

Back then, Sara had not been able to see the purpose of waiting. And even last summer, when her parents had wanted her to wait until the coming summer to get married, she had rebelled. Would that have made all the difference in their lives? She did not know, but she did know this one thing: how much wiser her parents were than she! Sara could hardly believe the difference between the way she saw things now and the way they had looked to her then.

But the past could not be changed. *Today I am Jacob's wife, bound to him till death. I will try to submit and live a Christian life, and possibly by doing this I will be able to win him to the Lord.*

Lord, I need Your help. It looks overwhelming, Sara prayed as she walked into her untidy kitchen several hours after she had left it. She set a teakettle of water on the stove, poked up the dying flames, and added another chunk of wood from the wood box. Dropping the lid with a deep sigh, she began gathering dirty dishes off the table. *Surely he is just going through a period of strong temptation,* she reasoned. *This is not the way Jacob really is. I will be careful not to anger him. I will encourage him in every way I can.*

The next few days did go much better. Jacob showed many little loving considerations to his wife. Sara believed he was trying to show her he was sorry.

Saturday came and Sara's heart was light. She had enjoyed rich fellowship with the Lord all week and now was looking forward to His blessing in worship on Sunday. She spent the day cleaning her little home until every corner was polished and every window shone. She refilled the wood box and carried in two buckets of water for over Sunday. She finished her baking and cleaned and dressed one of the old hens for Sunday dinner.

After six o'clock Sara began to watch the clock restlessly. She prepared stuffing for the Sunday dinner hen and peeled potatoes. After setting the potatoes in a kettle of fresh water, she began to pace the floor. Seven o'clock, eight o'clock, nine o'clock passed. Finally she sat in the old hickory rocker and opened her Bible. *Father, help me not to fret but to keep my trust in You,* she prayed with deep longing in her heart. *Help me to be able to meet Jacob cheerfully when he arrives and not to nag him. O Father, keep me close to You.*

Oh, where can Jacob be? What can he be doing this time of night? Troubling thoughts filled her young heart.

Dear Father in heaven, I want to read Your Word. Help me to turn my thoughts to You, to be able to concentrate on Your precious Word, to receive the strength I need . . . Sara read for an hour, one comforting passage after the other, and her heart was uplifted.

Eleven o'clock, twelve o'clock passed. Still not a sound of footsteps. Sara could not hold back the tears any longer. He had never come home this late. Perhaps there had been an accident. *Perhaps,* she thought, *I should run over to my parents and ask someone to go up the mountain and check. But . . .* Sara waited.

Finally she went to bed. Then he came. She heard his footsteps and ran to the door. Holding it open, she smiled a welcome home as great relief flooded her worry-tortured brain. Her husband was well, and he was home. He staggered in and leaned against the kitchen table to steady himself.

"You are very tired," she said compassionately. "I have kept the fire going, and the stew is hot. Come in and eat."

"I don't want to eat," he said with a thick voice. "I'm going to bed. And let me sleep. Don't wake me up till noon."

Sara's head reeled when she smelled her husband's breath. He had been drinking. Her husband was *drunk*! First smoking, now drinking! Sara regretted that she had not told him about finding the cigarettes. She had hoped there would never be any more, but his breath had told her more than once that there had been, though she had never seen them again.

Sara watched with an aching heart as her big, strong husband made his way unsteadily to the bedroom. She pulled the stew off the stove and followed him.

"Jacob," she said softly, "tomorrow is Sunday. Don't you want me to wake you at eight? You could sleep again in the afternoon."

"No!" he shouted. "I told you to wake me at noon. Did you hear? I know what day it is; that is why I'm sleeping in. I don't have the chance to do that any other day of the week." He glared at her. "And I hope that by twelve o'clock you will have a big dinner of ham or fried chicken ready for your hard-working husband."

Quick tears sprang unbidden to her eyes at his sharp retort. "But, Jacob, I can't possibly get home by twelve. I will have dinner on as soon as I can after church. If I put it in the oven in the morning, it will be ready to serve soon after I get here." Sara bravely tried to smile as she helped the tottery man to bed.

"Do you mean you are going without me?" he asked in an injured tone.

Sara was shocked to silence. The first several times he had refused to go to church, she had remained home with him. Later, he had told her that she could go if she wished to but that he was too tired.

His sharp tone again cut her to the quick. "Do you mean you won't stay home one time with your husband, to prepare him a good meal on time?"

"If it was necessary, of course I would," she

answered meekly. "Are you sick, Jacob?" she asked with concern.

Jacob laughed a hard, dry laugh. "Do I look sick? I can take care of myself. If you want to see that preacher more than the man you married, go on and see him first. If you can't bear to miss seeing him one Sunday, I can wait."

As Sara humbly surveyed the man she loved, she wanted to tell him, "Yes, you do look sick." But she held her tongue. No explanation was needed as to why she was going to church. Jacob knew that her love and devotion were for God. His insinuating accusation hurt deeply, but Sara did not speak as she prepared for bed.

Soon Jacob was snoring. Then Sara let the tears flow, and the sobs shook her body. *This is so different than I had planned. I refused to face reality, refused to believe it was possible for Jacob to be anything but the gentleman that he pretended to be!* There was no comfort in the thought, except that now she had seen her mistake and had found forgiveness with the heavenly Father. He had pardoned her and had drawn her close to Him, but she would have to live her lifetime with the consequences of the way she had chosen.

Sunday morning Sara wearily built a good fire in the cookstove. *That should hold till I return from church,* she decided as she placed the roaster pan with the stuffed chicken into the hot oven. She set the table and pushed the kettle of potatoes to the back of the stove.

I would be glad to stay if that would help, she reasoned. *But it wouldn't. I would soon lose out spiritually also.* Many unanswered questions churned on and on in her mind as she prepared to go to church. *How can I fill my place as a submissive wife and still give God first place in my life?* Sara was open now for help. Her high esteem of her own opinions was crushed flat. She was ready to listen to those older, more experienced, and wiser than she.

The guilt of her past rebellious and unsubmissive attitudes toward her parents and minister had burdened her until she had promised the Lord that she would confess it to them and to the church, and do whatever else was needed to clear the past. At last she was ready to humbly submit. But it was too late to change the awful plight in which she now found herself.

I will leave early enough so I can walk, she decided. She knew that her parents would welcome her going with them. It was a beautiful spring morning, and a walk would be invigorating to her troubled mind.

When she neared the Germantown Valley church and saw several families arriving, all her resolves suddenly fled. Sara was sorely tempted to retreat quickly to the woods. *I want help, and yet how I cringe before it!* she agonized. If only she could disappear, to find her way home again rather than face the many questions that were sure to come. Jacob's unconcerned absence still another Sunday would surely reveal what she had for so long tried to hide—that she had been deceived. While she contemplated these thoughts, a cheery "Good morning, Sara" came from behind her.

Startled, she whirled around and faced James.

"I decided to walk through the woods along the railroad track today," he explained, stepping out from between the trees. "The rest are with Father and Mother in the carriage. But where is Jacob?"

"At home," Sara stated simply, reluctant to say more.

"Is he sick? Or too tired to come?" James did not mean to be thoughtless. But Sara could not think of a justifiable reason to give him. With relief, she noticed her parents' carriage turn in just then. Father stopped near where she and James were standing, and Sara walked to meet them. She knew that her parents would ask the same kind of questions, but still she wanted to be near them.

"Jacob isn't with you?" Father asked in a disappointed tone, not requiring an answer.

"Logging is hard work. He is very tired," she managed to say. Father did not ask any more questions.

167

Sara walked in and sat beside Mother. Ruth squeezed between them.

After the service, Sara stayed long enough for Mother's greeting. "We are praying for you, Sara," Mother said, squeezing her hand. Sara smiled through teary eyes and then hurried down the aisle and out the door before anyone else had the chance to talk to her. She knew she desperately needed the fellowship of the saints. But the truth was just too painful now. She hurried home.

The house was quiet. It was quarter till one. She started toward the closed bedroom door, when suddenly an unsightly mess on the kitchen table arrested her attention. She had not left the kitchen in such a shambles.

Sara stared. Her mouth dropped open. She sank into the nearest chair. A sudden weakness overtook her. There was a sickening churning in her stomach as she took in the sight before her—four cigarette stubs and an empty whiskey bottle, all evidence of what had happened in her absence. Sara wept bitterly.

Her mind swept back again to a scene months ago: Brother Mast sitting across the room from her and saying, "Sara, he does seem sincere. We want to give him the benefit of the doubt. But it would be safer to wait. Give him a six-month proving period. If he is sincere and is seeking God's will, he will wait for you." And her own angry retort, "I don't believe it! I don't know why everyone keeps bringing up all these false reports against him, after he has repented!" Now her own undiscerning, unsurrendered will appeared to her as it really was, not as she had thought it was then.

At the time Sara had been hurt. Too hurt to recall that it was not like the Masts to hold anything against a repentant person just because of false rumors and gossip. She had often confided in them and found help and encouragement. Now she wondered how she could have so blindly assumed that they would accuse anyone falsely.

Sara also remembered the Saturday Father had come home from town and warned her of the things he had heard about Jacob. That time, too, she had defended the young man. It could not be true, she had thought. Why was everyone so ready to believe tales? Sara had been shocked that everybody could be so unreasonable. And when Father demanded that she break off her courtship with Jacob, she had rebelled.

She thought about how Jacob's record of good conduct, along with her defense of him, had finally cleared him. He was received into the church, and her parents had also lifted their restrictions for Sara's friendship with him.

Sara shuddered miserably. *And now it has taken only a few short months to learn to know*

Jacob as he really is! The young wife sat motion-less, too stunned to weep. Too many incrimi-nating thoughts crowded into her troubled mind to allow her to be able to think or do anything. Even when she shut her eyes, she could not erase the scene before her. She tried to think, to con-vince herself that she still trusted the man she loved. She wanted to believe that it was not true. But it was.

Blindly she stumbled to the bedroom. Jacob was not there. The room reeked with a nause-ating smell. The bed was a mess. Immediately she began rolling up the putrid bedding to be washed.

One evening during the next week, Brother and Sister Mast stopped for a visit. Surprisingly, Jacob was home. No longer did Jacob try to appear humble and repentant. He was loud and coarse and blatant, boastfully admitting the sins he was being accused of. Sara could only listen in heartsick humiliation. Jacob had deceived her, and he did not even care.

After his excommunication from the church, Jacob no longer tried to hide his sins from the small church community. He committed them openly and boldly. "It is what they expect of me," he laughed at Sara's grief and pleading. With no consideration for the one to whom he had pledged his love, Jacob plunged deeper and deeper into sin.

6.

Learning to Look to God

More months passed. Spring turned to summer. Jacob and Sara's first anniversary passed uncelebrated. Jacob celebrated in his own way, but it was not in remembrance of their wedding, nor would Sara have wished to be included. Sara's birthday passed unnoticed. More and more, Jacob came and went as he pleased, as much at home with his logging buddies as he was with his wife.

Soon afterward came another special day. Again Jacob was not there to share this very special occasion with his wife. Mother and Father Yoder came over in the evening to bring Jacob and Sara some baskets of fresh produce from their garden.

171

"Jacob isn't home yet?" Mother questioned when they were ready to leave later in the evening. "I notice that supper is still on the stove," she added.

"No," Sara replied wearily, her voice trembling. "And when he isn't here by nine on Saturday nights, he usually doesn't come until morning."

Father looked at Mother, deeply concerned.

"I will stay and spend the night," Mother said, casting an anxious eye toward her daughter. Father nodded his consent and went out the door alone, after noticing the look of relief on his daughter's face. Quickly Mother followed Father outside for a moment. "Father, you had better send James over so I will have someone to send for help if I need it. He can sleep on the couch in the kitchen. I will sleep with Sara."

Before morning a healthy seven-pound boy brought a new joy and responsibility to the Bender home. Sara gazed on the small, innocent gift from God with a feeling of great wonder. His lusty cry brought a mixture of joy and grief as her arm lovingly encircled him.

How can I bear for this dear child to grow up with a drunken father? she mourned. But nothing could change that now. The father of this innocent child was spending the night drinking, smoking, playing cards, and carousing with the rest of the loggers, up on the mountain at the logging camp. He was totally unaware that his son had been born.

When Jacob returned on Sunday morning, he was surprised and not a little disgruntled to find his mother-in-law in the kitchen. Without a word, the young husband walked straight to the bedroom. In his stupor, still not comprehending what her presence meant, he called hoarsely, "Sara, are you still in bed?" He walked into the room. "Did you know your mother is out there?" he asked in an aggrieved whisper.

Sara aroused from a deep sleep. "Oh, Jacob! Is it you?" Smiling, she drew the covers aside, revealing the sweet face of the tiny baby.

Her husband stood dumbfounded. For once he had nothing to say.

The following week, Jacob showed Sara the most benevolent kindness and consideration that she had enjoyed since they were married. Her hopes soared. Now Jacob would be different. The baby had touched a tender chord in his heart as nothing else had. *Yes, I can see he is truly sorry for the past months,* she rejoiced. *We will have a happy, godly home yet!*

Father and Mother Yoder and all the children came several times in the next weeks to watch the progress of the new baby in the family. How thrilled Ruth and Lois were to hold their tiny nephew and try to coax smiles out of him. Even the Benders came to visit. This was their first grandchild as well. Sara was happy that Jacob's family was interested enough to come. But she could not help but compare her own family, in their quiet demeanor, to the noisy and boisterous Benders.

So soon, it seemed, Sara's soaring hopes for Jacob's improvement were dashed into the same depths of sorrow that all her other dreams and expectations of the last year had been. The Sunday baby Samuel was four weeks old, Sara felt able to go to church. How eagerly she dressed her little one, hoping that Jacob would also go. But he soon made his intentions known. "Can't you keep him home one day a week for me to enjoy too?" he asked.

"Jacob," she pleaded, "you do want our son to have the opportunity to grow up to be a Christian man, don't you?"

"He can be a Christian man like his father, without going to church," Jacob replied irritably. "All right, go ahead and take him. When he is a little older, he will choose for himself whether he will go with you or stay at home with me."

The very thought struck deep pain and fear to Sara's heart. *Oh, my God,* she cried in distress, *somehow help me to be able to instill Thy fear in his young heart.* The young mother knew that she would be working against odds that were beyond her strength or wisdom. Her only hope was to commit her son to God and rely on Him.

174

Even though Sara knew she could only expect to reap the painful consequences of her rebellious heart and hasty actions, she still determined to do all in her power to bring this child to know and serve the Lord, regardless of the cost. *I dare not break down under the weight of my disappointments. I must be strong and live my life above reproach before this child.* Realizing that the task was too great for her, she turned to God.

After bundling her little one up for his first outing, Sara walked to her parental home that morning and rode with them to the Sunday morning service. The whole service was inspiring. How good it was to be in the midst of God's people again after having missed more than a month of services!

The message spoke to her heart in a special way that morning. Though Sara knew that God had forgiven her, she suddenly realized that her sinful rebellion must be confessed publicly. Her example had left a harmful influence and had brought reproach on the testimony of the church in the community.

After the sermon, when Brother Mast opened the service for anyone who had a testimony or confession to share, Sara rose to her feet, trembling, her little one in her arms. "I want to ask all the brethren and sisters to pray for me," she began. "I have been stubborn and rebellious and have taken my own way. I would not receive advice from my parents nor counsel from our faithful ministers. I thought I knew best. But I was mistaken. I'm very sorry. I hope you can forgive me for the reproach I have brought on the church by taking my own willful way. I believe that God has forgiven me and received me again as His child. But there is a lifetime of reaping ahead, and I need your prayers and help," she finished brokenly. She took her seat again with tears flowing freely.

Before he closed the service, Brother Mast also made a confession to the congregation. He confessed his laxness in guarding the church and using proper discipline and carefulness to keep sin out of the church.

After the service, Brother and Sister Mast met with Sara and her parents. "I feel a share of the responsibility for the situation Sara is in," Brother Mast admitted with regret. "I was not discerning enough. And I was too easily persuaded to receive Jacob without sufficient proving time."

"We too feel a deep remorse," Father said. "I am sorry, Sara. We should have taken a firm stand and never allowed you to begin that friendship in the first place. Jacob had obvious spiritual needs, and we all chose to ignore what was so apparent. We are at fault for our leniency. And because of our failure as parents, you have the reaping to bear." Father and Mother were both weeping.

"You are all forgiven," Sara said sincerely. "But it is finally my fault, not yours. I chose the way, and I will have to walk in it. You did warn me. I can thank God for forgiveness and believe that His grace will be sufficient for each day. But do pray for my dear husband. God is able to save his soul and deliver him from his life of sin. We must never give up."

As the weeks passed, Sara felt refreshed by regular church attendance, even though she needed to go without Jacob. Listening to God's Word being preached and sharing in the fellowship of the saints was so strengthening. The brethren and sisters kindly refrained from asking Sara about her husband. They were grieved for her sake and were deeply touched by Jacob's evident neglect of his young wife and child. Many offered words of encouragement and assured Sara of their prayers for her and for her husband's salvation. Sara felt the love of the brotherhood and was touched.

One Sunday after the message, Brother Mast again opened the service to anyone who wished to share anything with the congregation. In the moment of silence that followed, Sara was flooded with love and adoration for her Saviour and for His love and forgiveness. Joy welled up in her heart, thrilling her through and through. How thankful she was for the opportunity of repentance and acceptance with God. Past sins were forgotten, put away as far as the east is from the west. And she had love and acceptance from the saints as well.

Someone was speaking. Sara's thoughts were drawn again to the present. It was her dear friend Sadie, who was still in the group of young people.

"I want to confess that I have been guilty of the same sins Sister Sara confessed several weeks ago, and I ask your forgiveness." Sadie's words, though sounding contrite and sincere, cut Sara to the heart.

Why would she bring up my past sins again? Why not name her own? Bitterness threatened to rob Sara of her peace. Quickly she sought her Saviour's face for the enabling grace to forgive. Peace was restored in her heart, and Sara rejoiced, thankful if her confession could be of help to other struggling souls, to spare them going on to spiritual ruin.

The next couple of years brought no desired changes in the Bender home. Sara remained true to her commitment and kept her faith in God. Jacob continued in his sinful habits.

Then there was a change, one that Sara accepted as bittersweet. A little girl was born into their home. Two-year-old Samuel was delighted with a baby sister, but the mother was pained, realizing afresh what her children were missing in not having a Christian father.

Sara had found herself often comparing Jacob with her own father, the dear godly father under whose watchful care she had grown up, and she had tried to make up for the difference to young Samuel by careful training and a godly example. Nevertheless, she was realizing more and more the tremendous, overwhelming odds she was working against. And now here was another eternal soul to instruct in the fear of God. Would it be possible? *Only with God's help*, she breathed to herself, *and by relying heavily upon God's grace*.

One March evening several months later, Sara had just fed Rebecca and had tucked her into her small bed in the clothesbasket. There was a sudden commotion outside. Quickly she took Samuel's hand and went into the front room. What she saw made the frail young mother turn pale. Four big, burly men were coming across the porch.

The door burst open and Jacob entered, motioning his noisy buddies to come on in and join him. All four pulled out kitchen chairs and sat down. One pulled out a deck of cards and another a pack of cigarettes. From somewhere came a bottle of whiskey, which they immediately began passing around.

From the shadows where she had hidden, Sara had seen enough. Noiselessly she slipped back into the bedroom, the only other room in the house. *Oh, what will I do if all four get as drunk and unruly as Jacob alone does?* she cried in silent distress, knowing there was no outside door from her bedroom. *Father, protect me and my little ones,* she pled earnestly.

Instead of placing Samuel in his crib as she had intended to do a moment before, she drew him close and lay across the bed with him encircled in her arm.

"I will tell you another Bible story," she whispered to the wide-eyed, silent child. He nodded mutely. She felt him tremble under her arm and prayed that they could both be calm. "You be very quiet, and don't ask any questions this time. Just listen," she instructed. Samuel nodded again. He was always ready to listen to Mother's stories.

The bedroom was dimly lighted with one candle. Sara had left the kerosene lamp on the kitchen table, intending to put the children to bed and then go back to the kitchen to make a few more preparations for their Sunday meal. But after Samuel was asleep, Sara stayed hidden in her bedroom. *I will not risk being seen by that group of wicked men,* she reasoned, and knelt quietly beside her bed.

"Sara! Sara!" A call came from the kitchen. Sara lifted her head but had no desire to respond.

"Sara! Sara!" The call came louder and more insistently.

Sara glanced wearily at the clock. Eleven

o'clock. She had not slept yet. The time had been spent on her knees in prayer and communion with God.

"Sara! I say, come here!" Jacob's voice plainly declared that he had no intention to stop calling until she came.

With awful dread, Sara got to her feet and stepped quickly out the door, hoping the children would not awaken. Fearing that her trembling knees would not support her, she leaned against the wall.

"Don't just stand there staring," her husband ordered rudely. "It's getting cold in here. Put another log on that fireplace."

She obediently turned toward the fireplace. Quickly she stirred up the glowing embers and added three small logs.

"Don't be so slow," Jacob snarled. "We are hungry! Get the fire going in the cookstove and get us some supper." He was glowering at her. "Now get some supper," he repeated threateningly, "before I have to show you who's boss."

"I'm afraid the fire has gone out," she said hesitantly, not moving a step toward the kitchen end of the front room.

"Well, what's the idea? Letting the fire go out before I've had my supper. You had better get it going again, and be quick about it!" he growled.

The other men laughed raucously. "You don't expect her to treat us like company, do you?"

One man bullied him. "I'll bet she'd rather throw you out."

"I expect her to do anything I tell her," Jacob returned coldly.

He turned to Sara. "I want supper," he demanded menacingly.

Sara thought quickly as she walked toward the stove. *I'll use some of this beef that my parents brought over this week,* she decided, picking up a jar. *And I have noodles. Perhaps I can hang the kettle over the fireplace. That would be quicker.* She looked across the room and saw a good blaze in the fireplace, with lots of red embers.

"We aren't going to settle for any pot of soup." Jacob gave his stipulation angrily. "I want ham or fried chicken."

"There is no ham," she replied meekly. "And I didn't dress any chickens today, since my parents shared some beef."

"You heard what I said. I want fried chicken. And mashed potatoes and green beans."

When Sara hesitated, he bellowed, "There aren't any chickens dressed? Well, you know how to butcher a couple, don't you?"

Sara nodded incredulously. Did he really expect that of her at midnight? It was evident that he did. Quickly she hung the large kettle over the fireplace and filled it with water. She grabbed a handful of kindling and started the fire in the cookstove. Then, with the butcher knife and the empty water bucket in hand, she hurried out the back door.

Oh, I should have brought the lantern, she lamented, but she did not turn back. *The moon is bright. I can see.* She pumped the bucket full of water, ran to the chicken house, grabbed two five- or six-pound fryers from the roost, and began the job. After their heads were off, Sara returned to the house. She stuck several more chunks of wood into the cookstove where the kindling had caught.

The men paid little attention to her as they continued their filthy talking and jesting. Sara took the water, which was now boiling in the kettle over a crackling fire, to scald the chickens and hurried out again as fast as she could, thankful to get out of their presence.

As soon as the feathers had been removed and the chickens were cleaned and washed in the bucket of cold water, Sara returned to her once tidy kitchen, now thick with tobacco smoke. Quickly she cut up the fryers. She set the large black skillet on the front burner, adding a lump of lard. Then she rolled the chicken pieces in flour and laid them in the skillet to fry. She went to the pantry for a few potatoes from the family's fast-diminishing store and quickly peeled them. While they boiled, Sara turned the golden brown chicken pieces to the other side. She opened a jar of green beans and put them in a kettle to warm.

Sara glanced at the clock. Twelve-thirty. *Oh, I hope Rebecca won't awaken until I have this meal served*, she thought. The thought became a silent petition to the heavenly Father. Not a sound had been heard from the bedroom since she had come to the kitchen.

At one o'clock, Sara set four plates on the table and filled the water cups from the bucket in the dry sink. She hesitated before adding one of her fresh loaves of bread. She had baked only three yesterday because the flour was nearly all gone, but if she did not put bread on the table, Jacob would be sure to ask for it. She set the dishes of food on the table before the four men. They set to eating greedily while she retreated to the bedroom.

The delicious aromas followed her, and her empty stomach churned miserably. She had not eaten any supper. But she knew she would not have been able to swallow a bite of food even if she had had the opportunity.

When Sara returned to the bedroom, Rebecca was beginning to stir restlessly. Sara carried Samuel to his small bed in the corner; then she fed the baby and tended to her needs. It was almost two o'clock when she dropped onto her bed exhausted, to listen to two more hours of loud carousing, curses, and raucous laughter.

Finally everything quieted and Sara fell asleep.

When Sara awoke to the urgent crying of a hungry baby, the reluctant March sun was already shining over the eastern horizon. Remembering that it was Sunday morning, Sara quickly got up to feed the baby. She would have to hurry to be ready in time for church. Jacob had not come to bed, and the house was still and quiet.

Sara shivered in her threadbare nightgown, wondering why the house was so cold. Pulling a quilt around her, she finished feeding the baby. Then she dressed quickly and went out into the front room. *No wonder it's cold!* she thought. The front door was standing open, and the fire in the fireplace was nearly out. Hastily she built up the fire and hung the black kettle over it. Then she cleared away the remnants and confusion of supper, busily setting the house in order before getting Samuel up for breakfast.

She stirred oatmeal into the water in the kettle. While the oatmeal simmered, she got the little ones up and dressed. *Jacob won't likely be home for dinner,* she thought. *I will not start a fire in the cookstove this morning. I can fix something quickly over the fireplace for Samuel and me for dinner.*

   *   *   *   *   *

Nearly two years passed. Again it was a Sunday morning. And again Jacob was not at home. Sara dressed the children for church, eager to be with the people of God again for another Lord's Day worship service.

Just when Sara was ready to start out the long lane to meet her parents for a ride to church, they came driving in to pick her up. "Thank you, Father," she said, holding Rebecca up to Mother before she climbed up. James jumped down and picked up Samuel, hoisting him up into the carriage. Then they were on their way.

"You don't ever need to walk out with the little ones, Sara," Mother offered. "Just wait for us to come for you."

"I just wish my husband would take me to church," Sara said wistfully. "But of course we don't have a carriage, and now not even a horse." Recently Jacob had sold the horse he had used for several years to go up the mountain to his work every day. He had been saying recently that he planned to buy a car as soon as he could save enough money.

"We don't mind at all taking you along to church," Mother assured Sara.

Sara looked at Samuel. He was always happy to go along with Grandpa's to church. He was sitting contentedly on the floor between Uncle James and Uncle David. The aunts were good-naturedly arguing over whose turn it was to hold Rebecca, while Mother smugly kept the smiling two-year-old on her own lap.

"Our carriage is full," David remarked. "Maybe

we ought to get one of those cars like the ones we see going through Germantown now and then."

"Maybe we will sometime, David," Father said as he guided the horses toward the Germantown Valley church.

Sara noticed the twinkle in Father's eyes, and then James burst out, "Maybe in time for church next Sunday!"

While Sara's younger brothers and sisters were chattering about that surprising announcement, Sara turned questioningly to James.

"Father has decided to get a car, which is propelled with an engine and doesn't need horses to pull it. In fact, it is ordered already!" James explained, his excitement evidenced in his voice.

"That sounds like a good idea," Sara said. "I've wondered how long it will be till my family makes the change, since several others are already driving cars now."

"Since we got the tractor," Father added, "we don't need the workhorses. And a car seems practical so that we won't need to keep the driving horses either. It seems to be a good invention and will certainly be more comfortable, especially in bad weather."

"Jacob has sold our horse and is planning to get a car as soon as he can," Sara told her family. "He says he can get around a lot cheaper and faster that way."

One day not many weeks later, Jacob suddenly

seemed to have a lot of money. The new car was purchased, and he proudly showed it off to his family.

"Would it suit you to go shopping on Saturday? I'm off all day and would like to take you along," he offered.

"We need groceries and some other things as soon as we can afford them," Sara replied, thinking of the many needs the family had.

"Sure," her husband answered congenially. "Make a list, and we will get everything we need. The children are probably needing some clothes. I think we will go out to the larger city, because there are things I want to get that we can't get here at the dinky little Germantown store."

Sara nodded silently.

"Do you want to take the children along? Or shall we leave them with my mother?" Jacob asked.

"Oh, I'm sure Samuel would enjoy going along, especially since we have the car," Sara replied. "And Rebecca would rather go along too than stay somewhere else. In the car it will be easier to take the children."

"Yes," Jacob agreed. "It is a wonderful convenience. I don't know why I never thought of inventing a horseless carriage. Just think of the money we would have if I had been the inventor!" He laughed.

"Oh, Jacob, you earn plenty," Sara answered

modestly, never mentioning that very little of that money was used to meet even their simplest needs. *With the wages Jacob earns,* she continued to muse, *we should never have any needs. If only he would stop drinking and gambling with that crew of loggers . . .*

Suddenly Sara felt a qualm of conscience. Where had all this money come from? She was sure it was not from his wages, and he had no savings that she knew of. Should she ask him? No, that would not change anything and would only anger him. Sara's joy in the necessary things that they were about to purchase was dampened. Were some poor logger's wife and children going without necessary food and clothes because of a large bet that her husband had won? Her heart ached for whoever it might be. Sara earnestly sought God's will concerning their spending and what her responsibility was regarding the extra cash they had so suddenly and mysteriously acquired.

The Saturday trip did supply many things that the Bender family badly needed. It even supplied an extra that Sara had not dared to allow herself to hope for—lumber to build an addition to their tiny house. She had dreamed for months of how practical it would be to have separate rooms for their growing children. And now, to her surprise, they stopped at the lumberyard and Jacob ordered enough supplies to build two bedrooms onto their two-room house.

In the weeks following that shopping trip, Jacob stayed home every Saturday. And best of all, he stayed sober. With the help of his brothers and Sara's father and brothers, the rooms were soon finished. Four-year-old Samuel was pleased with his new bedroom. Later, when they were able to obtain a crib, Rebecca was moved into hers.

"Jacob, will you go to church with us tomorrow?" Sara pleaded after a pleasant afternoon of working together to finish the new rooms.

"If I wake up in time," he responded with a grin. "I haven't been working so hard. Sure, I'll go with you."

Samuel ran to his father and threw his arms around his legs. Then, looking at his mother, he asked, "Will you tell Grandpa that I can sit with my father tomorrow?"

"Surely you will sit with your father tomorrow," Sara assured her little son.

When James brought eggs over that evening, Samuel ran across the yard to meet him. "You don't need to come for us tomorrow. Father is going along to church."

"Wonderful!" James responded.

When James returned home with the good news, his father said, "We must keep praying. God is working."

Jacob kept his promise. He went with his family to church. But to Sara's deep disappointment, he spent the afternoon in bitter complaining. First it was about the sermon, and then the church's mistreatment of him, and finally, the hypocrisy he claimed he saw in the members, as well as a whole list of other grievances.

Sara's heart ached miserably. "Please, Jacob," she pled with him softly, "don't let the children hear you talking like that. Samuel especially is already picking up so much."

His careless response grieved Sara deeply. "He may as well learn it now as after he is grown," he retorted.

After the addition to the house was finished, Jacob again quit coming home on Saturday nights. Many other evenings he was away also, and the times he was home were often a terror to Sara and the children. Even Rebecca, at two, was growing fearful of her father. Sara noticed with deepening apprehension that Jacob was becoming more violent each time he came home drunk. She thought it seemed that he was becoming increasingly bitter and disagreeable since his one Sunday in church.

Sara appreciated the new rooms greatly. It helped so much to have a little more living space in the house. She was thankful for the added privacy she now had to entertain the children out of their father's presence when he came home drunk—or when he brought his buddies home for a night of card playing and drinking.

After such times, her heart was especially saddened. Would her children never know a Christian father? Sara continued to pray and endeavored to live a life above reproach. Could not a submissive and godly wife finally lead her husband to God?

It was summertime, and the days were very busy. One hot July day, Sara spent most of the time picking an abundant crop of green beans. Samuel helped all that he could until Sara sent him to keep Rebecca happy. Sara was hot and tired. With supper over and a canner of beans on the stove cooking, she went out to the garden again to try to finish her job. She finally finished the last row and plodded wearily to the porch. "I will try to snap these yet this evening," she said to herself.

Stepping up onto the porch, she heard Samuel suddenly cry out. She hurried into the kitchen in time to see Jacob swing his big, muscular arm, hitting the small child on the head and knocking him flat on the floor. "I will teach you to sing something different once in a while," he bellowed. "I told you I am tired of them Sunday school songs." He grabbed the boy roughly and stood him on his feet. "Now, do you want to sing it again?" He roared savagely in his face.

Shaking with sobs, Samuel shook his head. "No, Father, I won't," he choked.

Jacob laughed.

Sara's heart was sick. She felt numb with dread. Besides her sorrow for her children in their suffering, she wondered how she could ever train them. Day after day she was realizing more profoundly the importance of seeking God's will in every detail of her life. She felt totally unable to face life's perplexities alone. She had no godly husband to support her. In fact, he was working against her. The way she had chosen was a hard one.

As the summer progressed, Jacob was away from home more often than he was at home. Sara kept close to God. He was her constant companion. Though there was much grief to endure, she daily felt His sustaining grace. More and more their family life was revolving around Sara and the children. She no longer waited to eat until Jacob came home, but fed the children at the regular supper hour, had family worship with them, and put them to bed. If Jacob came home, she always had something prepared that she could fix quickly for his supper.

One evening soon after Samuel's unjust punishment, Sara called the children to come. "We will have our Bible story now," she said. Samuel took Rebecca's hand, and together they walked to the couch, where Mother sat with the Bible storybook.

After reading a story about Jesus caring for the

little children, Mother asked, "What shall we sing?"

"'Jesus Loves Me.'" Rebecca lisped her favorite song and joined in with Mother as she started to sing.

Samuel sat silent, a strained and tense look on his face.

"Samuel," Mother said softly, "help to sing."

He shook his head, stiffening up all over.

"You usually enjoy singing," Mother encouraged.

"Father doesn't like it," he said, scarcely moving his lips.

"Father is not here now, Samuel. You can sing."

When he still refused, Sara said, "Samuel, I am sorry that Father does not love God. But we love God. God is pleased when we sing. We want to sing to Him now, don't we?" She looked longingly at the tense child.

"I don't want to sing anymore. I am afraid I will forget and sing when Father is here."

Tears came to Sara's eyes. Should she insist that he sing?

"Let's pray first," the burdened mother suggested. "Then God will give us courage to do what is right." She poured out her soul to the loving Father in heaven and rejoiced as Samuel formed his little prayer.

Without any more resistance, Samuel helped as they all sang several songs, and the children went to bed with cheerful hearts. Sara rejoiced in God's provision for her and her little ones.

That summer, besides the garden to meet the family's needs, Jacob had planted an acre of corn and rows and rows of beans. Sara worked hard from early till late. There were always customers to buy vegetables, and there were always the leftovers to can. She had not counted on any help from her husband, but neither had she ever dreamed what an endless task it would be. Some days she was sure she would never be able to last till the end of summer. There was no choice but to neglect the children, much against her desire. But finally the first frost came and the truck patch was over.

One evening in October Jacob came home with bundles and bundles of strawberry plants. "If I get a piece of ground worked up this evening, do you think you could get these planted tomorrow?" he asked.

Sara sighed inwardly before she replied. "I probably could. But, Jacob, how will we ever harvest them in the spring? How will we keep them weeded, along with a big garden?"

"We'll worry about that when the time comes," he remarked carelessly. "You get these unloaded while I work some ground. I won't be in for supper till late."

After the new plants were unloaded and carefully placed in a shady spot, Sara prepared supper, fed the children, prayed with them, and put them to bed. She waited and ate with her husband when he came in after dark. Nothing more was said about the acre of plants to be set out the next day.

7.

Sorrow Upon Sorrow

Spring came again, and with it came the burden of overwork. The new baby, Dorcas, was only three weeks old when the large strawberry patch needed to be weeded. Sara looked ahead with a deep feeling of depression. What lay ahead she could not know, nor did she wish to know. One day at a time was enough to face, and she faced each one with dread, wondering how she could possibly go on.

Day after busy day passed, with Sara laboring to keep up with the weeds in the strawberries and the peas, as well as the rest of the gardening. In addition, Jacob had requested—rather *demanded*—that they pick and clean dandelion leaves too and deliver it to the Germantown store to sell, whenever they had some spare time.

Five-year-old Samuel did the best he could to help her and tend the younger children. Totally exhausted by night, the young mother would fall into bed to sleep for a few hours till daylight came again in the early morning. By Sunday she was almost too tired to appreciate the worship services.

Finally, worn to exhaustion, Sara faced her situation squarely. "I have gotten too busy," she decided. "I have neglected my time alone with God. There is no way that I can do everything in a day that has to be done, but I will not neglect my daily devotions."

She noticed evidences too that she was not spending enough time with the children. They were often quarrelsome and naughty. "I will not neglect the children," she determined further. "Their care and nurture shall have first place."

Having gotten her priorities straightened out, and committing all things anew to God, Sara felt she could go on with His help. She got up the next morning with calmness in her heart. She felt more rested than she had for weeks. Dorcas had slept better, and Rebecca and Samuel had both slept all night. She walked to the kitchen, picked up her Bible, and sat down in her rocker. She would not be pressured again into beginning her day without taking time to pray and meditate on the precious Word. She found sweet refreshment in this time that she spent alone with God before getting the children up and preparing breakfast.

Jacob was not at home, and he had not been home for over two weeks. He was beginning to be almost a casual visitor. Sara did not mind that he was not there.

As soon as the house was in order and tiny Dorcas had been fed, Sara wrapped the baby in a warm blanket. Then she laid her in the clothes basket and carried her along to the garden. Samuel and Rebecca followed.

Samuel helped to drop seeds into the rows for a while. Soon he tired of that and was happy to play with Rebecca to keep her satisfied while Mother covered the long rows.

When Sara was finished covering rows, she walked over to the children. She was just in time to hear Samuel say a naughty word. "Samuel!" his mother lovingly and sternly corrected him. "I told you that you would be severely punished if you use that word again. It is bad to talk like that." While she was talking, Sara broke off a little switch from the willow tree near the garden.

"Father said it one Sunday when he was mad," the small boy defended himself.

Sara was pained deeply. She knew full well where her son had learned his bad language, but she knew she must give the promised punishment. *Is it fair?* she wondered. *Yet Samuel must learn right from wrong. He must learn that doing wrong brings punishment.* And so she administered the punishment with an aching heart.

As Sara prepared lunch for her little family, troubling thoughts continued to tumble in her mind. Must she live with the remorse and reaping of her wrong choice all her life? And must her children also suffer the consequences of her rebellion for the rest of their lives? *How confusing it must be to one so young. He is suffering from the wrong choice that his mother made,* she reminded herself with deep regrets. Would it never be different? Would her husband always set a bad example for the children and finally lead them astray in spite of her best efforts to train them in the fear of God? How different their lives would be with a Christian father!

Never before had the youthful folly of taking her own way looked so serious to Sara as it did since her children also shared the consequences. Many fears plagued her; painful memories haunted her. Sara knew that the guilt was gone. For that she thanked God, but what about the results of her choice? Those would remain.

After a morning in the fresh air, the children were ready for naps after lunch. How Sara longed to join them! But she returned to the large garden to spend the rest of the afternoon.

All through that week she labored, pleased to be getting so much done before the weekend.

Friday afternoon came at last. She and Samuel were working hard to finish weeding the last of the strawberry patch. "Can you pull just a few more weeds," she encouraged when Samuel would have gone off to play, "so that we can finish the strawberries this evening?" She smiled at her little son. "Then we won't have to work so hard tomorrow and will be better prepared to worship God on Sunday."

All week Sara had planned her time well, working hard to accomplish her goals. She had even had time, with the help of her sister Lois, to clean two half-bushels of dandelion greens, which James delivered and sold for her. She felt a deep satisfaction with the results of her week as she sat reading to the children on Friday evening. That is, until Jacob came driving in.

"Not much garden planted yet," he observed, coming into the house after a brief look at the garden. "Have you sold any dandelion?"

He pulled out the cash drawer in the kitchen and quickly counted the small pile there. "Is this all of the money?"

"Yes, Jacob," Sara replied. "With all the weeding in the garden, I haven't had time to gather and clean much dandelion. And besides, it doesn't sell for much."

"Well, we'll have to get busy tomorrow and plant more beans and tomatoes." He made his stipulation plaintively. "I brought a thousand tomato plants home with me that must be planted tomorrow."

"Oh, Jacob," Sara protested, feeling weary to the core, "I don't think I can handle more."

Jacob stared at her long and hard. "Maybe we can grow less next year if the strawberries do well. But we don't have much choice this summer, with the children to feed and clothe all next winter."

Silently Sara wondered just how much of the crop cash would be left in the drawer until winter came again, regardless of how much she raised.

At four o'clock the next morning, Jacob called, "Sara, let's get started planting those tomato plants while it's cool. You can come in later and dress and feed the children. Just fix us some coffee and cooked mush quick now, before we go out."

Obediently, Sara got up, feeling dizzy from weakness and loss of sleep. Dorcas had not slept well, and even Samuel and Rebecca had cried out for their mother several times.

After eating a quick breakfast, she and Jacob worked in the garden until the sun had risen high in the sky. When Sara went back to the house, both Dorcas and Rebecca were crying brokenheartedly, and Samuel was sadly trying his best to comfort them.

"Hurry, Sara," Jacob called an hour later. "It looks as if it will rain today."

Again the baby was taken out in her basket

202

and set at the end of the rows where they worked. Rebecca fretted and played in the dirt. Samuel dropped row after row of tomato plants while his parents planted them.

By evening, everyone was exhausted. Sara sank down wearily to feed the baby before preparing supper.

"Come, Samuel," Jacob called, walking toward the kitchen door. "Do you want to go with Father to get something to eat? Then Mother won't have to cook supper for us." Samuel hesitated, and then went to his father.

Sara was alarmed. "Jacob, where are you going?"

"Into the city. It won't take long in the car. I'll have him back by bedtime."

Sometimes Sara wished they had never gotten the car. Where would he take their five-year-old son for his supper? What all would the young child encounter while away from her protecting care? In deep grief, the mother spent her evening in prayer, never thinking of her own need for food. She fed and put the little girls to bed and dropped into her rocker again with her precious Bible. Where should she turn for relief and consolation and guidance in this dark hour? God in His faithfulness drew His child to Himself, and her soul was flooded with hope and encouragement before she heard the Model T chugging in the long lane again.

The next morning, while Sara prepared break-fast, she also put Sunday dinner in the oven. When she went to awaken the children, Jacob, to her surprise was up also.

"Oh, Father," Samuel exclaimed, "are you going to church with us this morning?" He ran and grabbed his father's hand.

"Aw, son, I'm too tired. Why don't you stay home with me?"

Samuel hesitated. He loved going to church, and he scarcely knew his father. But he had had a good time with Father the evening before.

No more was said. Sara prayed fervently that the young child would not be bribed or—worse yet—forced to stay home.

After breakfast Sara quietly told Samuel to dress for church while she dressed the girls. He obeyed without question, apparently having for-gotten his father's suggestion. Jacob appeared to be asleep on the couch until Sara was just ready to walk out the door.

"You going to stay with me, Samuel?" Jacob asked, raising his head off the couch.

"Oh, Jacob, please . . ." Sara pleaded.

"You have him every Sunday. I don't often get a chance to enjoy my own son," he remonstrated. He turned to Samuel. "Will you, Samuel? We'll play some games."

Samuel gave in reluctantly and remained behind when his mother went out the door, her

204

tears flowing freely. Sara felt crushed, realizing anew that the choices she had made in her youth would have a very real bearing on the choices her children would also make.

For a while after that, it happened often that Jacob would come home for Sunday and persuade his young son to remain at home with him. Then Jacob began to drink more heavily, coming home less, and Samuel was no longer willing to stay at home when his father was there. Jacob never forced Samuel to stay with him, and for that Sara often thanked the Lord. She continually prayed for wisdom and strength to do everything she possibly could to teach and train the children right so that when they were older they would make right choices.

The summer was long and wearing for Sara and the children. By early June, there were strawberries and peas to pick. Although the strawberries did not bear as well as they would the following spring, the large patch still produced many hundreds of quarts. After the strawberries were over, it was only a short time until there were bushels of beans and tomatoes to pick. Many customers came to buy what Sara grew in the garden. What she did not sell, she canned for the family.

Soon the corn began to yield, and that also sold well. But in spite of all she sold, the cash in the drawer did not accumulate to any great amount. Jacob came home often enough to keep it to a small minimum.

One Sunday in late September, Sara arrived home from church, blessed and strengthened. God had been good to her, and she looked forward to the week ahead. She mused on the past summer, marveling at how God had supplied the physical strength she needed, and thinking how helpful and obedient the children had been. She thanked God that the strenuous summer days were behind her, and she looked forward to the winter for time to do some much-needed sewing.

As Father and Mother drove away, Sara walked toward the house. Jacob's car was there, so she knew he was home. Samuel, too, had seen Father's car and was ready to burst into the house. "Wait, Samuel," Mother said softly. She had heard voices and laughter inside. She moved nearer to the window at the far end of the kitchen. *That is a woman's voice, I am sure.* The knowledge stabbed her, wounding her afresh. In the instant that she stood there, she heard, "Don't worry. I'll tell her you're an old school chum that just happened by. Don't look so scared. Sara is harmless!"

Sara could hardly force herself to go inside. Her first impulse was to run and hide, or to quickly cross the fields to her parents' home. But she could not run so far with the children. Furthermore, Jacob had already seen her and would likely expect her to prepare dinner.

Stiff and tight-lipped, Sara stepped inside the kitchen, feeling like a stranger in her own house. Jacob made his explanation without a hint of uneasiness or guilt. Then he asked, "What's for dinner?"

"I don't have anything prepared," she replied in a faraway voice. "I was not expecting you." Her voice sounded ghostly to her own ears as her pale face looked at the two who were sitting on the couch. "I was just planning to get a little something simple and quick for the children and me."

"Well, you are going to have to change your plans," Jacob retorted. "We are here and we want dinner. We must go in about an hour. So fix something for us first."

Sara handed baby Dorcas to Samuel. "Take her to your bedroom and take off her coat," she instructed. "Rebecca, go with your brother. He will tell you stories until dinner is ready."

Samuel nodded and took his little sisters to his room and shut the door. Sara did not worry about them. Samuel was trustworthy.

A great weakness overwhelmed her as she set about the unpleasant task of preparing a meal for the man and woman lounging on the couch behind her. Their joking and laughing were subdued now. Nancy, as Jacob called the stranger, was obviously uneasy, and the high-pitched laughter that Sara had heard when she had first approached the house was silenced.

Somehow her task was accomplished, and they were gone. Sara was alone. She sank, exhausted emotionally and physically, into a chair. Finally, urged by her senses to her duty as mother, she got up unsteadily. *I must give the children something to eat.*

When she softly opened the door to Samuel's bedroom, her soul was blessed. There was Rebecca sitting in the middle of the bed, holding Dorcas, and Samuel was standing in front of them, telling an animated story of the Israelites. He had their attention, and the time had passed swiftly for the children.

"God did so many miracles for them," he was telling his audience as his mother entered the room.

"Yes, Samuel, He did," Mother agreed with a smile. "Before we go eat dinner, let's pray and ask Him to do a miracle for us and save Father," she suggested.

Late that night, after the children were in bed and Sara was still on her knees by her bed, Jacob returned alone.

"Jacob," Sara pleaded, "do you remember the happy evenings we used to spend together?"

Jacob hung his head. Finally he replied with a soft, "Yes."

"Remember how we planned together to have a godly home, a happy home?"

Without looking up, he nodded again. He was sober and very subdued.

"Jacob, that is still possible." Sara's voice was pleading. "Wouldn't you like to enjoy those pleasures we had looked forward to? Wouldn't you like to be at peace with God? He has abundant mercy to pardon and will give you victory if you will only turn your life over to Him."

Instead of answering any more of her heart-searching questions, he began asking questions of his own. "Sara, do you remember I told you I wasn't like you, that I wasn't worthy of you? But you thought you could reform me. You were willing to take the chance."

With tears streaming down her face, Sara said, "Yes, I remember. I thought you wanted to change; that you needed my help." How like a weak excuse that sounded now, even to her own ears! It was an awful chance she had taken and it appeared so much more awful now with three children involved. "I thought you wanted to change, to allow God to take over your life. I thought you wanted to be a true Christian," she repeated sorrowfully.

"Who says I didn't?" he asked sharply. "Maybe if you keep working at it you can convert me yet," he scoffed. Then he quickly changed the subject. In a completely different tone of voice, which told her that subject was closed for now, he asked, "Do you have any cash? I need some badly."

"Not unless there is some in the cash drawer," she answered honestly.

"Well, why isn't there any in the cash drawer?" he asked in an agitated voice. "I am desperate. Don't you have just a little stowed away somewhere after that productive and prosperous summer?"

"No," Sara assured him, "and what I did have in the drawer has disappeared." She dared not remind him where it went. But he knew already and did not ask any more questions.

"Well, if you don't have money, I know where I can get it," he declared mysteriously.

He went outside for some time. Sara saw the lantern in the barn and waited for him to come back to the house. Finally he came into the kitchen, rummaged in several drawers, and then went outside again. Soon Sara heard the car start. When the last *chug, chug* of the engine faded into the distance, she dropped into bed. *Father, she prayed, give me strength to meet each unknown tomorrow!*

That night their small barn burned. Sara awoke to the loud bawling of the cow and the startled cackling of the hens. As she sat up in bed, she could hear the crackling of a fire and see the brilliant reflection of the flames against the side of the woodshed. "Oh, no! Dear Father, help!" she cried as she realized what was happening. The rest of the night was a nightmare.

She remembered dashing into the burning barn to lead the cow out and frantically opening the door to the chicken pen so that the chickens could also go free.

Then her father and James were there, leading her back to the safety of the house. Other neighbors came, starting a bucket brigade from the pump to the burning barn. But little could be done, and from the porch Sara watched in horror as the roof finally collapsed into the building and the whole barn burned to ashes together.

For days afterward, Sara wondered what had started the fire. There was no fresh hay to heat and ignite spontaneously, and no lit lanterns had been left in the barn. Jacob came and went several times over the next few weeks, diligently filing claims with the church's brotherhood aid program for the loss of the barn. He padded his claims generously, Sara could not help but notice. But she knew it would only anger him if she mentioned such a thing.

And then came the incriminating evidence that Jacob himself had set the fire. Sara was totally shamed but not totally surprised. She remembered his statement the night the barn burned, "If you don't have money, I know where I can get it." She remembered also his strange behavior that evening.

When the church refused to pay on his claim, Jacob was indignant, threatening reprisal. His

211

bitterness increased so that Sara sometimes wondered if he could ever possibly be reconciled to God and the church. At such times of hopelessness, she could only fall on her knees, claiming grace and strength from the One whom she had always found faithful.

The church brethren helped to build a new barn for the Benders, making it very clear to Jacob that they were doing it out of consideration for his wife and family. Sara's and Jacob's fathers both helped to provide grain and hay until more could be grown during the coming summer. Church friends had kindly given them several heifers and a few pigs, so that now they had more stock to feed than before. Samuel was big enough now to help his mother take care of the animals, and he enjoyed the challenge.

*   *   *   *   *

Years passed, years of hardship and sore trial. Conditions changed very little, except that Jacob grew more and more hardened in the ways of sin and Sara grew daily stronger in the grace of God. She realized more and more her own weakness and insufficiency, prompting her to put her trust completely in God. There were many hard situations to face, but she was not alone. God was with her.

Sara's faith was sorely tried in many ways. Sometimes months passed during which Jacob seldom came home. But one evening he came home in time to eat supper with the family. Samuel eyed him hesitantly, and Rebecca cringed before this man from whom she had experienced only hurt.

After supper, Jacob left again. To go where, or to be with whom, she did not know. But this she knew—that what she faced was all the result of her own wrong choice years ago. How could she go on under such an emotional strain? The burden was suddenly too heavy to bear alone, and Sara knew she must get help. Leaving the girls in Samuel's care, she walked to her parents' home and asked them to please ask the minister and his wife to come to her.

Brother and Sister Mast helped the sad mother to find peace, encouraging her to be faithful in spite of what her husband did. "You cannot change the past," Brother Mast continued, "but be assured that God has forgiven you. Now you must forgive yourself and go courageously on from here."

"God's grace will be sufficient for all your present needs. Just trust Him," Sister Mast comforted.

"I hesitate to suggest this," Brother Mast continued. "But under the circumstances, I am wondering if you should take the children and go somewhere else to live, away from Jacob's evil influence. Jacob has not been faithful to you or even supported you financially."

"Oh, but I don't think I could do that," Sara replied brokenly. "I love him and still hope to win him if I remain faithful. Doesn't 1 Corinthians 7:10–13 encourage a faithful lifetime commitment in hopes of winning the non-Christian husband?"

"Yes," Brother Mast agreed slowly. "Maybe that was not a wise suggestion. But on the other hand, Sara, you really wouldn't be leaving him. He has already left you. That Scripture says, 'If the unbelieving depart, let him depart.'" Brother Mast cleared his throat and then added, "Of course you know that whatever you choose to do would not give you liberty to have another companion." Brother Mast made that point clear.

Sara was deep in thought. Yes, Jacob had left her, in a way, when he started bringing Nancy home with him and demanding that Sara prepare meals for them. Then there had been other women also. Her husband was seldom home, but as long as he returned occasionally, perhaps there was still hope of winning him for the Lord. Oh, how could she leave him? She did not want to consider such a possibility.

Whether or not Jacob was at home, Sara always called her children together every evening for a short period of worship and instruction concerning God. How she longed for her husband to lead out in these devotional periods. *I knew when we got married that he could not read or write,* she often thought. But she understood acutely now that it was his spiritual condition that hindered his leading out in their worship experience, not his lack of reading skill.

Jacob was home again for a few days. He occupied himself at the kitchen table while Sara read to the children and put them to bed. "Sara," he said when she came from the girls' bedroom, "come here and write something for me."

Sara had often written little business messages for her husband. Unsuspectingly, she walked to the table, where Jacob sat fingering a pretty, light pink piece of stationery. There was a matching envelope lying on the table.

"Here, put this address on that envelope," he ordered uneasily, shoving a little paper across the table to her.

Sara looked questioningly at her husband when she saw the strange name and address. How could she do it?

"Just sit down here and do as I say," he said impatiently when she hesitated. Without another word, she started addressing the envelope. Then he shoved the stationery over to where she sat writing. "I want to write her a letter. Write it word for word as I say it," he demanded.

Never had Sara had a harder assignment! The words she was writing for her husband were to go to some strange woman that he had met in his travels and with whom he wished to keep up a friendship. They were endearing words that should have been spoken only to his wife. But Sara obeyed. Many times in the future, this heartrending task would be hers.

Sara felt confused and began more earnestly to seek God's will in her circumstances. "How can I possibly fill my God-given place as a submissive wife? Is submitting to Jacob in such things helping him along in his sinful practices?" she questioned aloud one day as she knelt at her scrub board. "Should I have taken Brother Mast's counsel and moved out?" Jacob had been home just the night before with another letter for her to write for him. This one was to some tavern in the city, offering them gallons of home-brewed liquor.

"I can't write such a letter," Sara had protested.

"You'll do what I say or suffer the consequences!" Jacob had stated coldly, shaking her till it seemed her teeth rattled in her head. Then his manner had changed, and he had laughed boisterously. "I've found me a new way of making money fast," he had bragged as he pulled out a kitchen chair and sat down at the table. "And you ought to be thankful. It's a lot easier than growing produce to sell!" He had slammed a heavy fist on the table and laughed again.

I can't go on like this, Sara protested in her heart as she rubbed a pair of Samuel's dirty overalls on the rough board.

When Samuel came from the barn that morning, Sara felt even more reason to wonder what she should do next.

"Mother, when I was getting hay bales off the stack for the cows this morning, I found a whole lot of glass jugs stuck under the hay filled with something."

"Oh, son!" Sara cried, knowing exactly what they were. What should she do?

Inner strength flowed into her being from her faithful Father. "I want you to run across the field to the Hostetters'," she directed. "Ask Elmer to come help you. We are going to empty all those jugs." She felt too much shame to ask her own father or David to come.

"What's in the jugs, Mother?" Samuel asked innocently.

"It is wicked drink that makes Father and his friends drunk," Sara answered.

"Oh." Samuel took off on a run across the fields. Before long he was back with Elmer. For the next hour, Sara and the two boys diligently emptied the jugs of bootlegged liquor into the barn gutter. Then they rinsed the empty jugs and set them in a row along the barn wall.

Sara went back to her washing, her heart full of questions. She knew she had done the right thing, but still her whole being was atremble. What would Jacob ever do to her, or worse yet, to Samuel, when he came home and found out what they had done? Sara beseeched the Lord for grace to endure whatever Jacob might choose to lay upon her. Surprisingly Jacob did nothing when he came home again several days later. And to her knowledge, bootlegged liquor was never again stored on their farm.

During the next summer, Sara's health began to fail. Jacob paid little attention except to wonder on his occasional trips home why the truck patch was not being cared for as before.

"I have felt too weak and sick to keep after it," Sara explained patiently from the couch where she was resting.

"What's that big boy doing all day?" he asked, pointing out the window at Samuel.

"He helps all he can. But now that school has started, he has only the evenings to work."

"Well, if he got outside to work every evening right after school, he could get a lot more done," Jacob declared.

"He does work hard after school." Sara defended her young son. "Jacob, perhaps you could come home at five and help. The evenings stay light yet till nearly seven-thirty. It is too much for a ten-year-old to do."

"I do my work up on the mountain. The work here is for you and the children to do!"

"Then I think you will have to plant less," Sara suggested.

Samuel happened to walk in the kitchen door just then. He set a basket of beans on the floor.

"That all you did tonight?" his father asked angrily.

"No, I picked another basket besides this," Samuel answered meekly.

"Are there more to pick?" Father asked. When Samuel nodded, Father looked at Rebecca, who had followed Samuel into the house. "Tomorrow you pick the beans after school," he ordered, looking at Rebecca. "Then Samuel can pick the corn." Then, looking reproachfully at their mother, he added, "It seems to me that if you aren't good for anything else, you could at least teach the children to work!"

Tears streamed across Sara's face as she lay helpless. She knew that the children should work. She had taught them to work, and they were learning to take responsibility. But they were too young to be expected to do so much work alone!

"Jacob," Sara began courageously , changing the subject, "I have asked for anointing with oil for healing, according to James 5:14-16. In about an hour Brother and Sister Mast are planning to be here. I want the children to finish cleaning up the kitchen and then wait here until the service begins."

To her relief, Jacob did not object, or demand that the children go back to their outside work.

But he did mock, which did not completely surprise her. "I got some tractor oil out in the barn that I could pour on your head," he scoffed, "if you think oil will heal you."

"I don't," Sara replied. "But I think the Lord will, if we look to Him and do His will."

Jacob went outside, slamming the door behind him. Sara was grieved. She did not know if he would return that night or not.

Samuel and Rebecca obediently and quietly went about cleaning up the kitchen. Dorcas climbed up on a chair and dried the dishes while Rebecca washed them.

Soon the elderly minister and his wife arrived. Sara's parents and a few close friends also joined the group. Everyone in the small group assembled there believed that God was able to heal. They committed the need to Him, saying, "Thy will be done."

The following morning, when Sara awoke, she felt greatly strengthened, physically and spiritually. She got up and prepared for the day. Jacob, who had come in to bed after the others had left the night before, had already gone before Sara got up.

"Rebecca," Sara called after combing her hair, "I cannot find my covering. Can you come and help me look for it?"

Rebecca and Samuel both came and searched every corner of the bedroom. Then they went to the front room, where their mother had lain on the couch the past week. Sara searched with them. "I know I had it on last evening," she said. "I remember laying it here on the dresser when I put my night covering on. This one is so badly worn, but I will wear it until I find my good one," she finally decided, putting her night covering back on. Then she went to the kitchen to prepare breakfast.

When she opened the lid to put kindling into the cookstove, Sara noticed that the stove was warm. "Um, it is unusual for Jacob to start a fire before leaving," she mused aloud. Then suddenly something caught her attention. Hanging onto the edge of a slightly charred stick was a small fragment of white net material. Part of the hem and a couple of pleats remained, making it evident what had happened to her covering. It could not have gotten there by accident, Sara knew. She was deeply grieved that her husband would go to such an extent in opposing her.

Without telling the children what had happened to her covering, Sara prepared breakfast. As soon as the children left for school, she sat down at her sewing machine to make one more covering from the last small piece of material she had. She never mentioned the loss to her husband, and he never asked where she got her new head covering, though he must have noticed that she continued wearing one.

As the days passed, Sara realized that she had her normal health and strength again. God had chosen to miraculously heal her, and how God's Name was magnified as she shared this experience with her brothers and sisters at church. The service also made a lasting impression on the young children. But their father scorned the idea that it was God who had healed, and he continued to mock for many weeks to come.

Jacob was again staying at home more, and Sara allowed her hopes to rise that he might yet be saved. She tried to show her love for her husband at every opportunity even though he ridiculed her in every way he could.

As that fall and winter passed, Sara realized that eight-year-old Rebecca was not the sturdy, healthy child she should have been. She lost her appetite and often sat at the table silently while the others ate. She seemed to be increasingly insecure and fearful as well, especially around her father. Before long, Rebecca was not able to handle as much of the work as her younger sister could.

Occasionally her schoolteacher sent notes home for Sara. She also was noticing some emotional strain in Rebecca and was quite concerned. At times Rebecca's mental abilities enabled her to excel unexpectedly in school. At other times, she did not seem able to comprehend even the simplest concepts.

Sara was concerned and troubled. But Jacob was angered at the evident weakness in his daughter. One afternoon he looked out the window to where she sat at that moment under the apple tree, forlornly staring at nothing.

"Why isn't that girl busy?" he demanded.

"Please, Jacob," Sara pleaded, the alarm she felt was evident in her voice. "She is not well. Let me take her to the doctor next week. We must do something for her. She has been acting so strangely, and I cannot even get her to talk with me anymore. The child needs help."

"That child doesn't need anything that a good beating won't take care of," Jacob argued. "I'll see that she straightens up. She is just trying to get attention. If I give her the attention she needs once, she'll quit asking for it!" So saying, the angry father pulled off his belt and started out the door.

"Oh, Jacob, no! Please don't. You'll only make matters worse; she'll only be more confused." Sara clung to his arm as he kept walking across the porch. He flung her aside violently, and she slammed solidly into the house wall. Jacob jumped off the end of the porch without bothering to use the steps.

Sara stiffly pulled herself up to follow Jacob, determined that she herself would take the beating, and not poor Rebecca. But Jacob was already wielding the belt, and Sara turned back in hopeless despair. The poor child had already endured too many undeserved beatings. Sara dropped on her knees, imploring God to show her what her place was in protecting her sick daughter. Perhaps her sickness was mental rather than physical. But whatever it was, it was real and she needed help.

After that day, Jacob did not return home for a long time. Sara lovingly nursed her abused daughter while the bruises healed, but she could get no response from Rebecca. Rebecca's will seemed irreparably broken. She seemed confused and crushed. Finally, taking the last of the cash out of the cash drawer, Sara took Rebecca over to her parents and asked them to take Rebecca and herself to the doctor. They were glad to help.

The doctor examined Rebecca thoroughly. "This child has a serious emotional condition," the doctor told Sara after the examination. "I do not know what your home situation is," he began, pausing to look questioningly at Sara, "but it is apparent that she has been abused."

Sara drew a long breath and looked hesitantly into the doctor's kind face. "I have an ungodly husband," she offered brokenly, quite sure that she knew what the doctor was concluding. She herself had suspected the same. Oh, could she bear any more!

The doctor nodded understandingly as Sara

broke down in tears. "I think I can prescribe a medicine that will help her. But she should also be kept calm and away from any situation, as much as possible, that would put stress on her."

The medicine the doctor prescribed helped. Sara was pleased with how much better Rebecca seemed. She was not well, but seemed fairly normal. Samuel and Dorcas loved and pitied their sister and did all in their power to make her burdens lighter. It was also a big help, Sara felt sure, that Rebecca's father was seldom around.

School days continued to pass in rapid succession for the children, followed by busy, work-filled summers. Sometimes it seemed to Sara that no matter how hard they worked, there was never quite enough money to reach around.

Then, in the fall of 1937, Jacob started to come home more frequently. Rebecca's mental condition immediately started to worsen. It seemed that Jacob took all his frustrations out on the poor young teenager. In time Rebecca became unmanageable, and Sara needed to again seek medical help for her. Sara was broken-hearted when finally it became necessary to place Rebecca in a mental institution.

To add to Sara's sorrows Samuel at sixteen was also becoming rebellious, mostly toward his unjust father but also toward life in general. Why must the awful condition in their home continue when his dear mother tried so hard to provide a happy home for her children?

One weekend that fall when Jacob came home, Samuel told Mother about a decision he had made. "Mother, I'm leaving! I can't take this anymore," he said. "I am dropping out of school and getting a job. Then I will help to provide support for the family."

"Oh, son, I would rather you would stay with us," Sara pleaded, "even if many of our material needs are not provided for."

But Samuel had made up his mind. He would find a farmer in some nearby community where he could work for his board and have a little spending money besides.

8.

Good-bye

Dorcas suddenly found herself alone with her mother. The future looked bleak. Her sister was in a mental institution, and her brother had left home. One evening soon after Samuel had left, she helped Mother do the few supper dishes and clean up the kitchen before they sat down together on the couch for their evening devotions. How lonely it seemed!

"Mother, I'll always stick with you," the ten-year-old said, attempting to comfort her desolate mother.

Sara could not speak for a moment as the tears silently flowed.

"Mother," began Dorcas again after a while, "do others in the family sometimes have mental trouble because one does?" Her anxiety was evident.

Sara wiped her eyes, realizing that her daughter needed her now. "No, Dorcas," she assured her daughter. "You do not need to worry about that."

"But, Mother, I worry about other things too." The face of the child was drawn and tense.

"Like what?" Mother questioned gently.

"Well, like that we never seem to have enough to eat. And our clothes are nearly all patched. And . . . and you didn't get much canned this past summer because Father sold all the produce. And now we don't have Samuel or Rebecca to help us on the farm." She began to cry disconsolately.

Sara could have added a few more details—that both cows were dry and the chickens were not laying enough right now to be worth their keep. And she and Dorcas were starting the winter with very few potatoes and hardly enough wood chopped to last the first cold month.

Instead she gathered the child in her arms. "Dorcas, God has always taken care of us," she comforted. "We will keep committing ourselves to God and trusting in Him. You know how the church has often helped us when things got desperate. And you know that Grandpa's give us meat when they butcher. They are always willing to take us somewhere when we need to go away. We will make out all right." Mother tried to encourage her young daughter, wiping away the traces of tears on her face. "Why don't we sing awhile this evening before we have our Bible reading and prayers?"

The idea was readily acceptable to Dorcas. "But it won't go as good as when Rebecca and Samuel were here," she added hesitantly.

"That's all right," Mother encouraged. "We will still enjoy singing together." The rest of the evening passed pleasantly for the destitute mother and her lonely daughter.

Dorcas returned from school one evening several weeks later in great excitement. Dashing into the kitchen, she called breathlessly, "Mother! Come look!" The screen door slammed behind her. Mother came from her bedroom, and Dorcas waved an envelope before her eyes. "I picked up the mail before coming in our lane, and here is a letter addressed to you and me. It looks like Samuel's handwriting!"

Eagerly Mother took the envelope. Upon opening it, she found a five-dollar bill and four ones. She read the letter aloud.

Dear Mother and Dorcas,
    Mr. Baxter pays me ten dollars a month besides room and board. I kept a dollar to buy a pair of overalls. You and Dorcas use the rest however you wish. Sometime before winter I

may need to keep two or three dollars to buy another pair of shoes.

I want to come see you sometime soon.

Love,

Samuel

There were tears in Sara's eyes as Dorcas danced about excitedly. At last they knew where Samuel was. "Save the envelope," Mother instructed, "so we have his address to answer him."

"Will you answer right away? I will run it back out to the mailbox," Dorcas offered.

Mother smiled at her eager daughter. "It's no use to take it out before morning," she reminded her. "The mail won't go out before nine, so you can mail it on your way to school. You may write too," Mother suggested. "Samuel would enjoy hearing from you."

Dorcas had never written a letter before, but that evening after the supper dishes were done, she eagerly began the task.

Samuel saw his mother and sister only on rare occasions that year. But he faithfully sent his pay home to Mother, except for the little he needed for clothing. Sara was thankful for the extra income, especially since Jacob had not been home for several months.

Once Samuel went with Mother and Dorcas to visit Rebecca. Rebecca cried when her family got ready to leave again. "Couldn't we take her home for a while and try it again?" Mother pled with the administrator.

"No," the administrator stated firmly. "She is not ready for that yet. Maybe after another year or so. You need to allow us time to get her stabilized."

Sadly Sara returned home, leaving a tearful, pleading daughter behind.

For six months they did not hear anything from Samuel. Sara continued to write, always expressing thanks for the financial help he had given them and encouraging him to commit his life to Christ. Then another letter came.

"Mother, I ran all the way in our long lane!" Dorcas gasped in excitement.

"I see that you did." Mother met her at the door. "Why did you run so hard?"

In answer Dorcas handed her mother the special letter. Quickly Mother opened the envelope.

Dear Mother and Dorcas,

I am sure you have been hearing about the war our country is getting into. I don't remember World War I, more than just hearing stories about it.

Mr. Baxter has been telling me that he won't have work for me much longer. He is planning to retire.

He encouraged me to join the army before I am drafted. I can get a better choice of job and location. The pay will be double what I have been sending.

Mother's voice choked and her hand trembled. "Oh, Samuel, don't," she pleaded aloud as her tears began to flow. When Mother did not continue reading, Dorcas took the sheet, stained by Mother's tears, and finished reading.

So he took me in last week, and I signed up for four years. That way I will also have some educational privileges that I wouldn't get by just signing up for two years.

"Oh, Mother, is Samuel actually going overseas to fight?" Dorcas cried in distress. She had been hearing in school about Hitler and the conflict in Europe, so she knew what Samuel was referring to in his letter.

Mother immediately sat down to write to her son. How she longed to be able to talk to him.

Dear Samuel,

I am grieved that you would consider going to war. Do you know there is provision made for exemptions for conscientious objectors that your grandparents didn't have in World War I?

Please reconsider. Won't you give your heart to God? Live for Him, and even suffer for

Him, if need be. Think of eternity. Don't you remember how many of our forefathers suffered in World War I rather than fight?

We are praying for you.

Mother and Dorcas

Sara grieved and prayed and waited. For several months she heard no more, and no more money came from the farm. One day an official-looking envelope arrived. Sara was shocked when a check for forty-five dollars dropped out—Samuel's army wages.

Dorcas's eyes grew big when she noticed the amount of the check. "Oh, Mother," she breathed, "that much money will help us out a lot!"

Yes, their needs were great. And if it were not for Grandpa Yoder's help, she did not know how their needs would have been met many times. But Sara could not accept such a check, this check from her son who was somewhere across the sea involved in war.

"We will return it. We will not cash it," Sara said slowly. Her face was white and her hands trembled as she tucked the check back into the envelope. "I cannot use that money. I cannot."

"But, Mother . . ." Dorcas stared into her mother's troubled face. "How will we make out if we don't use Samuel's checks?"

"God will provide," her mother offered with a deep sigh. "We will not use the price of blood."

"At least we have a home. And we can earn lots in the summer and store food for the winter. That way we won't need much else. We don't need to buy fuel, since Grandpa and the cousins cut plenty of wood for the cookstove and fireplace." Dorcas spoke bravely, trying to encourage her mother. "And maybe I can quit school and get a job."

"No, Dorcas, please don't consider that yet. You are only fourteen," her mother pleaded. "I want you home with me. God will provide. He has always been faithful."

In the following winter months, Mother and Dorcas never received another check or letter from Samuel. They did not know where he was, or even if he was alive. Their prayers followed him into the unknown. Sara could only conclude that Samuel was offended by her refusal to accept his check. How she longed to hear from him.

Sara faced many burdens that winter—the loss of income, her wayward son, her oldest daughter so far from home, the need of salvation for her youngest daughter. Often she went to her parents or to Brother Mast and his wife. They were always ready to share her burden, give advice, or help with any financial needs. Sara meekly bore her lot, and even though her burdens were heavy, she had a ready testimony of God's faithfulness to her.

"Are things going better for you at home?" a

concerned sister asked Sara one Sunday. "Several of us have been noticing you seem more cheerful of late, as if some burden had been lifted. We wondered if Jacob is helping out more at home, or at least being more kind and considerate."

"No," Sara admitted slowly. "It is not that." She did not wish to complain, nor did she feel inclined to share the burdens and cares that had driven her to the Lord. "It is just that we are finding God's grace sufficient," she explained. "I have been convicted that my life is not pleasing to God, nor honoring Him, if I do not claim His abundant provision for joy in every circumstance."

*   *   *   *   *

It was a beautiful summer morning in 1942. The long winter was past again, and Dorcas went outside to the large garden to start the day's work in the truck patch. As she cleaned up the kitchen, Mother heard her singing . She was eager to go outside and work with her daughter before the sun got too hot. Quickly Sara dried the few dishes and put them into the cupboard. Then she swept the kitchen floor.

Suddenly she realized that Dorcas was no longer singing. Soon the kitchen door flew open and Dorcas burst into the house. "Mother!" she screeched in alarm. Her eyes were dilated in her blanched face.

"What is wrong, child? Don't scream that way,"

Sara calmly admonished her daughter.

"Mother, I'm scared!" Dorcas managed to say in a more controlled voice, her eyes begging for understanding.

"About what?" Mother questioned with concern.

"There is a drunk man staggering up the lane," she panted, "and I think it might be Father." She paused to take a deep breath. "I don't know if he will make it or not. He has already fallen several times." It had been a long time since she had seen her father, and now to see him returning in this way, if this was he, was completely unnerving.

It was Jacob. He remained at home for several days. On Saturday, after he was sober, Dorcas begged her father to go to church with them the next day. He refused. Then, turning slyly to Sara, he offered, "I'll make a bargain with you. You and Dorcas go with me tonight, and I will go to church with you tomorrow."

"Go where?" Sara asked slowly.

"Oh, out to the city to have some fun," was his evasive answer. "But you can't go dressed like that. Get that white cap off your head, and I'll buy Dorcas a new dress." He looked at his teenage daughter and winked.

Dorcas glanced at her mother. "Jacob, you don't want us with you tonight," Sara replied calmly. "We would not fit into your crowd."

Good-bye

"All right. All I want is Dorcas. Go comb your hair out and let it hang," he said, turning to his daughter. "I will buy you a new dress and some hair ribbons. You will make a big hit with my crowd."

Jacob laughed coarsely at Sara's look of distress. She clasped his arm and cried, "Oh, Jacob, don't!"

Dorcas stood petrified.

"Are you going to obey your father?" he asked gruffly, shoving Sara away rudely.

Dorcas remained motionless as her mother broke into tears.

"Okay. You go your way, and I'll go mine," the big, brusque man said angrily. "And don't ever ask me to go to church with you again." He watched Dorcas scornfully as she stood trembling before him.

Then, turning to Sara, Jacob spoke again. "I know where there is a little woman more to my liking, who will be glad to go with me. She's got more spark and fun and isn't all the time crying her eyes out about something!" He looked at Sara with scorn. "But if you don't go, you'd better not be around here when I return tonight with her."

What was Jacob saying? Sara stood beside the table, holding onto it for support. She felt dizzy with fear for Dorcas as well as for herself. Jacob cast another malevolent look at Sara. "I'll give

you till midnight to clear out, and don't ever
expect to return. I'm sick and tired of you and
your religion both!" By the time he had delivered this ultimatum, Jacob was shouting and his
face was red and bulging. Without another word
he turned and stomped out of the house.

Sara remained speechless, allowing the shock
to creep slowly through her being. It seemed
she could not think. Should she take his threat
seriously?

"Mother," Dorcas cried in tears, "what did he
mean? Don't we even have a home? Where can
we go?"

"Dorcas, calm down," Mother said quietly.
"We need to think logically." A moment later she
added, "We will need greater wisdom than our
own to make this decision." Sara had long ago
learned not to trust her own wisdom in making
important decisions, but to look to God for help.
He who had promised wisdom to all who ask
would not fail her. *If only I had sought His wisdom in my teen years!* She groaned deeply.

Together mother and daughter knelt and
prayed. When they arose, Sara's mind seemed to
have cleared. "Dorcas," she instructed, her voice
so tense with emotion that it was scarcely above
a whisper, "go over to Grandpa's and tell them
we need help to decide what to do."

Dorcas nodded wordlessly.

"Tell them, as nearly as you can remember,

all that your father said."

Again Dorcas nodded.

"Tell them too that if they want to consult Brother Mast, it is all right."

Dorcas turned and walked toward the door. Soon Sara saw her flying on swift feet down the lane and across the field to her grandparents' house.

Sara was alone. She walked slowly from room to room, reflecting numbly on the home that had been hers for nearly twenty-two years. Mingled feelings struggled in her aching heart. What memories rose from every part of the house: the kitchen corner where she had labored long hours to provide meals for her husband and family, the couch in the corner, where she had often gathered her little ones for spiritual instruction, and finally, the worn spot on the floor beside her bed that spoke of her sacred trysting spot. . . . She dropped, exhausted, in that same spot for one last time and shed bitter tears.

It had been hard to say good-bye to Rebecca when she had needed to be institutionalized. It had been harder still to say good-bye to Samuel when he chose to leave the protecting walls of home to make his own way. Now it looked as though she would be forced to say good-bye to the memories stored for many years in her little home. But what grieved her most deeply was the realization that now she must say good-bye to all her years of hopes and yearnings and inter-cessions for her husband's salvation. She must still keep praying for him. Sara's heart was sick. "Lord, give me grace to go on," she prayed bro-kenly. Once again she reminded herself firmly, *I am walking the way I chose.*

Sara thought of the daughter still with her. Was there any way to save Dorcas from the conse-quences of her own wrong choice? *I must con-tinually give Dorcas warnings and advice for the decisions that she will be making as she faces maturity,* she thought. *O God,* she prayed humbly, *You are faithful. Help me to be a faithful mother and train the one child I have left to seek Your direction for her life. Where I have failed, do work in her heart and help her not to make willful choices that will lead to a lifetime of regrets!*

Dorcas returned from Grandpa's and shared what Grandpa's had advised. Then, while Dorcas cleaned the kitchen for one last time, Sara went to her bedroom and began packing her own and Dorcas's clothes in a large cardboard box. Should she take anything else? She was not sure. A few treasured dishes that had been gifts to her went into the box and, of course, their Bibles.

Sara heard a car pull in the driveway, and she quickly closed the box and pushed it to the bed-room door.

Dorcas was holding the kitchen door open. "Come on in," she invited warmly. "Mother,

Grandpa's and Brother Mast's are here."

So Brother Mast's came too. If only I had consulted them twenty-two years ago, how different my life would he, Sara realized in fresh pain. *There are things I cannot change. The best I can do now is to help the children see the need of counsel. But, O God, have mercy; I'm afraid for two of them the time is already past!* Beseeching God's strength for the hour, she stepped out of the bedroom to greet her guests.

After discussing her problem from every angle, Father suggested, "Sara, I believe the best thing for you to do is to move home with us. It will, of course, need to be your decision. You cannot remain here; that is obvious. And I do not think it is safe for you to get a place where you and Dorcas would be alone."

Tears were streaming across Sara's cheeks. "Father, I do appreciate so much your offer," she faltered. "But I think it would be too much for you and Mother, now that your family, except for Ruth, is all raised and gone. Living with you would certainly have its advantages," she added truthfully. "I could get a job and help out with living expenses, while Dorcas would not need to stay at home alone." Sara considered Father's proposition from all angles. It would certainly benefit her and Dorcas. But how would it affect the rest of the family, especially Ruth, who at twenty-seven might be plenty set in her ways?

Would she resent the intrusion?

"We will all be glad to do this for you, Sara," her mother offered generously, as though reading her thoughts. "Ruth will not mind, and it looks as though she will soon be getting married too. If you want to get a job, Dorcas could help me a lot at home. I know you would rather have your own home, Sara, but this seems a wiser arrangement at this time."

"It's so hard to think of breaking up housekeeping and needing to rely on others," Sara admitted humbly. "But I will take up your offer if you are sure we would not be imposing on you too much at your age. I realize that in this situation nothing could work out better for us."

"And we will be happy to give you a home," Father assured Sara kindly.

Sara bowed her head and wept again. " I never thought I would leave my husband for any reason. I vowed to stay with him until death parts us," she said tearfully. "But now it looks as though it is forced upon me."

Brother Mast spoke gently and solemnly. "We do want to be Scriptural, even though it may mean suffering. But in your case, I believe leaving is justified, especially now that Jacob has demanded it. Really, as far as your marriage being broken, it is Jacob who has broken it. I feel confident that you are doing right to take your parents' advice."

It did not take long for the six of them to gather a few more things together. With those things, and the box of clothes that Sara had packed earlier, the move was made that night.

Living in with Grandpa Yoder's brought many adjustments for Dorcas, a lively fifteen-year-old who was used to having only her mother around. There were many adjustments as well for Grandpa's, who had gotten used to a quiet house in the past few years. Now they were faced with the responsibility of guiding and correcting an ambitious young girl in the absence of her mother.

However, it was finally Sara who needed to make the biggest adjustments. Not only had she needed to give up her home and her husband, but now also the daily care of her last child so that she could go out and work in another home as a maid.

Sara was grateful though to find work in a Christian home. There were eight children in the Moser family, the eighth being a new baby. Sara began working there the week after the baby was born. Sister Moser did not regain her strength after the birth of this last child, and Sara needed to take up the responsibility of the whole household as well as many outdoor chores. Although she did not have a big truck patch of her own to tend this summer, Sara had the Mosers' garden, with all the picking and canning.

She thought at times, as she worked in the Mosers' garden, about the little farm she had left. Who was tending the big truck patch there? Was it growing up in weeds? Was anyone tending to the animals? It was a relief to her when Sister Moser told her that she had heard that the Benders and their grandchildren were caring for the truck patch and selling the produce. And yet she could not help but wonder why, when she and Dorcas had done all the initial planting and weeding, some of that produce or the proceeds were not offered to them!

She was concerned also at times about the extra burden she must be placing on her elderly parents. Besides caring for Dorcas, there was the burden of extra work—the extra washing and cooking and gardening. But at least Dorcas, she knew, could help with those jobs. There were extra groceries needed too, but for those she herself was working and supplying some of the income.

Sara was humbled and submissive, willingly taking the advice and help of others. And so she let these small burdens also rest with the Lord. She did have so much to be grateful for in the way God was providing for them.

What burdened her more than the material things was the longing to spend more time with her daughter. Sara was away for long days, and she worried that her mother would not be able to cope with Dorcas. Since it was summertime and Dorcas was home from school, Sara's longing intensified to be able to work with her. But, she reminded herself often, she could thank God that at least Dorcas was safe in the care of her parents.

Fall came at last, but still the days at the Moser home were busy. As Sara canned the last of the corn one Saturday afternoon, her back ached and she was totally exhausted. She felt that surely her strength would fail if tomorrow were not Sunday. Every day that week she had canned corn, along with all the regular work—children to care for, three meals a day to prepare, and the huge family wash to put through the wringer washer and then to fold, mend, iron, and put away.

Wearily Sara pulled out the scrub bucket and mop. Sister Moser stepped into the kitchen. "It is getting late, Sara, and the girls are finished with the other cleaning. They can wash up the floor. You need to be going home."

"Oh, thank you," Sara responded sincerely. "But I thought I would try to finish this job yet. The children have helped so well today."

Tears filled Sara's eyes as she walked out to Grandpa's car. *How good the Mosers are to me,* she mused gratefully. *But, oh, how I long to work with my own daughter and give her more opportunities to confide in me.* As the sad mother's heart swelled with gratitude, it also nearly burst with longings that could not be filled. How she longed to be near enough to Dorcas to sense her every mood, struggle, or temptation. Now that Dorcas was back in school, Saturdays were the only days they could be together. And on that day too Sara must work.

One hard year followed another. Rebecca's condition did not improve, and it was necessary that she remain in the institution. Sara visited her as often as possible, sometimes taking Grandpa Yoder's with her, and sometimes only Dorcas. No word had come from Samuel during those years, and Sara had no idea where her son was, or if he was alive what he might be facing.

In the spring of 1945, Dorcas finished high school. "Mother, now that I am out of school, I'm going to get a job. Then you can stay home and help Grandpa's with the gardening this summer. That will be so much easier on you," Dorcas offered on her first day at home. "I have been so eager to help more."

"Oh, but, Dorcas, do you think you could handle the work at Mosers'? There is much more work there than here at Grandpa's."

"No, Mother, I don't plan to work at Mosers'. I don't think I could stand to work at such a place when it's too hard for you. I would get a better job."

"But where, Dorcas?" Mother faced her daughter. "It would surely be nice to just stay at home," Mother agreed. "The work at Mosers' is getting to be almost too much for me."

"All the Bender cousins are working in town, making more in a day than you make in half a week, and they don't work nearly as hard. The girls said they can easily get me a job. I could start next week, Mother. I want you to stop working."

Mother looked at Dorcas sadly. She had tried her best through the years to keep the children as much as possible from close association with the Bender cousins. But she guessed it was inevitable that they were often together in spite of what she could do about it, since they *were* cousins. "Dorcas, you know how I feel about your cousins working in town," Mother said, sorry to disappoint her daughter. "You may not do that. In another year or two, I will stop working and allow you to try it at Mosers'."

"Mother, I won't work at Mosers'! I can get an easier job. Please let me take a job in town. I am mature enough to behave myself." Dorcas's raised eyebrows and the high pitch of her voice spoke volumes more than she meant to betray about her desire.

"Dorcas," Mother said firmly, "I cannot allow you to work in town. Grandpa will not approve of it either."

"He isn't my father," Dorcas protested. "He

doesn't have any right to say where I work."

"Yes, he does, Dorcas. We are living in his home. And even if we weren't, I would still say you may not go to town and get a job at your age. You will be much better off spiritually working here in the valley among our own people, even if you earn less. I will work at the Mosers' a few years yet until you are older," Mother said again. "Then we will discuss the possibilities for you to get a job."

"Haven't I been trustworthy since I was saved last fall?" Dorcas argued. "I'm no child. You are overprotective, Mother. All my Bender uncles allow their girls to work in town. They are Christians, and some of them are not much older than I am. It hasn't hurt them, has it?"

"Don't be too sure," Mother cautioned. "But my responsibility is not to criticize them, but to watch out for your spiritual good. With the attitudes you are displaying, you have some maturing to do yet. I will work awhile longer until you are more ready to face the many temptations of the world."

Dorcas was moody for a while. She sincerely wanted to help her mother. She meant it well. Mother, sensing her disappointment, tried to help Dorcas understand why she was so concerned, sharing the seriousness and the long-lasting effects of wrong choices in youth.

"But haven't I always behaved well with the

other young people?" Dorcas protested a couple of evenings later when she and Mother were again discussing working away. "Oh, Mother, why can't you trust me? Other parents trust their children."

"I do trust you, Dorcas. But I also understand the immaturity of youth. You need to become more firmly grounded in the faith," Mother admonished, "and develop convictions that will help you grow into responsible adulthood."

Dorcas subsided into reluctant acquiescence. She understood her mother's concern and appreciated it. She respected her grandparents. And yet there was something in her that wanted to be more like her cousins on the Bender side. She knew that her Uncle James's girls did not work outside of Christian homes. But they did not need to, she reasoned.

"You can help the most, for the present time, by cheerfully doing all you can for Grandpa and Grandma," Mother encouraged.

Dorcas gave up her cherished dream to relieve her mother and put her heart into the work at home. She worked hard that summer and learned many household skills. While Dorcas went ahead with the household work, Grandma could spend time quilting and sewing for other people, thus earning a little extra money.

The garden did well and produced more than what was needed in the Yoder home. Grandpa allowed Dorcas to sell the extra produce and give her mother the proceeds. That money helped to provide clothes and other necessities for Sara and Dorcas.

"Dorcas, you have done very well. I have appreciated your willing help," Mother commended her one Friday at the end of the summer. "From now on, I'm going to be working only four days a week."

"Oh, good!" Dorcas exclaimed happily. There was a warm glow on her face. She had really helped to relieve Mother's load! "But is there work for all of us at home?" she asked.

"Grandma has more orders for sewing than she can keep up with," Mother assured her. "You and I will both help her this winter."

Sara was so thankful for the break from the work at Mosers'. Summer turned to fall as she and Dorcas worked together at gathering in and storing the last of the garden produce. Then together, with Grandpa's help, they raked leaves and hauled them to the strawberry patch to mulch between the rows. The days spent working at home with her parents and her daughter were much more leisurely than the long, hard days at Mosers'.

Dorcas was also thankful—thankful for the privilege of working with her mother. "Mother, it is so good to have you home some days!" Dorcas exclaimed one Friday morning in October. Then in a soft voice she whispered, "I

250

enjoyed working these past years with Grandma, and I appreciate all she has taught me. But it is so special working with you."

"Have you ever told Grandma how much you appreciate her?" Mother asked with a warm smile.

"Yes, I often have," Dorcas responded. "But I guess sometimes, especially when I was younger, I failed to show my appreciation as much as I should have."

"Dorcas, it does me good also to be able to be with you more. I'm thankful that we can share our thoughts and ideals and ambitions with each other. We have had some hard years, but God has been so good to us!"

"That is very true," Dorcas agreed. "He has always provided all we need, even though sometimes in my early years I longed for a more normal home life. Yes, God is good. Grandpa's were wonderful to take us in. But, oh, Mother, sometimes I've just longed to be able to confide in you and share my struggles. But when you came home in the evenings you were tired, or it was bedtime, or maybe it was just that the urge to share my problems had vanished."

"I'm afraid I failed you sometimes in my weariness," Mother said.

"Oh, no, Mother. You were always ready to listen when I came to you. But today is so special. You and I so seldom have the house alone. I'm sure it is special to Grandpa's to be able to go and come more freely too since I am older, and especially now that you are here Fridays and Saturdays. They still never like to leave me home alone." Dorcas laughed softly.

"I know they don't," Mother replied gravely. "I've always been so thankful for their carefulness in watching over my dear daughter. Now they are getting older, and we want to take good care of them."

"We surely owe it to them," Dorcas agreed. "And now, Mother, I'd better be doing something while I talk. It's especially good to have you here at a time like this, to help prepare and plan for our big weekend. Please tell me what should I be doing first?"

"What is there to do?" Mother asked.

"Everything!" Dorcas exclaimed with a laugh. "We've got the whole house to clean, all the food to prepare for the weekend, beds to make up, and . . ." Dorcas stopped and rolled her eyes. "It would've been a busy time for me if the Mosers wouldn't be giving you two days off each week now. But Grandma said she would have stayed home this morning to help me if you wouldn't be here."

Sara thought with longing to the next two days. How much she enjoyed these times of fellowship with all her brothers and sisters and their families. She had missed that so much in the years she lived with Jacob because he had seldom allowed her to attend the Yoder family reunions.

"Let's see, Uncle James's and Aunt Marie's families will be arriving this evening. Then Uncle David's and Aunt Lois's will arrive in the forenoon tomorrow. Aunt Ruth and her husband will get here just in time for dinner."

"So we will all be together for dinner and the afternoon," Dorcas said. "I'm so eager to see them all. We haven't seen Aunt Lois's new baby girl yet. She makes thirteen cousins now."

"Only Uncle David's and Aunt Ruth and her husband will be staying over Saturday night and for Sunday. So we need to plan the biggest meals for Saturday dinner and supper. But we want to get some food ready for Sunday too, so there won't be so much to do on Sunday."

"Why don't we both work at cleaning this morning. Then this afternoon we can fix all the guest beds and start preparing the food we will need. Grandma will be back by then to help with the meal planning."

Together mother and daughter swept and scrubbed floors and polished furniture. By lunchtime, Grandpa's house shone. After lunch they made up floor beds and set up extra cots in the bedrooms. "There, now there are places for everyone!" Dorcas remarked with satisfaction. "Imagine, there will be more than a dozen of us in this house tomorrow night." Her voice was high with excitement.

"It will be a lively place," Mother said happily, also eager to see her brothers and sisters again. "Grandpa's will enjoy having us all at home once again."

It was a busy, happy day. Grandpa and Grandma enjoyed the afternoon preparations with their daughter and granddaughter, and the evening activities after the rest started arriving.

The weekend passed too quickly. Precious memories were shared and relived, and encouragement and admonition given. Everyone was there except Jacob, Rebecca, and Samuel.

Late Sunday afternoon, Sara and Grandma and the aunts went to rest. The older cousins were enjoying a quiet game. An old pickup pulled in the driveway, and the driver blew the horn. Grandpa looked out. "Doesn't look like anyone I know," he commented.

"What a lot of nerve," Dorcas remarked when the driver blew the horn again before crawling out.

"I'll go see who it is and find out what he wants," David offered, starting toward the door.

"Wait," Grandpa called. "It's Jacob Bender. I'll go."

David turned back and faced Grandpa. "I didn't recognize him, Father. I haven't seen him for probably ten years!"

"None of us have seen him for four or five

years," Grandpa remarked as he opened the door and stepped out on the porch.

Dorcas tried to see the approaching man without being seen. A shudder went through her as she noticed how hard and sinful he looked. Her father stepped up on the porch, and he seemed to be very cross. She stood close to the kitchen window that faced the porch. From there she could hear his loud voice very easily, even though the window was closed.

"Where is Sara?" the angry man demanded. "I want to see her."

Grandpa stalled. "What do you want? Is there anything I can do for you?"

"No," Jacob said with a scowl. "I said I want to see Sara. Is she here? I understood she came back home."

Grandpa nodded.

"Is she here today?" Jacob continued, stepping closer to the door.

"We have guests today," Grandpa said slowly. "It is not suitable to invite you in now."

"Are Sara and Dorcas here?" the man asked again impatiently. "I want to see them. Sara is my wife. Tell her to come out because I want to see her."

"I understood you have a wife over in town," Grandpa answered in a soft voice, trying not to anger the agitated man.

"Will you tell Sara that I want to see her?"

Jacob asked in a pleading tone.

"No, I won't. You no longer have any right to her," Sara's father answered evenly and firmly, facing the man who paced the floor nervously.

Jacob's shoulders sagged, and he looked whipped. Heaving a deep sigh, he turned and walked off the porch without another word.

When Grandpa stepped back inside, Dorcas was trembling.

"Where is your mother?" Grandpa asked.

"Resting back in the north bedroom," Dorcas replied.

"Good," Grandpa answered, looking relieved. "It might be best not to mention the visitor to her today. I will tell her about his visit later. She is needing rest now."

Dorcas nodded, grateful that Grandpa was in charge and was trying to make it easier for her mother. She returned to her game, but her heart was no longer in it.

Sara submissively accepted her father's wisdom in turning away her unfaithful husband. Still she longed and prayed for his salvation and for a reunion of their family.

9.

The Separation

"Mother, I will be twenty in a few months," Dorcas said one winter morning a little more than a year later.

"Yes," Mother agreed, smiling at her eager daughter. "How well I remember that spring day twenty years ago. The forsythias were blooming in a blaze of yellow all around our little house, and the daffodils and hyacinths were especially lovely that spring. Every time I passed them going between the garden and the house, I had to think about how good God is to give us beauty in the midst of all our trials."

For a time Mother silently reminisced, and Dorcas waited. She had something very important to propose, but she would allow Mother time to pause and think. She would not rush into what she had to say, because she must make Mother understand!

When Mother did not say more, Dorcas took a deep breath and began again. "Mother, since Grandma is so feeble, I have been thinking you are the one who should be here with her now and I should take on the responsibility of providing for the family. Don't you think so?" The young girl waited expectantly.

Mother looked up. "Why, Dorcas, you have been doing a lot of that for the past two years. And besides, I am the one here most of the time anyway, since I only work at Mosers' two days a week anymore," she said thoughtfully. "Their girls are getting older, and probably before long I will be home all the time. I suspect they are just giving me work now because they know we need the income. Sister Moser will soon have plenty of help."

After a short pause, Mother added, "Did you have something particular in mind?"

"Well, I do," Dorcas began. "I have enjoyed working in church homes when young mothers needed help. But even working four or five days a week, as I have been doing the past couple years, I don't earn much. I'm still thinking about working in town. There I could earn enough for our support, and you could be here with Grandma all the time." Dorcas looked appealingly at her mother. "Wouldn't that be more relaxing for you? And really, I believe there should be someone here with Grandma and Grandpa all the time now."

"Yes," Mother agreed, "I have been concerned about leaving them alone. But Dorcas, I believe you could earn enough to meet our needs just working here in the valley. I always have, although I know the wages are not as much as you could earn in town."

Dorcas nodded, but went on unconvinced. "Darlene Bender told me on Sunday that there is an old lady living next door to where she works. Mrs. Woodrow is eighty-nine and needs someone to live in with her. There would be just light housework, and she is willing to pay fifty dollars a week, Darlene said. That would be quite different from the three dollars a day I am earning now."

"Yes, it would," Mother agreed, but she seemed doubtful that fifty dollars a week was necessary.

"Maybe we don't need that much to live on," Dorcas replied to Mother's questioning look. "But we could put some back in savings for a rainy day."

"I am wondering about the conditions in the home," Mother began thoughtfully. "Does anyone else live there? Would you be able to get home on Sundays for church? What would you be doing in all your spare time? We should think seriously about all those things."

"I already learned I could have all my week-ends off, Saturday afternoons and Sundays. There is no one else living there. I could work on some quilting or sewing in my spare time." Dorcas answered Mother's questions and waited eagerly.

"Who would be with Mrs. Woodrow over the weekends?" Mother questioned further.

"One of her grandchildren who lives a cou-ple blocks up the street," Dorcas replied. "I would really like to take the job. I don't think I'll have a better offer anywhere."

"You are so young to be away from home all week," Mother said with loving concern.

"Mother, you were married already at my age. You forget I am growing up."

"I know, Dorcas. You have grown up so fast. You have been a faithful daughter, and I have a lot of confidence in you. But who knows what temptations you will face in town? And how would you get back and forth to your job?"

"I could go in with Darlene on Monday morn-ings, and she said that someone from their fam-ily always goes to town on Saturdays. They would stop and bring me along home."

"I believe you and Darlene have this pretty well all planned, don't you?" Mother remarked, not sounding too pleased.

"But, Mother—"

"Let's pray about it," Mother interrupted kindly, "and talk to Grandpa's before we make a decision."

"But, Mother . . ." Dorcas tried again.

"Sara! Sara!" Grandma's frightened voice broke into their conversation, as she hurried into the room where Mother and Dorcas were talking. "Come quick! Grandpa fell in the yard and I can't get him up."

Dorcas and Sara quickly grabbed their coats. "Oh, Grandpa," Dorcas said as they reached the yard where Grandpa was struggling to sit up. "Just wait, we'll help you. You must stop trying to clean up these branches in the yard. I will get it done today."

Mother gently put her arm behind Grandpa's shoulders and raised him up, while Dorcas took his hands. Soon they had him on his feet again.

"Are you hurt?" Grandma asked, bustling around anxiously, trying to get Grandpa to lean on her arm.

"No, no, I just stumbled trying to drag a big branch. I am all right. This ground is so uneven, and I am not as steady on my feet as I used to be." He shuffled along toward the house, a bit unwillingly. "I could go on and keep cleaning up," he protested. "That ice storm last week brought so many branches down." But the three women insisted he come in and rest awhile. "No chance around here, one man against three ladies," he grumbled good-naturedly as he stumbled up onto the porch.

After Grandpa had a drink and had rested a few minutes, Mother brought up the subject that she and Dorcas had been discussing. "Maybe I should stay home all the time with you and just allow Dorcas to earn the living," she suggested.

"Maybe," Grandpa agreed. "But would that mean she would need to work in town? You were always able to earn enough to meet our needs just working here in the valley among our own people."

"I would be more comfortable with her staying here in the valley," Grandma agreed. "There is so much evil and there are so many temptations for young people to cope with in our day. Even in a Christian community one faces a lot, and how much more out in the world!"

Dorcas listened with drooping spirit. All the glamorous hopes of a life of ease and plenty began to crumble and disappear. Would she always have to live with the drudgery of everyone else's hard work? A wave of self-pity swept over her. Grandma and Grandpa and Mother all looked so serene and satisfied. They had no idea how much this meant to her!

Why must I earn a living for Grandpa's anyway? Why can't I earn big wages for myself as other girls do? Why? Why? Why? she thought bitterly. But then her conscience smote her. *Didn't*

Grandpa's sacrifice a lot to give Mother and me a home when we were so needy? Of course I owe it to them. Tears filled Dorcas's eyes, born of the conflict that waged within her.

But Grandpa began talking again, and quickly her attention returned to what he was saying. "Maybe it is time we share with Sara and Dorcas what we have been considering," he said, glancing at Grandma. He paused awhile before going on.

Grandma nodded. After heaving a deep sigh, Grandpa continued, "We have been considering moving to another area."

His words seemed to strike Dorcas dumb, and she watched him numbly. *Leave all my friends? Move to another area?*

"Of course we wouldn't do it without your opinion in the matter too." He was speaking directly to Mother. Dorcas watched Mother's face. It was sad, but submissive.

Why can't I be more like Mother? Dorcas mused. *She is always so meek and submissive, so loving and unselfish. That just seems to come naturally for her.*

Dorcas was startled at Mother's reply. "You mean because of the church situation?"

Grandpa and Grandma were both nodding. They must have talked this over before. Each of them seemed to know what the others were thinking. Dorcas felt confused.

"Perhaps we should share more with Dorcas before we consider such a move any further," Grandpa suggested. "She is almost an adult too." Grandpa turned to face Dorcas seriously. "Over the years, Dorcas, we—your mother included—have been concerned that our church is drifting into apostasy. Many things are being allowed among us that used to be spoken against." He waited for Dorcas to be able to absorb that much before going on.

"You have always taught me to respect the church and our leaders' decisions," she said uncertainly.

"That's right," Grandpa agreed, "and we trust you will still do that. We do not mean to imply that we do not respect our leaders. We always want to be faithful to the standards of the church to which we belong, and we want to lend our support and influence to stop harmful trends that may lead the church away from truth. But it seems the time has come here in our Germantown Valley church that our conservative witness is no longer appreciated. So we are thinking about areas where there are still churches seeking to live the whole Bible. We want to pray much about this before we decide. This decision will affect whether or not you would want to begin a new job."

"Where would we move to?" Dorcas asked.

Grandpa smiled. "Do you have any suggestions?"

Dorcas thought a minute. "The church where Uncle James's go seems to be living according to the Scriptures better than ours."

"Yes, they are, and we have considered that area," Grandpa admitted. "But we don't want to make any move quickly. We want to think and pray a lot about such a decision."

Grandma smiled at Dorcas and said, "We would need to make a few changes to meet their church standards. Could you feel at home there?"

"Oh, yes. But it would seem strange to leave this valley! I have lived here for all my almost twenty years."

"Your mother has lived here all her life too," Grandma put in. "And Grandpa and I have lived here ever since we were married, which is nearly fifty years. It would be hard to leave our home and friends here, but we want to follow wherever the Lord leads us."

"Even though a move wouldn't be easy," Grandpa continued, "we want to be where the church still honors God and His Word. That is worth any sacrifice."

Dorcas pondered this statement a long time. *"Worth any sacrifice . . ." It would mean giving up a good job, . . . being different, . . . changing locations for the sake of a faithful church. . . .* She knew that the sacrifice would likely be greater for Grandpa and Grandma than for her. They had raised their family here. They had built the house and barn. They had coaxed crops out of these fields for years and years.

And besides all that, Dorcas considered further, *they love the church here. For many years, they have helped to strengthen conviction. They have guided their family right and given direction to many other young souls. And still they are willing to move.* Yes, there was no doubt that it would be hard for them to leave it all behind.

Dorcas realized somehow that the move would not be as exciting for them as it would be for her.

"The separation from this group with whom we have worshiped for so many years would be painful." Grandpa's voice was heavy with emotion, confirming Dorcas's earlier conclusions. "But it may be necessary, to preserve the truth for ourselves and for those who follow us.

"For a long time we have noticed a growing laxness here in our group, and we became lax ourselves without realizing it. We notice this especially in regards to what is allowed among the young people. Parents and leaders have not taken a firm stand, but have been allowing things that have caused many of the youth to lose out with God."

"And many of the ones still in the church," Dorcas contributed honestly, "are doing things they shouldn't be."

"Many heartaches could have been avoided

if we as parents had given more firm guidance instead of allowing the young people what they wanted," Grandpa continued. "We believe that our young people do desire God's will, but they are undiscerning. We should have given them more direction as well as more restriction. We have many regrets."

Dorcas listened to Grandpa with deepened understanding and a new respect. She knew he had a lot of reason for concern, especially when she thought of how the young people's socials were conducted. There were many times when she had simply stayed at home rather than going and being involved in things she knew her mother and grandparents would not approve of.

A few weeks passed without any definite decisions being made. They were all praying daily for God's leading. Dorcas's twentieth birthday in April came and went.

*   *   *   *   *

"Dorcas," Mother whispered softly. It was very early in the morning. "Dorcas," she repeated with urgency.

Dorcas rolled over and opened her eyes. "Yes, Mother, is something wrong?" she asked as she glanced at her clock. It was three o'clock in the morning. Mother would not call her at this time of the morning unless there was an emergency.

Mother sat on the side of her bed. "Grandpa called me awhile ago," she said softly. "I went to see what he wanted. He said that something had awakened him—he wasn't sure what—but when he turned the light on, he noticed that something seemed strange about Grandma."

Dorcas sat up. "What's wrong? Is she sick? She was feeling well last evening wasn't she?" The words rolled out rapidly as Dorcas tried to gather her wits.

"Grandma is gone," Mother went on soberly. "She has gone to be with the Lord. When I went to check her, I noticed how still and colorless she looked, and I realized life had gone. She must have gone on without a struggle, so peacefully and quietly that Grandpa did not even realize it. Yes, she was well last evening. She fell asleep normally and woke up this morning with the Lord." Though tears stood in Mother's eyes, her voice was triumphant.

"Mother, I can't grasp it. Grandma! She can't really be dead; surely not. Did you try to awaken her?" Dorcas was climbing out of bed.

"Dorcas, Grandma has gone to be with the Lord. It is an awful shock, being so sudden and unexpected, but we can be thankful that she didn't need to suffer pain for many years. Grandma was ready to go. I am sure she was glad to go in this way."

Dorcas burst into uncontrolled sobs, and Mother drew her back on the bed beside herself. "Dorcas, you will miss her. She was more than a grandmother to you. She was also a mother. Let's kneel and pray for Grandpa; he will miss her greatly. They shared so many things together for so many years. Then we should get dressed and go out and join him. We will need to help Grandpa with the many arrangements that will need to be taken care of."

After the funeral was over, Uncle James's family remained for a few days.

"Father, have you and Sara given any more thought to moving into our area?" Uncle James asked the morning before they left. They were all relaxing at the kitchen table after a hearty breakfast of fried mush and chicken gravy.

"Yes," Grandpa replied as he absent-mindedly moved his teacup in circles, "we have all talked it over and prayed much about it. We will have to do something soon. I believe that the Lord is leading us that way. Sara and Dorcas are both agreed. Maybe now is the time to begin looking for something."

"You may not have to look very far," Uncle James replied with a twinkle in his eyes. "Do you remember Sister Benner from our church? She is the widow who has a little store attached to her home. Actually, her 'store' is just one room of her house where she sells dry goods since she lost her husband and has needed to earn her own living."

"Why, yes," Grandpa answered, the teacup

THE WAY SHE CHOSE

coming to a sudden stop. "We remember her. Grandma always went there when we visited in your community."

"It is up for sale," James informed them. "I wondered if Sara might be interested in running the store. That way she could stay at home and earn her living. The home is very reasonably priced. It has three bedrooms, a kitchen, a dining room, and a living room, besides the room she uses for her store."

Dorcas looked at her mother, who was smiling her approval. "That sounds exciting, a store in our house!" Dorcas exclaimed. "And that would be less than a mile from Uncle James's, wouldn't it?"

"Yes." Uncle James smiled, turning to Mother and Dorcas, who were smiling broadly.

Grandpa was still considering. "I don't know where I'd get the money to buy a place," he said slowly. "But if it is for us, I know that the Lord will provide a way."

James encouraged his father. "If you sold your farm here, I believe you could handle buying her place and have more than enough left over to buy out the inventory in the store too. Sister Benner is eager to sell; she isn't able to handle the business anymore and plans to move in with her daughter as soon as she can close things out there."

Sometime later, James and his family had the

car loaded and were ready to pull out. "Think about Sister Benner's place," he reminded Grandpa. "I will tell her you are interested. I will come back sometime next week and take you over to see the place. You can decide if it is what you want."

"I have a feeling it won't take much more thought," Grandpa replied. "It looks as though the whole idea is an answer to prayer, as well as being very acceptable to Sara and Dorcas. There we would have a church we all could be happy with, plus a home, and a job for Sara. Would there be likely places for Dorcas to work several days a week if she wasn't needed at home?"

Dorcas looked gratefully at Grandpa. He was so thoughtful to consider her wishes too.

"Oh, yes," Uncle James replied. "Our girls never have trouble finding housework, since we are in a larger church community. And if Dorcas wants a change from housework, one of our members, who has a butcher shop, is always looking for help. Our Rachel is working there now. It pays a little better than housework, and we feel it is also a safe environment."

By early summer, the move had been made. Sara enjoyed running the little dry-goods store. Customers were few, leaving her plenty of time for the housework and gardening. The income was sufficient, with Dorcas able to supply her own needs. Grandpa helped a little around the house, but he was becoming more feeble and spent much of his time just watching for customers and notifying Sara.

Dorcas soon got a job at the butcher shop and enjoyed the work there. The thousands of chickens they butchered each week kept many workers busy. It was an interesting change for her from housework. She also enjoyed learning to know her cousin Rachel better.

The changes Dorcas needed to make in her dress and lifestyle were not hard; she was happy to change to be like the other girls. She soon had convictions of her own and wondered why she had ever rebelled about such things before. *It was because I didn't want to be different,* she decided. Dorcas had not realized, as her grandparents and mother did, how far their church had drifted from Bible truths. She had grown up thinking that the way they did things was the way it had always been. The older folks remembered the time when the church had tried to live close to the Bible.

And so many pleasant months passed and winter came again.

"Mother," Dorcas began one Friday evening as she helped Mother get supper, "there is a new worker at the butcher shop. His name is Mark Wangard."

"Yes." Mother looked up with interest from turning the frying chicken. "I don't recall meeting any Wangards at church."

"No, you probably haven't. His family isn't from around here. Mark is Brother Lewis's nephew, and he is living with them. He just arrived last week and was looking for work, so our manager hired him. He works right next to my station."

"Yes," Mother said again, giving special attention to this information.

"He is a pleasant person to work around, very friendly and outgoing. But he has his sober moments too," Dorcas hastened to add. "Sometimes he even seems troubled. He is very courteous and helpful to the other employees. He seems to be a good worker and eager to do what is right."

"Where is this Mark from? And what church does he belong to?" Mother asked, her concern deepening as she realized Dorcas's evident interest in the stranger. Her mind could not help but go back almost thirty years to the stranger that had moved into her girlhood community.

"He is from the Hilltop congregation, which apparently is much like our church. You will probably meet him on Sunday. He said he is thinking about transferring his membership here, since he plans to live with his uncle for quite a while." Dorcas rambled on, apparently already quite familiar with the new worker at the butcher shop.

"How old is this Mark?" Mother asked. "You

have evidently had quite a bit of conversation with him already to know so much about him in one week."

"He works right next in line to me," Dorcas explained, "and our job doesn't require much concentration once you've learned it."

"How old is he?" Mother repeated.

"He is nineteen, a little more than a year younger than me. But he is so mature; you'd never guess he is younger than I am. He is very manly, built big and strong." Dorcas laughed. "I know he is strong, because he is doing the heavy lifting for me—which is very nice!"

"Dorcas," Mother said seriously, "remember your reserve! Mark is a stranger in this community. Of course you should be friendly to all the workers, but don't get too familiar with a young man. Give him time to prove his spiritual interests before you form too many conclusions about him. Being big and manly doesn't amount to much if his spiritual life is puny and dwarfed!"

"Oh, Mother, I do think you are the most cautious person I've ever met!" Dorcas declared, laughing. Then, seeing Mother's hurt look, she added quickly, "I appreciate your interest and concern, Mother. But don't be overly anxious. I will soon be twenty-one, and am mature enough, I hope, not to fall for anyone without some caution myself. It's just that it's so pleasant to have someone so congenial to work with. Not all the workers are that way. Mother, can't you be glad for me that my workplace is a pleasant environment?"

"Yes," Mother responded with some reserve. I am glad of that, but I have an even greater concern that it be a safe spiritual environment."

"I believe you can have that confidence too," Dorcas replied easily. "All of the workers are from our church families."

"That is a good situation," Mother agreed, "but not necessarily a sure guard against all temptations. Where a number of young men and women work together, there is always potential for temptation. Satan is busy, ready to appeal to our carnal appetites and lead us astray in whatever way he can. That is why I remind you to be reserved, modest, and quiet. And especially so with strangers!

"I have confidence in you, Dorcas, but I also know our human tendencies and weaknesses. You have a friendly, outgoing personality, and there is nothing wrong with that. But you must be careful lest you attract the kind of attention that can cause problems. Your friendliness may mean more to another person than you mean to express. Likewise, you also may be reading more into another's friendliness than he intended to convey. Do you see what I mean?"

"Thank you, Mother. I needed that reminder. I realize I am sometimes impulsive. Then later I regret that I didn't think more seriously before I spoke or acted."

A few months passed. Winter was over, and the glorious buds of spring asserted themselves everywhere. Mother and Grandpa were glad for the opportunity to get into the garden once again. And Dorcas was still very much enjoying the work in the butcher shop. For her it was a pleasant change from all the years of not having much association with other young people. Much as she enjoyed her small family, she had the normal longing for broader friendships.

One Sunday afternoon, there was a knock at the door. Mother answered.

"Why, good afternoon, Mark. Come in," she invited.

Dorcas remained in the living room. She had wondered if it might be Mark at the door, but she did not want to appear too eager.

"Good afternoon," Mark said in his friendly way. "Is Dorcas home? There is nothing going on over at Uncle Lewis's, so I thought I'd drop in and visit awhile."

"Sure. Just step into the living room," Mother said. "Dorcas, we have a guest," she added as the two of them entered the room where Dorcas sat reading.

"Perhaps you don't want to be bothered," Mark said hesitantly. "What are you reading?"

"Oh, I was reading some stories from the

Martyrs Mirror," she replied. "Stories about all that our forefathers endured for their faith. But that can wait; I'm ready for a change." Dorcas laid the heavy book aside.

"How about a hike?" the young man asked.

Dorcas was watching Mother, who was soberly shaking her head. Her disapproval was evident.

Mark paused for one awkward moment, and then added quickly, "Or a game of Scrabble? Or— maybe you don't have that new game yet."

Dorcas hopped to her feet. "Oh, yes. Mother got it for me for my birthday. And I enjoy playing it." She quickly got it out of the cupboard and came back to him. "I am always ready for a challenge," she said, laughing, "and with your quick wit, I don't doubt but you will be one!"

"Oh, I'm not the best speller. But I do enjoy Scrabble."

"Let's go out to the kitchen table," Dorcas suggested. The afternoon passed pleasantly. For Dorcas it was a welcome change from the normal quiet afternoons with Mother and Grandpa.

"Mother," Dorcas whispered. She had slipped into the living room, where her mother sat reading. "May I ask Mark to stay and have supper with us?"

Mother hesitated. "I wonder if we should. No doubt his uncle Lewis's are looking for him. He has been here all afternoon." Mother glanced toward Grandpa. He was asleep in his hickory rocker.

"It would only be Christian hospitality," Dorcas urged. "It is suppertime. You have often invited visitors to stay if they are here near mealtimes."

"I guess we could," Mother finally conceded. "But it won't be anything special."

When she saw how exuberant her daughter was, Mother wondered immediately if she had done the right thing. *I must be more cautious and encourage more reserve in Dorcas. Then we would have no need to make such quick decisions,* Sara chided herself as she slowly joined her daughter in the kitchen.

"Will you ride to church with me tonight, Dorcas?" Mark asked. He lingered at the door after the supper dishes were put away.

Dorcas looked at her mother, and then quickly turned to Mark. "Not this time," she said. "That would leave Mother to drive tonight, since Grandpa never drives at night. Mother could, but she would rather not."

"Would she mind?" he asked. Then, after an awkward silence, he turned and left, saying, "I have enjoyed the afternoon very much."

As soon as he drove out the lane, Mother turned to Dorcas. "Were you expecting Mark?" Mother asked.

"Not really," Dorcas replied. "He had said

something this week about coming over sometime. But I didn't know when."

"I wonder if you aren't encouraging his
friendship too much," Mother cautioned. "I wish
you would be more reserved around him and
not encourage any special friendship until he
has been here for six months or a year."

"Oh, Mother, he is just lonesome." Dorcas justified the young man's actions. "He didn't mean
anything by his coming over here today. Besides,
I'm not interested in a special friendship with
him. He's like a brother at work; that's all."

"Dorcas." Grandpa's words were slow and
decided. "He didn't ask you to ride to church
with him just because he is lonesome. If you
don't have any special interest in him, you don't
have any right to encourage his attention. If your
mother is in agreement, I am going to ask you
not to see him anymore, except at your work,
until he has been a church member here for at
least six months and proven himself a faithful
Christian."

"I agree that would be wise," Mother said,
relieved to have her father's help and advice in
directing her daughter.

"Grandpa, I am twenty-one years old. I have
waited longer to start courtship than most girls,
and you won't even allow me this friendship. He
hasn't even asked for a special friendship. He is
just interested in being friends."

"Dorcas, I see more in it than that. Please trust my judgment. I mean it for your good. I don't want to allow something that you will suffer for the rest of your life, and that I will regret the rest of my life. I have not asked you to wait any longer to begin courtship if God leads and you have the opportunity. I am only asking you to wait in relation to this Mark so that he can have a time of proving, since he is a stranger here." Grandpa's firm but gentle voice spoke much more to her than the words he had said. His lifetime of caring and sharing were proof of his love and concern for her.

Dorcas did not say any more. She felt too grown up to argue and fret as a child would. But the color rose in her face as she turned and walked back to her room. "I'll talk to Mother about it later," she resolved, trying to subdue the rebellion rising in her heart. She knew they were right, yet her independent spirit cried out to show them she was no longer a child. She could handle the situation and would be cautious until she knew him better. Mark was really attractive, and his witty manner had captivated her. She could not deny that, and she did not want to. He was lively and full of fun, and she enjoyed being with him. *If only I had a brother or sister to chum with; then I wouldn't have this craving for someone on my own level,* she decided, thinking that her reasoning justified a friendship with Mark.

After Grandpa went to bed after church, Dorcas again opened the subject on her heart.

"Dorcas, I know how you feel," her mother assured her. "I felt just as self-sufficient when I was young. But I want to spare you what I have gone through."

"Mother, you are forgetting that I am three years older than you were when you started courtship," Dorcas argued. "Besides, Mark is a church member and my father was not."

"Dorcas, I realize there are a lot of differences, but there are also some things that are the same. You are young and inexperienced. You are unwilling to take advice. You think that you know what you are doing and that no one understands. If Mark wants your friendship, waiting six months will not hurt either one of you. If he is not interested in courtship, then you'd better not be spending time together playing games and riding around." Tears shone in Mother's eyes as she expressed her concern.

Dorcas was touched. "I'm sorry, Mother. I don't want to grieve you. And I do intend to profit by your advice because I know you are much wiser and more experienced than I am. It's just that it seems such a little thing to make a fuss over. We work together and enjoy a comradeship because we are both the only young person in our homes. Don't you see what I mean?" Dorcas pleaded for understanding.

"Yes, I think I do," Mother agreed thoughtfully. "But I also see where a relationship like that could soon mean more than you intend. That is the reason for the caution. After he is here longer and we all know him better, we trust that he will prove to be the kind of person we would feel comfortable to have you share a close friendship with. But there is no hurry."

A long silence hung heavily between Mother and daughter as they sat together on the living-room couch. "Dorcas," Mother began again, very tenderly, "you know what I have been through because of my own willful decision. I thought I had a right to choose my own way. I chose it, and you see where it led me.

"I am grieved for your sake that our home has not been ideal. I am grieved for Rebecca's sake, and for Samuel's. Much of what they are suffering is because of the way I chose.

"Now as I look back on the ungodly influences that wrecked their lives, I can see that Brother Mast's counsel to take the family somewhere else to live was good advice. At the time, I thought I could not do that, but I see now that our family could have been saved much heartache if I had heeded the counsel of my spiritual leader instead of relying on my own understanding.

"I trust that you will seek God's will for your life and be surrendered to it, so I will not have to experience still more grief from my unwise choice. Your evidence of self-will scares me, Dorcas. I fear for you." Mother paused for a time as she regarded Dorcas soberly. "You can still choose right, even though much in your past has contributed to your independent desire to make your own decisions. You do have one advantage I did not have—nor your older brother and sister. The church we are in today is much more careful in teaching and discipline than the one I grew up in. I would not have gotten by, here at Pine Grove, with what I did back at Germantown.

"Talk to our ministers, Dorcas, before you go any further with this friendship. Let them learn from Mark's former ministry what kind of young man he is. I am sure such advice would be very helpful for you. Consider also that our ministry requires a six-month proving period before granting membership. That is for a good reason. They would surely discourage beginning courtship also during this proving period, and you will do well to honor the church's decision in this. You can be thankful for a church that cares enough to establish such guidelines and use discipline if they are not followed.

"I am here to warn you, Dorcas, that if you go against what our faithful ministry has decided, you are asking for trouble. I learned the hard way. And even though I didn't always get the right direction from the church, I did have faithful parents. And if I had listened to them, it would have changed the course of my life."

"Mother, I think you are overly cautious, but I do appreciate you and Grandpa. I do intend to seek God's will for my life, so don't worry about me. I will try to be good." Dorcas turned teary eyes up to Mother. "Good night," she said softly, "and thank you. I'm glad we can talk things over."

Several more weeks passed, and much as Dorcas had determined it would not, the friendship blossomed between her and Mark. It was so noticeable that even the ministry talked with her about it. "We don't know this young man very well, Dorcas," Brother Benner cautioned, "so we are asking you both to wait until his six-month proving time is satisfactorily past."

"Thank you for your concern," Dorcas said. "I appreciate it and want to profit by it." But little changed.

Mother and Grandpa were disappointed in Dorcas's response. "I really want to do right," Dorcas assured them, "but it is hard when we work so close."

"Then you should quit your job," Grandpa suggested finally. "You could find work someplace else."

"Oh, no, no, no!" Dorcas resisted this suggestion emphatically. "That is not necessary. I will be more careful."

"You trust your own ability much too far,"

Grandpa warned. "I strongly suggest that you find another job."

Dorcas was determined to prove that she could control herself without having to find another job. *I can't go back to housework,* she decided. *And they don't want me to find work in town. So I'll just have to be more reserved around Mark, even though I do so enjoy talking with him.*

She felt confident that no one would oppose their courtship after Mark had proven himself. *I must be patient and wait, though I have confidence in him now,* she resolved. *He is impulsive, but if I ask him to wait, I'm sure he will. We don't want to spoil things.*

Dorcas could understand Mother's concern, knowing how her own life had turned out. *But she doesn't seem to realize that I am older and more mature than she was. Besides, there is a vast difference between what Mark is and what my father was. But I must be patient . . .*

As time went on, Sara and Grandpa could see that Dorcas was trying to comply with their wishes. But they were not entirely satisfied with her still working beside Mark on the job.

Dorcas and Mark were not courting, but Dorcas had made up her mind that if anyone else would ask her, she would refuse. After sharing her feelings about this with Mark, he was willing to wait. He did not come to visit anymore at the Bender home, but that did not keep him and Dorcas from sharing at work.

One evening, sometime later, Dorcas had some news that she enthusiastically shared with her mother, "Several of the Bender cousins stopped in at the butcher shop today, Mother. They are having a family gathering on Friday afternoon and evening because Samuel is coming home—"

"Samuel!" Mother gasped eagerly. "Samuel! So he is alive! Oh, I wish I could see him again. Is he coming here? Did they say?"

"They said that he didn't know if you would welcome him or not with his new wife."

"New wife?"

"He is married to a divorced German girl. I think they said she had two children and now she and Samuel have one together. He wrote to the Benders, they said, because he didn't know our address since we moved."

"Oh, how much I would welcome him," Mother said sadly, "even though we do not approve of the way he has taken. So he married another's man's wife. . . . I wish he had let us know where he was, so I could have kept in touch with him." Mother was in tears. "Oh, I hope he will come see us while he is in the area. Did they say if he is home to stay?"

"No, he isn't. He is only visiting for a little while. They said he has signed up for twenty years in service so that he can draw a big pension when he is out."

"Oh, how sad," Mother sighed. "He was so young when he joined the army. I do wish we could help him. We can only pray."

"Mother, would you object if I went over to see him? The cousins said you would be welcome too, but they didn't know if you would want to come. Father will be there too, and all the married Bender children."

Mother contemplated the situation silently. "You may go," she said at last, "but I won't. But please tell Samuel to come home while he is here. Oh, how I wish he had not married a divorced woman. There would be more chance of helping him. He knows what the Bible teaches, but he has turned his back on it."

It was a sad evening for Sara, while Dorcas enjoyed eating supper and spending the evening with her brother, her father, and her cousins. Dorcas felt timid at first. It had been a long time since she had spent time with her Bender relatives. It seemed like years and years since she had left Germantown Valley. Now there was a much bigger difference between herself and her relatives than she had expected.

Her father, with the woman he was currently living with, spoke kindly to Dorcas. Samuel was overjoyed to see her. He was dressed in full army uniform and looked very manly. Dorcas tried to visualize her brother, now twenty-seven, as a young boy working on the farm. How he had changed.

"Meet my family," he said gaily. "This is Nora, and our three little girls, Lucy, Susie, and the baby, Nancy."

"I am glad to meet you," Dorcas said awkwardly. She was not sure how she was expected to greet this worldly woman whom her brother had brought into their family.

After a lot of feasting, playing, and catching up on family news, the Benders began to disperse for the night. Glancing at the clock, Dorcas said to Grandma Bender, "I believe I should go home. Thank you for the pleasant time."

Then, moving nearer to her brother, she said, "Samuel, Mother would like very much to see you. Won't you come home awhile?"

"If I come may I bring my family?" he asked uneasily.

"Of course," Dorcas answered readily.

"All right, how about tomorrow? We will spend the day."

"Good," Dorcas said with a happy smile.

"Grandma Bender says you don't have a very big house, so we will come back here for the night. I want to spend some more time here anyway," he explained. "We will be here yet over Sunday. I have to get back to base on Monday. We'll be shipped overseas again next week."

The following morning, an hour before
lunchtime, a fine New York car drove in. Mother
and Dorcas stepped out onto the porch to meet
Samuel and his family.

While she fried chicken and prepared mashed
potatoes, the loving mother visited with her son,
deeply grieved at what she was seeing in his family. Nora was restless in the afternoon and spent
a lot of the time out in the yard. After supper,
Grandpa Yoder went to his room to be alone and
rest. Dorcas called Lucy and Susie from their
quarreling. "Come; let's take a walk," she suggested.

"Go with Aunt Dorcas," their father sternly
ordered when the girls hesitated. Nora took
Nancy and plopped her onto Samuel's lap. "I'm
going too. I've got to get out and do something,"
she declared in an irritated voice.

Sara welcomed the opportunity to have a few
minutes alone with her son. Going to Samuel,
she held out her arms to the baby. "Will Nancy
come to me?" she asked.

Samuel handed the little girl into her grandma's willing arms. Sara cuddled the child gently
against herself as she rocked her back and forth.
"Samuel, I have prayed for you every day since
you left," she said.

Samuel hung his head. "I am confident of
that," he replied hoarsely. "I have often felt your
prayers." He seemed more humble and broken

since his wife was not there. The proud confidence was gone while he was alone with his godly mother.

"Won't you reconsider and give your life to God?" she pled earnestly. "Don't you remember your simple faith and trust in God when you were young, and the joy it brought to you? Are you forgetting that the day is coming that you will stand before Him in judgment?"

"Mother, I know all that. It plagues me night and day. But please, please don't ever mention it to me again!" Samuel spoke almost fiercely. "I have chosen the wrong way, and I know it, but it is too late to do anything about it now," he finished in a subdued tone.

"No, son, it is not—"

Before his mother could finish her sentence, Samuel held up his hand to silence her. "Don't!" he said sharply, cutting more deeply the wound his mother already bore.

Sara was shocked. Was this really her son, the tender boy who had sung songs of Jesus and loved the stories from the Bible? The young man who had faithfully helped to support her? He seemed to have become so hardened since she had seen him last.

Samuel got up and paced the floor. Finally he returned to where his mother sat silently rocking, waiting on God's leading and her son's return. "Mother," he began with deep emotion,

"let's change the subject, or I will leave immediately. All I want to hear is how you are getting
along. Is Dorcas helping like a faithful daughter?
Do you have needs that aren't being met?" He
paused momentarily and then said, "I love you,
Mother."

"And I love you too, son," Mother assured him
softly. "I do not have needs. God has been good
to us, providing us a home here. I stay home and
take care of the store and Grandpa, while Dorcas
works five days a week at a butcher shop. We
have everything we need."

"Dorcas is of age," Samuel said slowly. "She
will most likely soon be leaving you. Will you be
able to make it then?"

"The store provides a fair income, and God
is faithful to supply all our needs. The church
here is also alert to any hardships, like medical
expenses, and is ready to assist in a Scriptural
way. When Dorcas had her surgery a year ago,
they helped to meet those expenses, even helping to make up her lost pay until she was able to
work again. We are well provided for," Mother
assured him.

"Will you promise to let me know if you are
ever in need?" Samuel offered. "I will leave my
address with you."

"I will continue to trust the Lord to meet my
needs as He sees best," Mother stated cautiously,
wanting to leave a true testimony, and yet not

wanting to offend this son whom she loved.

The door opened, and Nora and two excited children entered. They were followed by Dorcas, who was carrying an armload of pine cones, a bird nest, and other treasures they had gathered on their walk.

"You must have had a hike in the woods," Mother exclaimed, examining the things the children had gathered, while Dorcas got them each a paper bag.

"You aren't carrying that junk back to Grandma Bender's," Nora said sullenly.

When the children began to protest, Samuel interceded. "Oh, Nora, Great-grandma Bender will be just as pleased to see their treasures as Grandma was."

"Well then, let them take it! But I'm ready to go," Nora stated with finality. She took the baby from Grandma's arms, and she and the children went out to the car, the children clutching the bags with their treasures.

Sara turned to face her tall son, who was still standing in her kitchen. "Will you come to church tomorrow morning?" she asked.

"If Nora will," Samuel answered, placing a hand lovingly on his mother's shoulder. "You may keep on praying for us," he said softly near his mother's ear.

"I will," she said. "And I will write, now that we have your address again. You are always on

292

my mind, son. The separation was very, very hard."

"I know, Mother. It was hard on me too."

Mother and Samuel walked out to the car, where the others were already waiting. Samuel slid into the driver's seat, and then with one last look at his mother they were gone.

To Mother's surprise and pleasure, Samuel and his family were in church the next morning.

"You will come with us for dinner, won't you?" Mother asked after church.

"No, I guess not. Grandpa Bender's are looking for us, and you know we have Darlene and Joyce with us. They are expecting to go back home for the day. Father is planning to be there too, and he thought I should come back there, since I spent the day with you yesterday. We will be leaving for home tomorrow morning." Samuel looked fondly at his mother. "Why don't you and Dorcas come over with us. I know you'd be welcome."

Mother shook her head. "Your father will be there with another woman, Samuel. I would feel very much out of place."

"I'm sorry, Mother," Samuel said with regret, seeing the pained look in his mother's sorrowful eyes.

Dorcas spoke up from where she was listening. "Mother, I think I'll go along to spend some more time with Samuel."

Mother and Grandpa went home alone.

Those few hours spent that weekend with the Bender cousins brought about a drastic change in Dorcas's life. Mother immediately sensed a coldness when her daughter returned on Sunday night. The atmosphere was strained for the next few days, and when Mother tried to get Dorcas to open up and share, she held herself aloof.

"Mother, I have quit at the butcher shop," Dorcas announced quite unexpectedly the next Friday evening. "Don't look so shocked," she added, laughing. "That's what you and Grandpa have been wanting me to do, isn't it?"

"Well, yes, depending what you are planning to do instead," Mother agreed.

"Well, I have a job in the factory where Darlene works," Dorcas said smugly.

"But you will have so far to drive," Mother began to protest.

"I thought of that. And I don't want to keep the car all the time so that you won't have it when you need it. I'm planning to move back over to Germantown and ride to work with Darlene."

"Oh, Dorcas, please don't do that. You may use the car. I don't need it. I'd rather you'd go to work from here, if you are sure factory work is what you want to do."

"But Grandpa Bender's offered me a place to board. They have plenty of room, they said, and would warmly welcome me to stay there."

294

"Must I be separated from my last daughter too?" Mother sighed.

"I won't be too far away to come home often," Dorcas tried to cheer her.

"You will surely be home over weekends," Mother stated rather than asked.

"Oh, sometimes," Dorcas replied carelessly. "After I save enough to buy a car, maybe more often."

"But, Dorcas, you will want to come here to church. You know how worldly the Germantown Valley church is getting."

"Yes," Dorcas agreed with a nod. "It will be different going there again, but for a short time it may be necessary."

Grandpa Yoder also tried to persuade Dorcas to change her plans, but it was no use. Her mind was made up.

10.

Sufficient Grace

Sara continued to grieve over her youngest daughter's decision to move back to the Germantown Valley. She knew also that boarding with Grandpa Bender's would not do Dorcas any spiritual good. After Dorcas had been away for a month, not attending Pine Grove for either fall counsel service or Communion, Sara realized that her fears for her daughter were justified.

"It is true that Dorcas does not have a car, but she knows I would gladly drive to the Germantown Valley to bring her home," Mother said to Grandpa.

"She may need to learn some things the hard way." Grandpa grieved with Mother.

"'The way of transgressors is hard,'" Sara

quoted. "I will always regret taking my own way in my youth. Oh, how I hoped that Dorcas would not need to also learn by hard experiences If only I could spare her the painful reaping. If only I could somehow help her to understand the value of taking advice from those who have more experience, and who care so much about her eternal welfare."

Grandpa just shook his head sadly.

During her years of sad experiences, Sara had learned to turn to God, her only hope. Again she felt utterly helpless as she saw devastating changes in Dorcas. "Father of mercies," she cried out, "thank You for saving my soul. And now I pray for Dorcas. Spare my dear daughter sad years of reaping. Bring into her life whatever it takes to make her turn to You." Sara prayed from a broken heart, knowing that God is able and willing, but knowing also that He forces no one against his own will. Dorcas would have to give up her self-will or suffer the consequences.

No amount of remorse could change the circumstances that Sara's long-ago choice had forced upon her family. Sara knew that their undesirable home life had influenced Samuel to leave. And now that same influence was working in Dorcas. *But they do not have to let the past influence them*, Sara reasoned humbly. *They can yield to God and find grace to live above the things that are a hindrance to them.*

At Grandpa Benders, Dorcas found herself in a whirl of activity. She enjoyed the Germantown Valley young people and her new job. She enjoyed the freedom of making her own decisions. But when she went to bed at night, she often lay awake feeling guilty. She knew she was disappointing her mother. But even more than that, she was disappointing her Lord and His faithful church.

Mark began making the drive to the Germantown Valley to see Dorcas every Sunday afternoon. Before long, he found work in the Germantown area and made plans to also move there.

"Mark, I simply must spend one Sunday with Mother soon," Dorcas told him after the fifth Sunday away from home.

"You'll wish you hadn't," he remarked casually. "All she and her father will do is try to convince you to give up our courtship. You know I have fallen out of favor with your church, don't you?" He laughed dryly. "Your preachers started inquiring back at Hilltop and found out I wasn't exactly appreciated there." When Dorcas looked at him questioningly, he hastened to assure her, "Oh, I'm planning to apply here at Germantown Valley, so I'll still be a church member."

"Yes, but I won't be, if the preachers at Pine Grove hear we are dating!" Dorcas exclaimed. "Which I'm sure they will very soon!"

"No problem," Mark said breezily. "Just join Germantown Valley with me.'

Dorcas was sobered. As much as she was enjoying some extra freedoms here, she was not sure she would want to change her church membership. "I have a high appreciation for our church," she said slowly, "even though in some things I think they are too strict."

"But if they knew some things you are doing and wearing," Mark reminded her, "you would be in trouble too. Oh, well, what's the difference? We all have to make up our own minds. We could move our membership here and still live on a higher standard than most of them, if we chose to."

"I don't know . . ." Dorcas stalled, not sure how she should feel.

She was not surprised when Brother and Sister Benner sent a note, requesting a visit with her the next Sunday afternoon. She had learned to know Brother Benner as a minister who faithfully discharges his duties.

Nervously Dorcas called Mark from the factory the next day. "I am going to be at home this Sunday," she informed him. "So don't come over."

"Why not? Sooner or later they will know that we are seeing each other anyway. They probably do now. Everyone else does."

"But it won't suit. We will have to skip our visit this Sunday. You can come to see me on

Friday evening if you wish. I will be going home on Saturday for the weekend." She did not mention her appointment for Sunday afternoon to Mark. He would not understand and would try to convince her to refuse the interview. He had not learned to appreciate the Benners as she had.

Dorcas tried to keep their time together on Friday evening lively, not only to drown out her own forebodings, but also so that Mark would not ask any questions about Sunday.

The next morning, Mother arrived soon after breakfast to take her home. As Mother drove home, Dorcas felt torn between her present lifestyle and what she knew was right . They did not talk much. Mother looked worn and sad. Dorcas was tired after a short night of sleep, and pretended to rest. But her thoughts were too busy to let her sleep. *I wonder if Mother knows about Brother Benner's coming over. I wonder if she knows that Mark and I are disregarding their advice. I wonder if she has heard of other changes I have made.*

Dorcas's thoughts troubled her more and more as she neared home. But as soon as she acted awake, Mother wanted to talk. She knew she should be happy to talk with her mother and share all the things that had happened during the last six weeks. But somehow Mother seemed like a stranger.

Grandpa Yoder looked more feeble. He was

very quiet and Dorcas's heart was touched. For a fleeting moment she wished everything could return to normal. *Give up Mark, go work for the church families . . .* But she steeled herself against it. *I will go back to Grandpa Bender's and decide later; I won't make any impulsive decisions.* She had forgotten the impulsive decision she had made six weeks before.

"Dorcas, I am sorry to see that you are not responding to the church as you used to," Mother said late Saturday evening. She and Dorcas were visiting together after Grandpa had gone to bed.

"Mother," Dorcas protested, "I have enjoyed so much being home again, and we have had such a splendid day together. Let's not spoil it before we go to bed. We will talk about our differences tomorrow. Did Brother Benner's tell you they are coming over to visit tomorrow afternoon?"

"Yes, they talked with me about it," Mother replied soberly. "And, Dorcas, whether or not you like it, I must talk to you; it is my duty as your mother. The changes we see in you, and the fact that you are ignoring our wishes for your courtship, cause us much concern. How can we make you realize you are making the most important decisions of your life? Now, more than ever, it is of utmost importance to submit to the church and to God's leading. Oh, Dorcas, I wish you would consider the way you are taking."

THE WAY SHE CHOSE

Dorcas made no comment. So Mother knew she and Mark were dating, and Brother Benner's likely did too. *But surely there can't be anything wrong with pursuing a courtship at twenty-one years old!* she reasoned silently. Yet a dread and uneasiness continued to grow on her.

"I'm going to bed now, Mother. I'm so tired. We can talk tomorrow." She gave Mother a weak smile and went to her room. But she felt sick. She could not sleep.

If there were reports about misbehavior on Mark's part, I could see their reason for concern. But everyone seems to think highly of him, except his former minister maybe. But Mark says that was just a misunderstanding between them. I don't want to be hasty or ignore warnings, but—well, this seems so different from Mother's situation. But I guess that is why they are overly cautious. Mark is a true Christian, or I wouldn't even consider him! If only they'd understand . . . For much of the night, Dorcas tossed and threshed all the pros and cons around in her busy mind.

Brother Benner's visit on Sunday afternoon proved very unnerving to Dorcas. It seemed no one tried to understand her point of view.

"It appears to us that you are rebelling against counsel from your mother and the church. Your decision to not come home for Communion convinces us of your disloyalty." Brother Benner spoke kindly and sadly. "Until we see signs of repentance and change of heart, you will need to be under church censure. And if you persist in the way you are taking, it will eventually affect your membership with the church."

Dorcas burst into tears but did not have a word to reply. She had never dreamed it was this serious.

"We do not wish this, Dorcas," Brother Benner added quickly, his voice mellow with compassion. "We trust that you will respond to the help we long to give you, so that further action will not be necessary. We aren't doing this to punish you, but to help you realize that rebellion is serious and will bring you to eternal ruin.

"We are also suggesting, for your good, that you come home and live with your mother." More admonition and advice was given from the concerned heart of Brother Benner.

"We want to hear from you within a week. We are praying for you, Dorcas." After an hour of visiting and sharing concerns, the Benners left, giving Dorcas time to think things over.

Dorcas went to her room with serious thoughts. She had not expressed herself to Mother or to the Benners. Her thoughts were too turbulent, and she wanted time to sort them out. Suddenly she realized that her uppermost concern was "What will Mark think?" rather than "What is God's will?" She still, however, did not heed the warning that she must stop seeing Mark, as Brother Benner had suggested. She would talk with Mark about it; that was the only fair thing to do. They would decide together.

Having made this decision, Dorcas returned to the living room, where Mother and Grandpa were resting and reading. Mother looked up with a smile, though Dorcas could see signs of recent tears in her eyes.

"Mother, I should be going back to the Germantown Valley this afternoon, if it suits you to take me now."

"I thought you would stay until after church tonight," Mother said with longing.

"I know you do not like to drive alone after dark, and if we go now, you will have plenty of time to drive back during daylight hours. They are looking for me too, so I'd better go. Then you will have plenty of time to get back for church."

"I have asked James's Lavern to drive us to Germantown Valley after church so I won't have to return alone," Mother informed her daughter, hoping she would change her plans. "Lavern doesn't mind."

"But I already told Grandpa Bender's that I'll be back early."

As Mother drove Dorcas back to the Germantown Valley, she felt again the pressing need to remind Dorcas of her responsibility in relation to Brother and Sister Benner's visit. "Dorcas, I trust that you will take to heart what you have heard this afternoon." Mother spoke softly.

Dorcas nodded. "I will talk it over with Mark tonight," was her reply.

"You had better send him a note instead of spending an evening with him," Mother warned. "I'm not sure that you can withstand his entreaties if you are with him. Also, If you send him a note, he will know you are intending to respect the authority of the church."

Dorcas remained quiet.

"Did you hear what I said, Dorcas?" Mother questioned.

"I think Mark wants to be true to God as much as I do. It is only fair that we talk it over together," Dorcas stated firmly.

Mother stopped at the end of Grandpa Bender's driveway. "Good-bye, Dorcas. Please pray about all this before you make any decisions, and be sure your will is submitted to God," Mother pleaded with her youngest daughter.

Dorcas did not reply as she got her small satchel out of the car. She hurried to the house with a wave of her hand.

Sara drove home with a burdened heart. Again she turned to her only Source of hope and help. There she found comfort and sufficient grace to go on trusting and rejoicing.

THE WAY SHE CHOSE

Back at her grandparents' house two hours before church time, Dorcas quickly rang Mark's number. "I'm back," she said hurriedly. "I wonder if you could come over a few minutes before church."

"Sure, I will be right over," he replied readily. "I had planned to swing around by there to see if you were back. Our evening will be too short at best, since I didn't spend the afternoon with you. I'll see you soon!"

While she waited, Dorcas remembered with a twinge of conscience her resolve to spend time in prayer before calling Mark. *Now I must get freshened up and dressed*, she decided. *Then I can pray in the time that's left.*

When she knelt to pray, her mental powers seemed frozen. No one understood her. Would God? She found herself unable to make one plea for help or guidance before she heard the tires crunching on the gravel below her window. As she rose to her feet, a silent voice intruded into her consciousness: "Perhaps you don't want the Lord's leading. You only want your own way." Dorcas felt alarmed. She was not sure what she wanted most. She did know that she was not ready to meet Mark. She should have waited until she had had time to think.

Dorcas walked out into the front room as Grandma Bender was inviting Mark into the house.

Their visit began on a strained note. "I want to hear all about your visit home, Dorcas," he said at last. "But not now. There are too many around. We will talk after your grandparents leave for church. It looks as if they are going this evening."

"We can talk on the way to church," Dorcas suggested pensively.

"Were you planning to go this evening?" he asked, surprised.

"Of course. We always do. Why wouldn't we tonight?"

"Because we didn't get to spend the afternoon together, and I think we have lots to talk about. It would get too late after church."

"Mark! You can't mean it," Dorcas chided him. "Don't talk like that."

Mark was grinning in his carefree way. It seemed to Dorcas, just then, that he did not take anything seriously. And yet she admired his unruffled ease in any situation. *If only I could take things more calmly*, she thought. *I let everything bog me down so. I suppose he has noticed that I am troubled.*

"We have a perfect record of regular attendance. No one will notice if we miss one Sunday evening."

"Someone would," Dorcas disagreed.

"Who?" he countered. "Your mother is miles away, and your grandparents here surely couldn't care less."

"God would," Dorcas reproved him. "It won't take me long to tell you about my visit this afternoon, Mark." Her eyes pleaded for understanding. "I believe we should quit seeing each other. Just for a while," she added quickly, noticing the sudden change in his facial expression. "I don't want to hurt you, but we are not respecting the advice of our church leaders."

"That is why I think you should change your membership back here to Germantown Valley. I will apply here also, and we can continue our friendship as usual. After we are married, we will go over and join the church your mother attends, if you wish." The solution was just that simple to Mark.

Dorcas's mind whirled. What should she do? It would be pleasant to stay home and relax. She had had a strenuous weekend.

While she was trying to decide, Mark continued, "You don't have much to say? Well, I do. I was afraid this would happen if you spent the weekend with your mother. I wish I had known the Benners were planning to see you. I would have been there with you."

He regarded Dorcas thoughtfully. "And that is all the more reason for staying home tonight," he added. "Those people have gotten you all stirred up."

Noting Dorcas's negative reaction, Mark changed his tactic. "We could read and study a chapter together. Wouldn't that be a profitable way to spend the evening?"

"Yes, any evening except time for a service at church!" Dorcas was not used to missing church, and the idea repelled her. "The Bible says, 'Not forsaking the assembling of yourselves together.'"

Mark laughed. "Oh, Dorcas, you're too serious-minded."

Dorcas was hurt. "Too serious-minded, Mark! Really?"

"Dorcas, don't look at me like that!" he scolded. "Do you realize your family has you all confused and upset? We will go to church together another time. You aren't in any shape to go tonight. I am staying right here to take care of you and to help you settle down." Mark spoke in his most affectionate voice.

Dorcas hesitated. *Should I? Oh, what shall I do?* Her thoughtful brow puckered. *It would surely be pleasant to spend the evening here relaxing in the cozy living room, with the fire crackling in the fireplace . . .*

"All right," she agreed, surprising him. "We will stay this once."

"Thanks, Dorcas." Mark was plainly pleased with her decision, but Dorcas was troubled. Had she done wrong to give in? It would give them a more relaxed situation to talk things over and make some weighty decisions. Mark had always seemed to enjoy going to church before. It was not that he was disinterested, but some circumstances, of course, make a difference. With her conscience eased, Dorcas enjoyed a pleasant evening. The proposed chapter study turned out to be a very short part of the evening. The minutes passed quickly.

The Benders returned. Grandpa Bender walked into the front room for only a minute. "Ah, ha! So this is where you two spent the evening," he said with a laugh. "Now give account of yourselves: what have you been doing while we were out of sight?" Chuckling, he walked away, saying, "Have a good time. You're only young once."

Dorcas could not avoid comparing his reaction to Grandpa Yoder's, and she knew where she felt the most secure.

The following Sunday evening, after a leisurely stroll through the woods, Mark said, "Let's go for a ride instead of going inside."

"We hardly have time." Dorcas hesitated. "By the time we get a bite to eat and get dressed for church, it will be time to go."

"Are we going tonight?" Mark asked.

"Are we going? Of course we are going!" she replied emphatically. "Of course we are going to church. We are not going to start missing church regularly."

"We were there this morning," he answered indifferently. "Let's go for a ride, just this once."

"No, of course not," she answered, "not on Sunday evening."

"Why not?'

"Mark! You know why not. Because we should be in church."

"Dorcas, will you go for a ride just to please me?" He waited for her answer.

Should I? Dorcas struggled with her conscience. *Maybe if we go for a ride, I will have an opportunity to talk to him about his negligence. It is almost church time. I can't talk to him seriously when we are hurried.*

As Dorcas toasted some cheese sandwiches for supper, he repeated his question, "Will you go for a ride just to please me?"

"Yes," she answered at last, "just this once."

"Dorcas, you give me great pleasure." His happy voice was all the reward she could ask for, for her sacrifice.

The pleasant evening passed so quickly that Dorcas never got around to discussing anything serious. A lot of the evening was spent trying out the new radio that Grandpa Bender's had just purchased.

Months passed. Mark and Dorcas applied for membership at Germantown Valley and were received into fellowship. The leaders there did not reprove them for their indifference and questionable conduct. Several times Dorcas had determined to talk to Brother Mast about things that troubled her, but Mark objected. "He's only the senior bishop. He's no longer active. You should discuss your problems with Brother Lane, since he is in charge here now." But somehow that idea never appealed to Dorcas. She had not gained the confidence in Brother Lane that she had always had for Brother Mast. And so she struggled on alone.

Grandma Bender began to express her disapproval about various things—Mark and Dorcas's habit of missing church, their questionable courtship standards, their following the trends in the church, and so forth. But Dorcas ignored her concerns, just as she had ignored the admonition and advice she had received earlier from her closer loved ones.

When some of the sisters began cutting their hair and wearing their veilings only for church, Dorcas finally became alarmed. Now the gradual drift away from God's Word stood out in bold relief to her. She thought back over the months of her and Mark's courtship. Then she began to realize that the drift in her own life, though not quite as apparent, was just as real. Their courtship was not becoming to those who professed to be Christians. And more often than not, they missed Sunday evening services for some other form of entertainment.

After several very touching letters from her mother, and the following nearly sleepless nights,

Dorcas finally came to grips with what she must do. "I have done wrong," she conceded aloud. "I can see that our friendship has come between the Lord and me. I can't go on like this."

She sat in thought again. *I will return to the Lord and to my mother's church. It was there that I was at peace with God and myself, knowing that I was living in obedience to the Word. But first—*Dorcas drew a deep breath and shuddered in fear *first I must end my friendship with Mark. That will not be easy, but I cannot go back like this and lose out with God!*

Having decided this, Dorcas sat down with determination to write to Mark. *Mother was right months ago when she said I should write to him instead of seeing him again. She knew I would not be able to withstand his entreaties.*

"Dear Mark," she began. *How shall I tell him? He won't understand. He will want to talk to me, but I am afraid he would convince me differently. I want to be true to God at any cost.*

"I have enjoyed seeing you and spending our Sundays together, but . . . ," she continued. That did not sound right. Dorcas stopped again, puckering her brow in deep thought.

"But what?" Dorcas crumpled that sheet and started again.

I feel that we have not been giving God
first place in our lives. We have been seeking

only our own pleasure. I am going to ask you not to come and see me this Sunday. Let's pray about it and seek the Lord's will for our lives. We have been neglecting church attendance and have spent very little of our time together enjoying spiritual things. I cannot feel that our friendship has been for our spiritual good, so it must end. Good-bye.

Dorcas

That sounds so final. I wonder if I should leave it that way. If he changes, I may see it differently later. After contemplating awhile, she decided to leave the letter as she had written it. She could consider dating him again later, but only if he changed.

The letter was mailed on Thursday, and on Friday after work, Dorcas drove home to spend the weekend with Mother and Grandpa Yoder. She knew she was welcome without needing to let them know she was coming.

    *   *   *   *   *

In the Yoder home, one discouraging day had followed another. Sara's grief for her youngest daughter was uppermost in her mind. Soon after Dorcas had been excommunicated at Pine Grove, she had come home and told Mother she was again a member at Germantown Valley.

Sara's mind had often traveled back over the years, back to her own youth. Her father and mother had warned her about the course she was taking, admonishing her to consider the end of the road. At that time, she had not been able to see what she could now see so clearly—that the choices she made would also have profound effects on the lives of her children.

Sara had had such high hopes for this last daughter, and now those hopes seemed blasted! She had tried to warn her daughter to come back, to make peace with God and with the church. But then Dorcas had not come home anymore, and all she had been able to do was write and pray. She had prayed with increasing zeal, especially as the reports she heard from Germantown Valley became more and more alarming. And she had written. But even though she had sent a loving letter each week, she had never received one in reply.

Father in heaven, Sara prayed earnestly, *I have made many mistakes, but You have been faithful. Now I commit my loved ones to You. I want to go on rejoicing and trusting so that my life from here on can be a better testimony for You. I cannot do it alone.* Sara prayed as she worked. She tried to count her blessings rather than dwell on the discouraging things of life.

As she shoveled out the ashes from the black pot-bellied stove in the living room, Sara sang joyfully, "'Praise God from whom all blessings flow; / Praise Him, all creatures here below . . .'"

The ashes were messy and very dusty. Sara shoveled them slowly into the ash bucket, filling it only three-fourths full to carry outside. Grandpa was no longer able to take care of these little tasks about the house that he had always done so faithfully and cheerfully. Now Sara needed to be responsible for the heavier chores when her own strength was waning.

Besides carrying the bucket of ashes outside, there was always the mess and dust to clean up where some ashes had been spilled. *It is just like my life*, Sara mused. *My life is like the ashes, useless, black and messy, dirty and ugly, leaving its blight on my dear children.*

Dear Father, it is enough that my sins are forgiven. She sighed heavily, thankful for God's mercy and yet remorseful for past failures. *I must be content and spend the remainder of my days praising Him.* As she mused, she dumped the heavy bucket on the end of the garden, where she would later rake the ashes around those plants that would profit from the extra potash and acidity.

Sara stopped abruptly, and a slight smile crossed her face. *Ashes are good for something!* She considered what her father had taught her about certain plants which do better with wood ashes around them. *Maybe, just maybe if some good can come out of these dirty, ugly ashes, God can even yet get some glory from my life if*

I am faithful. I will allow Him to use me as He sees best. Sara knew that would mean, first of all, that she must be cheerful, ridding herself of her gloomy disposition!

A verse she had read in Genesis that morning flashed through Sara's mind. Abraham was feeling his unworthiness before God when he pled the cause of his nephew Lot. "I have taken upon me to speak unto the LORD, which am but dust and ashes." It was his faith that was imputed to him for righteousness. Sara's heart was encouraged. "Lord, increase my faith," she prayed in sincere undertones. "Let my life yet glorify You."

The thought was an encouragement to the discouraged mother as she turned and walked toward the house. Dusk was already falling on this November evening, and Sara knew it would soon be time to get some supper for Grandpa and herself.

A car pulled up in front of the house. Sara strained her eyes to see who it might be. "Dorcas!" she exclaimed, hurrying toward her daughter, who was just emerging from the unfamiliar vehicle. "I am so glad to see you. Come; let's go inside."

"No," Dorcas replied, "first let me help with whatever you are doing. I came to spend the weekend."

"Oh, I'm so glad," Mother said sincerely, casting another glance at the dark blue car. "I didn't recognize your car at first," she said. "Is this one yours? Were you having problems with your other one?"

"Not mechanical problems. But I felt more and more convicted about its color and style. So I traded it in when I saw this one at a reasonable price."

"This one is much more becoming to a simple, Bible way of life," Mother agreed. "And I'm glad you chose the color you did."

"Thanks, Mother. I'm glad you like it." Together Mother and daughter walked toward the house. "But what were you doing outside?" Dorcas asked. "I want to help you finish whatever work you were doing."

"I am finished outside. I did the chores earlier, and just now emptied the ashes. I still need to clean up the mess around the stove before it gets tracked through the house. Then we will get supper. The rest of the cleaning can wait until tomorrow."

"I may as well bring my things in then," Dorcas said as she ran lightly back to the car. Sara held the door as Dorcas squeezed through with her arms full of bags.

"I should have helped you! Such a load!" Sara laughed, pulling the door shut behind Dorcas. Dorcas dropped her bags on the floor and followed her mother to the living room.

Sara set the ash bucket by the stove and

brushed up the ashes on the hardwood floor. "At least next spring some plants will be more beautiful and fruitful for the work of the ashes on the ground," Sara mused aloud, her thoughts returning to her former comparisons.

"What was that?" Dorcas asked, grinning. "Are ashes good for something?"

"They surely are. The Bible even speaks about the beauty that can come from ashes—'beauty for ashes, and the oil of joy for mourning.' That verse is in Isaiah 61, I believe."

"What does that mean?" Dorcas questioned. "Does it have anything to do with the big, luscious blueberries and those bright pink azaleas growing over there in the wood ashes?" She was remembering some of the gardening knowledge that Grandpa had shared with her in days gone by.

"Come to the kitchen. While we get supper, we can talk about beauty for ashes," Mother suggested.

"By the way, where is Grandpa?"

"He is resting right now."

"How is he?"

"He seems to be getting weaker all the time. He spends much of his time lying down. He still gets around some, but he needs to use his cane to walk."

"Dear Grandpa," Dorcas mused regretfully. She was realizing how much she had missed his kind and gentle ways while she was away.

"Here, you may peel potatoes, if you will," Mother instructed, handing a bowl of potatoes to Dorcas. "I will fry a chicken I have been keeping for just such a special occasion."

"Now, tell me about beauty for ashes," Dorcas reminded her mother.

"Well," Mother began reflectively, "when I was taking the ashes out, I was feeling rather discouraged, thinking what a failure my life has been. I thought of my life as typified by the ashes in the bucket I was carrying. Then the Lord brought the wonderful thought to me that just as ashes make fruitful plants, so the ashes of my life can also bring forth fruit for His glory. That is the great desire of my heart!"

Tears stood in Dorcas's eyes as she rinsed the potatoes and put them in a kettle on the wood stove. Furtively, she brushed at her eyes. *No wonder Mother must often have felt like a failure*, she chided herself, *when even her youngest daughter would not listen.*

Dorcas looked up when she heard the slow *tap, tap, tap* of Grandpa's cane crossing his bedroom floor.

"Well, well, our Dorcas came home," the old man said in a cracked voice from his open bedroom door. Slowly he entered the front room and sat down in the rocker.

Dorcas went to him. "I'm glad to see you,

Grandpa." Dorcas spoke softly, taking the wrinkled hands in hers.

"It has been a long time," he replied, straining his eyes to see his granddaughter.

"I know." Dorcas's voice was heavy with regret. "I will try to do better."

It was a happy evening in the Yoder home. Soon after supper, Mother helped Grandpa retire for the night.

When Mother returned to the living room, Dorcas was carrying in more boxes and bags. Mother looked questioningly at the procedure.

Noticing her puzzled expression, Dorcas asked, "Is my room still empty? Can I find a place for some of my things? Or maybe you are using the room for something else now."

"Indeed, you can find room for anything you wish," Mother assured her. "I have stored a few things in there while it was empty, but I will find another place for them."

"Never mind. Don't start moving them tonight. I see there is room for me."

However, Mother was already removing a big box of quilt scraps and rearranging a few other things.

Dorcas set down the box that she was holding. "Here, let me help you move that," she offered. They pulled the large box into Mother's bedroom. "Now, please, Mother, don't move anything else tonight. Let's just sit down and talk awhile while we have the evening to ourselves."

Mother was only too glad to accept that offer. There was nothing that she wanted more!

Dorcas had a quieter, more subdued air about her, as different from her former self as her car was from the former one.

"Mother," Dorcas said after a short companionable silence, "I am quitting at the factory in six weeks. Do you know of anyone in the community who may need my help by then?"

Mother sat up happily. "Oh, Dorcas!" she exclaimed. "I am so glad. You will be coming home to live then? And coming back to our church?" The eager questions poured out along with tears of joy.

"I don't know of anyone just now who needs help," she continued, "but I will look around. I am sure that by spring there will be some family glad enough to find a hired girl."

Dorcas returned Mother's loving smile. How cruel she had been to go away and grieve her mother as she had! How could she ever make up to her mother those long months of sorrow? "Yes, Mother, I would like to come back to live. But I suppose I will need to stay at Grandpa's as long as I am at the factory." She glanced at the calendar. "Six weeks will take me almost till the middle of January. Then I plan to come home to stay."

"What about Mark?" Mother asked.

"I have quit Mark. More and more I have been

realizing that our friendship was not spiritually upbuilding."

Mother was nodding her head seriously. "That was wise, Dorcas. It is so important to seek God's will in everything we do."

"I want to," Dorcas replied. "I have been too careless about doing that."

"How did Mark take it?" Mother asked. "Is he agreed?"

"I don't know. I didn't talk with him. I tried several times, but he would always talk me into keeping up our friendship." Dorcas drew a long breath before going on. "I just wrote a letter. He probably got it today. I don't know if that was the right thing to do or not, but it was easier than trying to face him again with my concerns."

"I think you did right, especially if you had tried to explain before and he would not accept it. Yes, I think writing a letter was the best thing to do."

When Dorcas broke down and started to cry, Mother waited a moment. Then she asked, "Is there anything I can help you with? I know it must have been hard, but there is so much at stake."

After a few more minutes of silence, during which the only sounds were Dorcas sobbing softly, Mother asked, "Is there more you would like to share?"

Dorcas wiped her eyes and blew her nose. "I

am planning to start again and to try to live differently. Do you think I can be a member here again, where there are more safeguards? I guess I see how much I need them."

Brushing tears from her eyes, Mother began in an unsteady voice, "Dorcas, of course you can be a member with us again. That is, if you are truly sorry and are willing to submit to the church. But first of all, you must surrender your all to the Lord and rely on His help to make a new start."

"I know, Mother, and I want to do that."

"Dorcas, this gives me more joy than you can realize. Let's just spend a little time in prayer together right now, to seek God's help and direction in our lives."

After spending time on their knees beside the couch, mother and daughter rose with new hope in their hearts. Sara went to the kitchen to get a drink for them both before going to bed. When she returned to the living room, Dorcas sat with a troubled look, staring off into space.

Sara stopped suddenly. "Is something else worrying you?" she probed kindly.

"Not really. It's just that I dread returning to the Germantown Valley on Sunday afternoon."

"Couldn't you just stay here?" Sara begged as she set the glasses of water on a side table. "The temptations there will be so strong. I wish you could move home right away. Be sure to pray for

God's leading in this." Sara's voice trembled.

"I am, Mother, and I intend to be true. With God's help I can resist the temptations. It will be only for a few weeks, and I will come home every weekend."

"I realize that you owe it to the factory to give them several weeks' advance notice before quitting," Mother agreed. "But if only you could live at home during that time."

"It would hardly be practical," Dorcas pointed out soberly. "I had thought of that. But, Mother, I'd be driving two hours a day to and from work."

"No, that wouldn't be practical." Mother sighed. "We will be praying for you. God's grace is sufficient, and He will keep you if you faithfully keep your heart yielded to Him."

"Yes, Mother, I have often seen God's sufficient grace at work in your life." Dorcas smiled as she took a sip of cold water. "I have learned a lot about His grace through your continued testimony of trust even in the hardest trials." Dorcas shook her head and put a finger on Mother's lips as Mother began to remonstrate. "You don't realize how much your life speaks to others," Dorcas went on with conviction, "because you don't see it as others do. Remember how I could see the beautiful blueberries and azaleas when you saw only the ashes? I have seen such beauty in your life also when you were seeing only ashes. 'Beauty for ashes,'" Dorcas murmured.

Mother reached for her well-worn Bible. "Let's look that Scripture up in the Bible," she suggested.

Together they found the passage in Isaiah 61. "This whole chapter is such a blessing to me. Let's read all of it together." Mother and daughter bent their heads together over Mother's Bible and read the stately passage verse by verse.

"'He hath clothed me with the garments of salvation, he hath covered me with the robe of righteousness,'" Mother repeated fervently. "What more could I ask for? Thank You, dear heavenly Father. May I now cause Your praise to spring forth!"

Dorcas looked at the joy in Mother's face and was suddenly seized with conviction for all the hardship she had caused her mother. "I am so sorry for the grief I have caused you and Grandpa, Mother. Can you forgive me?"

"Of course you are forgiven. I am so thankful to God for answering my prayers," Mother responded sincerely.

"Tomorrow I want to ask Grandpa's forgiveness too. He has been like a father to me. He seemed so glad to see me home again."

"I think that would bless his heart," Mother encouraged her.

Dorcas smiled as she looked back at the passage in Isaiah. "'To appoint unto them that mourn in Zion, to give unto them beauty for

326

ashes, the oil of joy for mourning, the garment of praise for the spirit of heaviness.' What is that talking about?" Dorcas asked thoughtfully. "It sounds like a wonderful exchange: beauty for ashes, joy for mourning, praise instead of heaviness."

"Yes, it does," Mother responded. "God's mercy is so great, giving us many things we don't deserve. He is always ready to bestow on us something much better if we surrender all to Him, even making beauty out of ugliness. Isaiah is prophesying what blessings God has waiting for His people, if only they will return to Him."

"I am intrigued by the thought of ashes being used in the Scriptures as a comparison to beauty, to bring out the vast difference," Dorcas mused. "That comparison must be suggesting the vast difference between a submitted life and a selfish one."

"Why don't you get the concordance and look up other references about ashes," Mother suggested.

After looking up several other verses on the subject, Dorcas was greatly impressed and inspired. "The ashes from the Levitical sacrifices were dumped outside the camp so the Israelites' dwellings would not be contaminated," she noted. "And the psalmist spoke of eating ashes and mingling his drink with weeping when he was in distress. Ashes proclaimed to others that one was in deep grief."

"God's people in the Old Testament would sometimes clothe themselves in sackcloth and ashes to show their unworthiness and unfitness to receive God's mercies," Mother added. "It was part of their submission to God and recognition of their need for cleansing and forgiveness. God was always merciful to all who humbled themselves and repented. Then God wanted them to put away the signs of mourning and rejoice!"

Dorcas was still paging through the Bible. "Here in Genesis is a reference about Abraham recognizing that he is but dust and ashes . . ."

"I was just thinking about that verse this morning," Mother injected. "It was in the context of his intercession for Lot in the city of Sodom. God honored Abraham's faith, and He still honors true faith today! That is a precious thought."

After they had spent more than an hour together in Bible study, Sara stood slowly to her feet. "We will have more time to share tomorrow. Maybe we should be getting to bed tonight."

"Oh, Mother, this has been rich!" Dorcas exclaimed. "I want to remember that I am but dust and ashes. But, Mother, I don't believe that God would want us to just dwell on the 'dust and ashes' aspect or to continue grieving over past mistakes. He wants us to remember that He will give beauty for ashes. 'He will beautify the meek with salvation.' We want to let the beauty of Jesus be seen in us." She closed the Bible and stood up.

"Good night, Mother," she said sincerely. "Thank you for the wonderful time of Bible study and sharing tonight."

Sara went to bed with such an overflowing heart that she could hardly sleep. She spent much of the night in praise and prayer, rejoicing in the mercies of God and beseeching His help for them all in the coming days.

11.

Singing God's Praises

Saturday was a pleasant day of working together, preparing food for Sunday and cleaning the house. Happy laughter often filled the house throughout the day.

Sara could hardly wait for Sunday morning, when the opportunity would be hers once again to have her daughter go to church with her. Her joy overflowed as Dorcas talked with Brother and Sister Benner, requesting membership again at Pine Grove.

The minister and his wife rejoiced, encouraging Dorcas to faithfulness. They explained to her the need for a public confession and a six-month proving period, to which Dorcas readily agreed.

Dorcas went home with Mother for the afternoon. Her heart was lighter than it had been for many a month.

Soon after three o'clock, Mother lay down to rest. Dorcas decided to take a walk through the orchard to relive some of her old childhood experiences. Grabbing a coat and boots, she was soon out in the fresh air. *It is so good to be home again*, she thought, breathing deeply of the crisp coldness.

She was out wandering through the trees in the orchard when she heard the sound of gravel crunching on the driveway. Dorcas turned to see if it might be someone she knew and was shocked to see Mark spring from his car. Oh, where could she hide? But he had already seen her and was heading her way.

Oh, if only he hadn't seen me. Then I would hide until he knocked at the door and got Mother up, she thought in desperation. *I don't want to see him alone.*

But it was too late. He had seen her. She could not hide, nor could she get around him to the house before he reached her.

Frantically, Dorcas tried to collect her thoughts. She had not even thought of this possibility. The reason she had come home for the weekend was so that she would not have to meet up with him at Germantown.

But now here he was, and what was she to

do? While she was still trying to decide how to approach him and what to say, Mark called out cheerily, "Hi, Dorcas! You really gave me the slip, didn't you? Not even telling me where I could find you."

Coming a few steps closer, he stopped short, seeing her obvious displeasure. His self-confident eagerness was quickly changed to a crestfallen soberness. "Dorcas, I received your letter, and I've come to talk to you about it." He waited for her reply.

Dorcas took a deep breath. "I don't have anything more to say," she said in a soft but firm voice.

"Well, I do," he said almost impatiently.

"Let's go to the house, Mark," she invited hesitantly. By passing him on the path and heading toward the house, Dorcas plainly told him of her intent to refuse to discuss the matter further at this point.

Reluctantly, he followed. "Dorcas," he pled, "wait. I would rather talk out here. Then when we have come to an agreement, I will come in to spend the evening, if you wish me to."

Dorcas turned and stared blankly at Mark. Had she not made her decision clear enough? "Mark," she said, turning back toward the house, "I have said all I have to say. There is nothing more to discuss."

When she kept on walking, he followed her.

"That isn't fair, Dorcas. Can't we at least be reasonable enough to talk it over together? Then I will go if you wish," he added in an aggrieved tone.

"Dorcas, really, understand me. I was touched by your sincerity in the letter. I want to do different too. I want to be all that you want me to be." His tone was as pleading as he could make it.

"But, Mark, we have talked it over before, and we cannot come to an agreement that satisfies both of us. No, this time it is final."

Dorcas stepped up onto the porch just as Mother stepped out the door. Mother stopped abruptly, looking from Dorcas to Mark. "I thought I heard a car drive in and came to see who it is," she explained. "Were you expecting a guest?" she asked her daughter.

Dorcas shook her head and stepped toward the door.

"Dorcas," Mark called after her, "will you please wait just long enough for me to express myself?"

When Dorcas stopped beside her mother, he continued, "As I said, I was glad for your letter. I was deeply touched by it. I have been doing some serious thinking myself. I would like to talk this over, and then I will step out of the picture if you wish."

While she hesitated, he added, "It is only

reasonable. You have not been fair with me."

"No," Dorcas replied. "I do not think I have been unfair. I have let you know before how I feel. You have often had opportunity to answer for yourself. But if you wish to say something more, you may come inside. I don't think Mother will object. But I refuse to come out there and discuss it further."

Seeing her reserve break down that much—that at least she was willing to listen—he decided to take his chances on asking for just a little more. "Dorcas, if I may express myself, I would really rather talk with you alone. Will you please go for a ride with me? I will bring you back as soon as you wish. But really, I have every right to request a private talk, since we are engaged."

"All right," she agreed reluctantly. "I will go with you for thirty minutes, until you have time to say what you have to say. I want to be back here in time to go to church with Mother."

Mother looked questioningly from Dorcas to Mark. Until now she had not interfered. Seeing that Dorcas was flustered and confused, Mother intervened, speaking first to Mark. "If you want to talk to her, there is the front room. You are welcome to come in for a few minutes. I would rather that she not accept your offer to go for a ride until she has had time to think it over and pray about it. She has stated her convictions to you and has found that they differ from yours."

334

Dorcas was obviously very unnerved. "Wait, Mother," she began uncertainly, stepping inside and motioning her mother to follow. Looking back, she said, "Just a minute, Mark."

Mother closed the door behind her.

"Just this once, Mother. I am not changing my mind, at least not until he proves himself. But I believe he is right that it is only fair that I give him opportunity to express himself."

"Dorcas, I do not think such a step is wise! Haven't you done that several times already?"

"Just this once more," Dorcas pleaded. "I am not starting to date again. I don't want to leave him with hard feelings. I think he is really considering my views, since he is convinced I am serious."

Mother was shaking her head. "He may come inside, but do not go for a drive. One of these times it will be once more too often. You are in no shape emotionally to talk things over right now."

"Mother, just this once more? Please give your consent. Then this will be the end."

Mother only shook her head again.

In his slow, shaking voice, Grandpa entered into the conversation. "I consented to your mother's wishes against my will once, just once, and I have regretted it ever since. Honor your mother, Dorcas."

"Mother, he is waiting. What shall I tell him?"

"To come in if he has anything he wants to say," Mother replied softly, unmoved by Dorcas's pleading.

"I want to be fair."

"You were when you wrote. Tell him firmly and kindly that nothing has changed."

Dorcas opened the door. "I will hear what you have to say," she said tremulously. "But don't expect me to change my mind."

Mark smiled and started toward the car, taking her answer to mean that she had consented to go along.

Dorcas looked bewildered, hesitated, and then followed.

Forgetting supper, Mother and Grandpa had a season of prayer together for Dorcas. It was time to go to church. They waited. "Soon we will be late," Grandpa said patiently.

"What shall we do?" Mother asked, her heart longing for her daughter. "I guess there really is no reason for waiting any longer. If they want to come to church, they will. If they don't, there is no value in our missing it too." She walked to her room for the keys. Just before the first song, she helped her father into the already full church.

Mark and Dorcas did not come. Sara helped her father to the car soon after dismissal. She must have a good talk with Dorcas yet tonight. However, when they arrived at home, her car was not there. Entering the house, they realized that she had come and left again. Sara determined to drive out to Grandpa Bender's on Monday evening to speak with her daughter.

Dorcas was not home, and Reuben Bender had no idea when she would be. Nor did he know where she had gone. "I'll tell her you are eager to talk with her," he offered.

There was no need to wait. Sara sadly drove home. Day after day she waited for some word from Dorcas. The following weekend, she waited expectantly. Again her hopes were blasted.

On Sunday afternoon, the Benners drove to Germantown, to see if they could find an opportunity to talk to Dorcas. Again she was not at home, and the Benders had no idea where she was or when to expect her back.

Sara reflected many times on the pleasant weekend she had spent with her daughter. She thought of the beautiful truths they had gleaned from Isaiah 61. Bravely she tried to keep a joyful heart and a cheerful countenance. She truly did want to bring forth praise for God's glory!

In great disappointment Sara waited expectantly for three long weeks. Then a letter came.

"Dear Mother, I love you," the letter began in Dorcas's hurried handwriting. Sara wiped her eyes so that she could see to read.

I hope I am not disappointing you, but after Mark and I talked things over, we decided to go ahead and get married this spring. That will make it necessary to keep our membership here at Germantown Valley Church if we want to have a church wedding, which we do. We intend to serve the Lord faithfully. I hope you and Grandpa will come to the wedding. Grandpa Bender's said they would be glad to have the wedding to save you the expense.

Your loving daughter,
Dorcas

Sara wept. How she longed and prayed for her daughter in the three months before the wedding.

At first Mark and Dorcas came home about once a month after they were married. But their visits were strained, and soon the time stretched further and further between. After the first year, Sara seldom saw her daughter and son-in-law, and when she did, it only added to her grief as she saw the changes in them. It was very obvious that they were not happy together.

Then little Sara was born. Grandma Sara made the trip to see her little granddaughter. Sara's feelings were bittersweet as she held the tiny namesake in her arms. "Mother, I named her for you," Dorcas said fondly. "I want her to grow up to be just like you." But as Sara gazed at the innocent little face, her heart ached. Dorcas and Mark frequently argued and did not seem to have a godly respect for each other. What a home for an eternal soul to be born into. *Must the wrong choice of my youth continue to affect the following generations?* Sara mused sadly as she drove home.

Before many months passed, Brother Benner made an announcement that tore at Sara's already bleeding heart.

"We have been strongly recommending that our parents do not allow their young people to associate with the Germantown Valley young people at their social functions. We want to reinforce that today," he began. "To the young people: we will hold you accountable if you are found to be taking part in any of Germantown Valley youth activities. It will be made a test of membership. We have learned that they are inviting worldly young people to their gatherings, and at these functions they are participating in dances, social drinking, and many other evils of the world, from which we must keep our church free."

Now Sara could better understand why Dorcas had not come to see her these past months and why, when she did come, they seemed to have so little in common. So the Germantown Valley Church had actually gone that far? No wonder that Dorcas and Mark were involved in the many worldly things that they were.

Sara thought about those older members

whom she was sure would not approve of the situation but could do little about it. She thought about faithful old Brother and Sister Mast. How grieved their hearts must be.

Later that same week a letter came from Dorcas. Sara opened it eagerly. Letters were so scarce from her dear daughter. Included in the short letter were a few sentences that Sara read with aching heart. "Mother, Mark and I are no longer living together. We stayed together for eighteen months, though we were not happy. He is asking for a divorce, but I refuse to sign it."

Sara, as was her habit, fell on her knees to beseech the Lord in a renewed way for the spiritual needs of her children. She arose, again refreshed by the promises and presence of her heavenly Father.

For the past months, Grandpa Yoder had been steadily growing weaker. Sara lovingly tended him, but finally his care became more than she could handle alone. Her brother James began coming to help at night.

Two weeks before his seventy-fifth birthday, Grandpa went to be with the Lord. For two days, Sara tried without success to contact Dorcas. When Reuben Bender learned of Grandpa Yoder's death, he sent word to Dorcas.

Dorcas came home with six-month-old Sara, a plump, happy baby. But Dorcas looked distressed and haggard.

Sara looked at her daughter with longing heart, but there was little opportunity during the time of the funeral to spend time alone with her. Dorcas did share, before leaving again for the Germantown Valley, one bit of news that was heartening to Sara. "Mark has come home. He would have come to the funeral, but he could not get off from his job."

"Are you happy he has come back?" Mother asked kindly.

"Yes," Dorcas admitted. "I do love him. Oh, Mother, pray for him," she added. "He is so discouraged."

"What about yourself?" Mother inquired lovingly as she shifted baby Sara to her other shoulder.

Dorcas broke down and cried. "I know that neither of us is right with God. But, Mother, Grandpa's passing and the service today have really spoken to me."

"I have kept on praying," Mother said softly.

"I know you have. And at times I feel such conviction that I think I will go crazy. I think that is why Mark left me. That and the church situation at Germantown Valley. He made the remark about the church there, that if he can sin and be part of it, he may as well sin and be out of it."

"Aren't you going to church anywhere? Dorcas, you don't want this innocent daughter of yours to grow up like that."

Dorcas paused as she wiped her eyes. "No, neither of us has been to church since Sara was born. Mother, we've had some rough going, and we both know we need to get right with God. But Mark says he will not join the church at Germantown Valley again. When I suggested we come over here, he agreed that he would rather do that. I think he would come with me some-time soon if I could convince him that he would be welcome."

Mother's eyes shone through her tears. "Welcome?" she said happily. "Certainly he is wel-come. Will you come next Sunday for dinner? Come in time for church in the morning."

"I will tell Mark about your invitation, and we just might come. We do want our child to grow up in a Bible-believing church."

"I will be prepared for you," Mother said with a happy smile. "And I will surely continue to pray."

"Please do that. We need it," Dorcas said with emphasis.

Sunday arrived, and with it Mark and Dorcas and little Sara. Grandma Sara rejoiced, commit-ted her loved ones to God, and clung to His faith-ful promises.

"We saw we were in time to drive here first and take you along to church," Dorcas informed her mother, handing the baby to her.

"I am so glad," Sara rejoiced as she cuddled the little one. "I guess we should leave about right away. We will have lots of time for visiting later."

When dinner was over and Mother and Dorcas had put things away, they found Mark in the rocker with the little girl sleeping in his arms. An open Bible was before him. "That was a good message this morning," he began immediately. "I had forgotten what it's like to hear a good message! Oh, God forgive us, but we had just about wrecked our lives!"

"God does forgive," Mother said gently.

"He has," Mark said humbly. "We have both repented and intend to make a new start."

"Be sure you join a Bible-practicing church," Mother encouraged them. "It is too hard to try to find your way alone."

"You're right. We do intend to," Mark and Dorcas both agreed. "You can see we have already made some changes in our dress," Mark added.

"Yes, I noticed," Mother replied.

"We are no longer going along with the social activities we were involved in with the Germantown Valley and community young people. We ourselves often had dancing and drinking parties in our home," he continued. "But we began to realize that such looseness was wrecking our marriage, and we want nothing more to do with it."

"Couldn't you move into this area and be away from the temptations there?" Mother wondered. "I'm sure you could find work here."

"Mark's parents offered that he could take over their farm when they are ready to retire," Dorcas injected. "They go to Hilltop, which is a church much like Pine Grove. But that is so far away." She looked longingly at her mother.

"And they may not be ready to retire for another ten years," Mark added. "They are not much more than fifty-five now."

"Why don't you talk to Brother Benner?" Mother suggested. "He could give you good advice."

"Let's do that," Dorcas said soberly.

"I'm agreed. We need to make a lot of confessions and clear our past here, no matter what we do from here on."

Mother Sara felt as though her heart would burst with joy as Mark went right to the telephone and called Brother Benner.

Brother and Sister Benner were willing to come right over. What an afternoon of tears and confessions and prayer. Sara did not know if she could dare to hope again or not. But surely her daughter and her husband did seem sincere this time.

Mark and Dorcas came home every Sunday, attending church regularly with Mother. They faithfully proved the sincerity of their commitment and complied with all the church standards. Within a year they moved into the Pine Grove area and were also received as members into the church.

Peaceful, happy years followed for Grandma Sara, years comforted by the cheerful little granddaughter named after her as well as several more children born into Mark and Dorcas's home. Still, much more than the comfort of faithful children, her years were brightened with the blessing of God on her life.

In the midst of Sara's happiness, there was still some cause for grief. In 1961, her daughter Rebecca, who for all these years had been an unresponsive sufferer in the state hospital, passed away. Soon after that, a letter came from Samuel, bringing great joy to Sara at its arrival, but deep concern at the contents. He wrote,

Mother dear,

I am embarrassed by the many years of silence. I did not wish to grieve you by the story of my life. Now I feel as though I need to tell it all to you.

Soon after joining the army, I married Nora, whom you met some years ago. She was a divorcee with two children. We had one child together, but we didn't get along very well and soon split up.

Two years later, I married a young woman who deceived me, took my money, and left me after only three weeks of marriage. I have not seen her again.

Now I am married again to a divorcee, but

we get along well. With this marriage, I have two more children of my own. I am sorry I had not let you know, but knowing your scruples against remarrying, I hesitated to tell you. Now I want to tell you everything before I die. Joel is six years old now, and Jeremy is eight; and I hate like everything to die and leave these two young sons.

I would like to come see you, but I am not able. I was determined to complete my twenty years in service to gain a substantial pension for the rest of my life. But things have changed.

In another six months I would have accomplished my aim to retire and live at ease. Instead, I had a massive heart attack and have received an honorable discharge. What good does that do me? It isn't fair. There is no pension, because I did not serve out my twenty years, and I am completely disabled.

I am writing from a veteran's hospital in New York. Come see me if you can. I regret that I did not come to see you when I was able. It is too late now.

Sara cast her burden once more on the Lord, pleading for her son's salvation. She sought God's will in planning to see Samuel. When Dorcas heard about the letter and Samuel's need, she was ready to go with her mother to see him.

They made arrangements to fly to New York the following week. Plans were made to leave ten-year-old Sara and the four younger children with Uncle James's family. Mark would take his wife and mother-in-law to the airport and would pick them up the following evening.

The visit with Samuel was heart-rending. He was suffering and bitter. There was no evidence of repentance. And it was quite apparent that his life was coming to a close.

"Oh, how sad!" Dorcas cried as they left the hospital early in the afternoon. "If only we could do something. But he will have to make his own choice."

"Gladly I would give my life for him," Mother agreed, "but that would not save him. One life has been given for Him, and unless he accepts that, there is no hope."

Mother and Dorcas went home saddened.

A few months later, Samuel had another massive heart attack and never recovered. As far as anyone knew, he died as he had lived, estranged from God.

"How sad when our goal is earthly possessions and a life of ease," Mother reminded Mark and Dorcas as they gathered to comfort her. "Now Samuel has lost all his hopes for this life, with nothing to look forward to in the future. There is nothing so important as preparing for eternity. God has made all the provisions for our salvation. We only need to accept them."

A few months after Samuel's funeral, Mark and Dorcas moved to his parents' farm near the Hilltop church. The parting was hard. How Sara would miss their being nearby, and the grandchildren often popping into the house for a little visit. Yet Sara had deep joy in knowing that these dear children were faithful.

Sara continued to be able to provide for herself with the income from her little store business. She got along very well and daily rejoiced in God's goodness to her. Many were the opportunities she had to witness and offer encouragement as she waited on customers. Seldom were there more than one or two customers at a time, and so she learned to know many of them personally.

Mrs. Bailey stopped in nearly every morning when she brought her two little girls to Pine Grove's church school. "I'm so glad you have accepted my children into your Christian school," she told Sara one morning. "I see the biggest difference in them since they are attending here. It may be partly because we had to get rid of our television to be able to send them here. That was a blessing too."

"Yes," Sara agreed. "I am sure there are a lot of parents who would realize a big difference in their children if the children didn't have that corruption to feed on every day."

"The influence of the school has been a blessing in our home," Mrs. Bailey continued. "And making friends with Christian children has made a big difference too, I am sure."

"Well, our young children are not Christians," Sara contradicted her carefully. "Until they give their hearts to the Lord, they are living according to the fallen nature too. But they are greatly helped by the training of Christian parents. There are times when they need to be punished, according to the Bible method," she further explained. "The Bible says that 'foolishness is bound in the heart of a child'—and that means our children as well as yours. But the Bible tells parents how to control that: 'The rod of correction will drive it far from him.'"

"I know that the Bible says all that, even though many people do not believe it," Mrs. Bailey said. "But your children behave themselves, and I'm thankful mine can be with that kind of influence."

"We are glad your children can come to our school, and that it is a blessing to them."

"Well, Mrs. Bender, I must be going," Mrs. Bailey said, seemingly reluctant to leave.

"Keep searching the Word of God," Sara encouraged her with a smile. "There you will find the answers to all of life's problems."

"You people have it so nice. You are always happy. It must be nice to have a Christian home."

There was longing in Mrs. Bailey's voice and eyes.

"We have our trials too," Sara said, "but we know where to go to find comfort."

"But one can see on your faces that you have had an easy life: there aren't the lines of worry and fear that some of us have," Mrs. Bailey continued, convinced that Sara had not seen the troubles non-Christian families have.

Mrs. Bailey left. Sara wondered what she would say if she knew all Sara had been through in her lifetime. *She need not know,* Sara decided. *Thank You, Father, for giving me peace and a clear countenance that speaks for You,* Sara prayed as she waited for the next customer, who was now crossing her porch.

"Good morning, Sister Leah," Sara greeted her neighbor cheerfully. "What can I do for you today?"

"Oh, I need a few supplies. Fred's are coming this weekend. Most of all, I need some cheer to carry me through the hubbub of the weekend with six children tearing around in the house," she said a bit disconsolately. Then she added quickly, "Oh, I'm glad they are coming, but I am always glad when they leave."

"Read Psalms 34 and 37," Sara suggested, "and meditate awhile on Psalm 127:3–5."

Sara continued a cheery conversation while Sister Leah slowly gathered a number of items together. Finally she left and Sara was alone. She went back to the quilt she was working on. *I hope that I can finish this one this week,* she sighed. She had felt so tired the last several months. Sometimes she thought her health was failing faster than it should be for a woman who was only sixty-seven years old.

Another year passed, a busy year for Sara as she tended her little store and kept up with her few household chores. She was sitting at her quilt again one winter morning when the mailman stopped at the mailbox. As soon as he drove away from the mailbox, Sara eagerly donned her coat for the walk out the short drive. Mark and Dorcas were very busy on the farm and did not write nearly often enough to satisfy the lonely grandmother's hungry heart. Still she searched the mailbox every day, hoping.

"Thank You, Lord!" She spoke aloud to the twittering bluebirds in the fence row. "A letter from Dorcas!" She clutched the mail eagerly and hurried back to the house.

Dear Mother,

I don't have time to write much this morning, but I have some news I want to share with you. You will remember Samuel's son Jeremy, I'm sure. Remember, we met him for just a few minutes in the hospital the day we visited Samuel, several months before he died.

I had asked him for his address that day

and have contacted him several times in the years since then. Recently we had a letter from him, asking if he could come and live with us. His mother married again, and the stepfather doesn't want him around. Jeremy is sixteen now. Jeremy thought it might be because he looks so much like his father, and the step-father resents that. He says his stepfather does not seem to resent Joel, who is fourteen.

Anyway, Mark called and contacted them. His mother agreed to his coming to live with us, so we are going to New York for him. I hope he fits in well with our family.

When Mark called him, he said he had become a Christian. He seemed very sincere. When we get back, we will be eager to bring him to see you as soon as we can. If he is as sincere as he seems, I know it will bless your heart!

Sara bowed her head and wept tears of joy. Again she thought of the beauty for ashes. "God is so good!" she exclaimed aloud. She repeated that phrase often over the next weeks as she shared the news of her grandson with everyone she met.

Several weeks later, her brother James stopped by one Saturday afternoon. Sara met him at the door. "Well, what a nice surprise," she exclaimed with a happy smile. "What brings you here to see me so unexpectedly?"

"First of all," he began, "Joy wanted me to

invite you for dinner tomorrow."

Sara thought about the many lonesome Sundays that she spent alone. "Why, sure, I'd be delighted to come," she returned happily.

"But I also come with some sad news," James continued.

Sara looked up startled, suddenly realizing that he had not responded in kind to her own cheerful spirits.

"Joy had a phone call this afternoon, just before I came over here."

"A phone call? From where?" Sara's face was etched with concern.

"There was actually some good news and some sad," he added. "First I'll give you the good news. Mark and Dorcas and the children plan to be at Pine Grove tomorrow."

"Then they are all right. But what has happened? Is Samuel's Jeremy all right too? Will he be with them?" Sara waited patiently. Her will was submitted to God's, accepting whatever He allowed as a gift from His hand for her good. She was submitted, but still in her mother heart was a deep concern for her family.

James cleared his throat. "Jacob died last night in a drunken fight. Dorcas is all torn up, of course, about her father. She wants to stop by and see you tomorrow. Then they will go from here to the Germantown Valley to be there for the funeral. She said you would be welcome to go with them, but she doesn't suppose you will want to be there."

"No, I do not believe I could bear to be at the funeral," Sara concluded thoughtfully. Then tears began to flow freely as the awful truth of the situation sunk into her heart—the heart that had once thrilled at the young man's love, and later had suffered bitter cruelties at his hands. "If he had left that cursed drink alone, he could have been a good man," she said through her tears.

James wept with her, reliving too the many years that he had been a silent observer to the abuse that his sister suffered. "Sister," he said finally, "we can only leave Jacob in the hands of our righteous God. We cannot let his passing rob us of our joy."

"Oh, James, I know," Sara sobbed. "But I had continued through all these years to pray fervently for his salvation. And now all hope is gone."

"Sara, you must remember that he had many years and many opportunities to repent." James attempted again to comfort her. "We must not think God unjust. Finally, every person must make his own choice. And he has made his, nevermore to change it."

"Yes, James, you are right. God is merciful, and He gave Jacob plenty of opportunities."

James stood up. "Can I get you something to eat, Sara?" he asked kindly. "You look pale and worn out."

354

"Thank you, James, but no. I will be all right."

"Just a cup of hot tea?"

"Perhaps I could handle that," Sara replied. "Yes, I will have a cup of tea. But, come; sit down in the kitchen. I will make it myself—and one for you too."

Dorcas's visit comforted her mother. Seeing Samuel's son, who seemed to her as her own Samuel rejuvenated, put fresh life into her flagging spirits. But most of all, she was comforted by Jeremy's devoted commitment to Christ. Though the heartache of Jacob's passing weighed heavily upon her, seeing one more of her descendants on the straight and narrow way was a tremendous encouragement to Sara.

Jeremy's love for this grandmother that he had never learned to know before seemed instant and spontaneous as well. Sara rejoiced in his seeming delight in just being near her. She loved to hear him talk, and loved to gaze on the face that took her back thirty years to the time when her own son was a teenager.

"I'm sorry we can't see you more often, Mother," Dorcas said as they left the next morning. "Mark is very busy on the farm, and it is hard to get away. I just wish you would sell out here and come live with us." Dorcas looked lovingly upon her mother.

"I will keep going here as long as I can, Dorcas. But I do thank you for the offer."

Sara looked longingly after Mark's car as it drove out the driveway on its way to Germantown. She struggled with mixed feelings. Had she made the right decision to not go to her own husband's funeral? She had talked with Brother Benner's yesterday, but they had not told her what she should do, only that she should do what she felt comfortable with. It was certain that she felt more comfortable staying away, not subjecting herself to such stress again.

As the years passed, Sara gradually became weaker and weaker until she was unable to keep up with all the responsibilities that living alone entailed. Her brother James had been encouraging her to sell the store, or at least close it, and come to live with him and his family. His children were all gone now, except for the youngest two. "We have plenty of room," he urged her.

At last Sara gave in and sold her home and store. Giving up her own home was hard, but she was not so attached to any earthly possessions that she could not give them up and go on living cheerfully wherever she was. James and several of his children helped to move a few of her things into a couple of spare rooms in their house.

Sara's presence in the Yoder home proved to be a blessing. She found many little jobs to keep herself occupied with. When there was no mending to do, she kept her hands busy with small pieces of embroidery work or crocheting. In the summer, she was often found helping with stemming, shelling, snapping, peeling, or whatever was involved with getting fruits and vegetables into jars for the winter. During the winter evenings, shelling nuts was a favorite pastime. Many were the guests in the Yoder home who commented on the cheerfulness of Aunt Sara.

"Yes, she always seems happy and content, although we know she has many heartaches," Joy, James's wife, replied to such comments. "I enjoy very much having her with us, and James counts it a privilege to help his sister. The children also benefit by her consistent, godly life and cheerful acceptance of all that comes to her. She is living evidence of God's wonderful grace. She is an example of beautiful old age."

On hearing this comment once, Dorcas added, "'Beauty for ashes.'" She knew her mother often struggled with the temptation to be discouraged over the dark and dirty stains of her present experiences, brought on by the rebellion and self-will of her youth. She knew too that God's love and power was able to give her mother the oil of joy for mourning and a garment of praise for heaviness. Her mother had submitted to God's will and had kept the heaviness hidden beneath the garment of praise so that she would glorify God's Name.

12.

Beauty for Ashes

"Aunt Sara, how are you feeling this morning?" Joy asked softly, entering the elderly woman's bedroom.

"Oh, I don't want to complain, but I did not sleep well. I am very weary today. I guess I should get up, and maybe I will feel better."

"No, Aunt Sara. You don't need to be in a hurry to get up. I just wanted to check if everything is all right," Joy said, lovingly straightening the covers on the bed. She fluffed up the pillow, trying to make her husband's sister more comfortable. The bed showed evidence of a restless night. "Why weren't you able to sleep? Are you having pain?" she questioned further.

"I do have a lot of pain. Oh, I am such a bother

to you that I don't want to be complaining about my aches and pains yet. Sometimes I used to wonder why Grandpa would often heave such a heavy sigh. When I worked hard and was very tired, it seemed he was just trying to let me know how weary he was. I thought that if I am ever old and helpless, I would not burden others with my weariness. I would bear it quietly. Now here I am, always worrying you with my suffering!"

"No, Aunt Sara, you have been very patient. You hardly even let us know how you are feeling. You must share some of that with us, so we know how to care for you."

Joy tenderly cared for Sara, trying to meet all her needs. "I wonder if you should see your doctor," she said one day soon afterward. "Maybe he would have something to help with your pain. James said you worked very hard in your younger days, which probably ruined your health."

"Well, I hardly know about seeing the doctor. There is so little money left, and I don't have any means of earning more. I don't want to burden James."

"Aunt Sara, you know that James has taken you in as one of the family. He is happy to pay any bills for you. We have a good income from the farm now. The children are mostly raised, and we have few expenses. Don't hesitate because of the cost. We are glad to help out wherever it is needed. The church is glad to help also with the needs of our widows and the helpless. I think we will go ahead and make an appointment for you, if you are agreed to that."

"I guess I really should let you do that," Sara said hesitantly. "And God bless you. You have been so good to me."

"It is my pleasure," Joy returned with a smile. "You know I don't have a mother to care for. I lost her when I was young. Now I am thankful for another mother to take her place. You must remember that you are a blessing to us too."

"Well, I don't know about that," Sara replied uncertainly but gratefully. She looked fondly at her sister-in-law, only ten years younger than herself but still healthy and strong. Joy was like a loving daughter to Sara in the absence of her own children.

Sara was able to get some relief from her pain by the medication that the doctor gave her. However, she continued to suffer many ailments due to the emotional stress and physical strain over the many years of mistreatment from an unfaithful husband.

James entered his sister's room one summer evening soon after he came in from doing his chores. "Well, how's it going today?" he asked with sincere concern.

"Very well," Sara said, returning his smile.

"I heard you singing this afternoon while I was working in the shop," he continued.

"Oh, I will have to tone down," Sara replied, chuckling. "I didn't realize I was disturbing the neighborhood!"

"You certainly weren't. I am glad to hear you singing more again since you are feeling better. Joy said you were shelling her beans while she was out picking the raspberries. That really gave her a lift."

"I'm glad for something to do," Sara returned, "And I'm thankful to do what I can to help," she added modestly.

"I came to bring you some good news," James continued.

"Well, hurry up and tell me," Sara responded playfully.

"Dorcas called and said that they are planning to come in this weekend."

Happy lights brightened Sara's wrinkled face. "Are they all planning to come?" she asked happily. "All the children still at home?" Two of Dorcas's children were married, including her namesake, Sara. The oldest son helped Mark on the farm at home, which made it possible for Mark's to get away from home occasionally.

"They plan to bring the youngest two, as well as Jeremy and his special friend."

"Oh, thank the Lord, I will get to meet her." Sara knew that Jeremy had been courting a girl from Hilltop for the past two years. She had often wished to meet the girl who would likely become Jeremy's wife.

Friday evening came at last, and with it came Mark and Dorcas. Sara rejoiced at the lovely, godly girl whom Jeremy presented as his wife-to-be. *Kind heavenly Father,* she breathed humbly, *I'm not worthy of any blessings from You. But, oh, dear Father, I rejoice in the blessing of Jeremy's faithfulness to You.*

Dorcas insisted on relieving Aunt Joy of the care of her mother over the weekend. "You get to take care of her all the time," she reminded when Joy did not want to give up the privilege. "For these few days it is my turn!"

On Saturday morning, as she sat with her mother snapping beans, Dorcas had a coveted opportunity to share. "What a blessing to be here with you," she said. "It has been so hard to not be able to come more often. But the farm work has us tied down. Now that Mark, Jr. is married and doing more of the work, we can get away more easily."

"What does Jeremy do?" Sara asked.

"He usually helps with the farm work too," Dorcas explained, "along with our younger boys. But since you hadn't met Linda yet, we thought they both should come along this time."

"I was so happy to meet her. She seems like a very special girl."

"She is, Mother. She is a very spiritually-minded girl and will be a real stabilizing influence for

Jeremy. Not that he is not stable," Dorcas hastened
to add, seeing her mother's questioning look.
"Jeremy has applied himself to living the Christian
life in a way that puts some of our own young men
to shame. Linda began courtship with him with
the blessing of her parents and our ministry."

"Oh, I'm so glad," Sara said with a sigh of
thankfulness. "Just another of the wonderful
blessings of a wonderful God!"

Mother and daughter snapped beans in companionable silence for some time. "It is so good
to be here with you, Mother. I just wish you
would come live with us." Dorcas looked longingly into her mother's face. "You know, our offer
is still good."

Sara smiled at Dorcas. Yes, Dorcas had often
written that Sara should come live with them.
But this community was home.

"Wouldn't you consider it?"

"Dorcas," Sara replied, "I belong here. I am
very fortunate to have a brother to look after my
needs, and I have a faithful church. No, dear, I
appreciate your offer, but this is home to me.
Nearly everybody in your community would be
a stranger to me. And you have your family near
you there, plus several still at home. Your aunt
Joy doesn't have any children that need her care
anymore. I am well cared for here. But thank you
anyway."

"Mother, I want to tell you one more time

how beautiful your life of contentment and joy is to me. Remember the ashes?"

Sara nodded as she smiled at her daughter. "I remember that special weekend so many years ago when we studied into that subject."

"And remember the beautiful blueberries and azaleas you had the summer that you so liberally acidified the ground around them?" Dorcas continued.

Her mother nodded, reminiscing with a far-away look in her eyes.

"You have a good memory for a woman of seventy-five!" Dorcas complimented with a laugh.

"Better from my earlier life than from the past few years," her mother chuckled. "That is where my loss of memory catches me. But one of these days I will have a new body that will function perfectly in every way."

"Oh, Mother, don't talk about that." Dorcas turned her face away to hide quick tears.

"Why, Dorcas, that is what I have been looking forward to all my life! It is the day I have lived for! It is what has made all life's hardships and trials worthwhile." Her voice was so triumphant that Dorcas could not help rejoicing with her mother that the longed-for day might be near.

How different from my father's and my brother's death, both of which caused us untold grief, she mused thoughtfully.

As Dorcas returned home, the challenge of

her mother's godly life went with her very force-fully. Could she leave with her children the same godly heritage and example her mother had left with her? The pure joy, holiness, and content-ment that were evident in her mother's life con-tinued to encourage her to commit her life and her loved ones to God. It was He alone, the Almighty God, who could give beauty for ashes, the oil of joy for mourning, and a garment of praise for heaviness.

Dorcas knew well the heaviness her mother had endured, and she never ceased to marvel at the joyful praises that filled her life. The burden of lost ones was still heavy; but soon, very soon, her dear mother would be relieved of even that. No, Dorcas could not wish her mother to remain in this suffering body longer. She would be missed, greatly missed; but when God granted her eter-nal rest, Dorcas felt she would rejoice with her.

Life lingered on wearily day after day for the elderly child of God. Her saintly attitudes and patient suffering made Sara a pleasure to care for. Each day she grew physically weaker and less able to care for herself. Sara did not complain, and did everything she could to make it easier for Joy to care for her. However, the time came when Sara's care became too much for Joy alone.

"Joy," James said thoughtfully one evening, "You are tenderly caring for Sara, and I appreci-ate it deeply. It means so much to me to see her receiving your loving care. My heart has often gone out to her over the years.

"But you are working too hard. You aren't young yourself. I wish I could help more. I talked to the girls today, and they think they can start taking turns coming home to help. They will come nights when their husbands are home to care for their children. Our single girls can take turns at day shifts. I felt it would be too much for them to care for her day and night."

Until now Joy had not heard anything about her husband's plan. "Oh, but I have been so glad to do what I can," she answered at last. "Sara is a very dear sister to me." Joy heaved a deep sigh. "It may be hard on her to have so many others working with her, since her mind isn't so clear anymore. Considering the condition she's in, she won't be with us much longer. I want to do what I can."

"I know you do, dear," James agreed. "But you are close to seventy yourself and are not up to giving her all the care she needs."

Joy thought for a while. "All right, James. I do appreciate what you are suggesting. We can try it awhile and see how it works."

James nodded his head. "As you said, it may not be much longer; we don't know. I thought a year ago that it would not be much longer. So I have decided to get more help, since she needs constant care and so much lifting. You need some

366

undisturbed nights and can still help with her care during the day."

The arrangement worked out very well. Not only James's girls, but also several sisters in the church helped in the months that followed. Working together in this way proved a blessing to the whole church.

Just before her eightieth birthday, Sara passed on to her eternal reward. She is gone but not forgotten. The beauty of the ashes of her life continues to live on to bless the lives of faithful family members.